Healing Depression by Degrees of Fitness

The Brain Health Guidebook

To Corey and Becky, good
friends, good neighbors,
and good people

Bob
9, SEP 2019

Robert S. Brown, Sr., MD, PhD

Cristy S. Phillips, PT, EdD

Robert S. Brown, Sr., MD, PhD
COL, Medical Corps, USAR, (Ret.).
Dr. Brown retired 2016 after 45 years of psychiatric practice. He was Clinical Professor of Psychiatric Medicine and Neurobehavioral Sciences and Professor of Education, UVA where he received the William James Research Award, the Distinguished Alumnus Award, and the 2017 Walter Reed Distinguished Achievement Award.

Cristy S. Phillips, PT, EdD
Associate Professor, Arkansas State University
Associated Faculty, University of Tennessee Health Sciences. Dr. Phillips works to integrate therapeutic lifestyle interventions and personalized medicine in the treatment of neuropsychiatric and neurodegenerative disease. Her articles have appeared in several top-tier journals and Global Medical Discovery.

Table of Contents

MIRACLE OF EXERCISE FOR BRAIN HEALTH

Physical Activity Improves Brain Health

You may know that 150 minutes of weekly aerobic physical exercise is good for your heart because the American Heart Association has drummed it into every generation for the past 75 years. You may not know that the same amount of physical exercise has an even more favorable effect on your brain, the fundamental message of *Healing Depression by Degrees of Fitness, The Brain Health Guidebook.* Whether depressed or not, regular physical exercise actually fine-tunes your brain, improving brain health to a remarkable degree.

Muscles Talk to Your Brain

Muscles activated during periods of physical exercise can't keep their secret from the brain, the control center of the body and mind. Exercise is hot stuff. The movement of muscles uses energy to contract and in the process produces heat, changes that cause muscle fibers (type III and IV) to convey information to the hypothalamus by the vagus nerve, one of the longest nerves in your body. Both the muscle and vagus nerve fibers directly communicate news of changing body needs to the brain via electrical impulses that are sent via the fast track. Within seconds, the vagus nerve conveys news of chemical, thermogenic, and mechanical changes to the hypothalamus, thereby serving as a body to brain relay station.

At the same time, moving muscles trigger the release of factors called *exerkines* into the bloodstream. *Exerkines* are anti-inflammatory peptides, metabolites, and RNA transcripts that travel to the brain in blood vessels via the slow track. The slow route factors sneak across the blood-brain barrier at a special place where crossing is easier (the circumventricular organ). Then slowly, the factors make their way to various regions. Thereby, exerkines released in the body during movement affects the function of the hypothalamus, hippocampus, and frontal cortex. BDNF (Brain Derived Neurotropic Factor) is a well-known exerkine that affects the hippocampus. Another exerkine that gets a lot of attention is IL-6, a factor that is formally known as interleukin-6. What makes IL-6 particularly important is the fact that it conveys news of changing metabolic and immune needs to the brain.

The Brain Talks Back to the Body

Upon hearing from the vagus about the news of changing body needs, the brain talks back to the body by initiating a stress response. The hypothalamus secretes CRH (Corticotrophin Releasing Hormone). CRH is carried in blood vessels to the pituitary gland in the brain. It causes the release of ACTH (Adrenocorticotropin Hormone). In turn, ACTH causes the adrenal glands to release cortisol and epinephrine from the adrenals. Thereby, exercise triggers an autonomic system response that induces physiological changes in a number of end organs in the body, changes that are a part of the fight-or-flight response.

At the same time, this party-line conversation is heard by the hippocampus, which alters the level and function of neurotransmitters, BDNF (Brain Derived Neurotropic Factor) release, and communication between brain areas, changes that help the brain become more aware of surroundings and primed for foraging or aversive maneuvers.

BDNF is released from specific nerve cells. Remarkably, BDNF converts stem cells in the brain into new brain cells. BDNF also creates new connections between brain cells. This activity takes place in the hippocampus of the brain, a region that influences, among other activities, autobiographical, particularly emotional, memories.

The Owner of the Brain

The owner of the brain benefits from all this activity at the structural and molecular level. As electrical signals are conveyed to relevant brain areas, the activity induces increases neurotransmitters, and BDNF promote synapse communication, formation, and strengthening, occurrences captured well by the sentiment that neurons 'that fire together wire together.'

At the molecular level, all the signaling changes prompt the nucleus of cells in the brain and body to keep notes about the changing environment for basic safety and survival purposes, notes that are transcribed by the placement or removal of chemical tags on DNA. The DNA tags either promote or inhibit the expression of genetic information, ultimately effectuating changes in the production of key mediators in the body. For example, tags on DNA control the synthesis and breakdown of neurotransmitters, hormones, cell receptors, peptides, and proteins. Thus, alteration of tags on the portion of the DNA that code for the BDNF protein helps the brain keep track of environmental situations that affect neuronal health to ensure that neurons stay in tune with changing circumstance.

During physical exercise, the owner of the brain feels and thinks better because brain wave rhythms prompt activity that release rejuvenation substrates, particularly neurotransmitters, hormones, and BDNF. At the same time, excess stress hormones are converted to inactive forms, which enables a relaxation response after exercise.

Over time, regular physical activity prompts the hippocampus to form stronger connections with other parts of the brain that put the brakes on the stress system, particularly the frontal cortex. The hippocampus also builds strong connections with parts of the association cortex that are in charge of memory storage and retrieval, a process that is important for autographical memory and identity. As the connections grow, so does the girth of the hippocampus, building resilience by strength in synaptic number (less vulnerable during stress because it can lose a lot and not dip below the critical 80% threshold number).

"I Feel Pretty…"

What causes the brain owner to think he/she looks better after becoming fit? Blood flow and neurotransmitter shifts in the brain alter activity of information in a way that positively biases the processing of positive information. Interestingly, endorphins and BDNF that are released during exercise loosely mimic some of neurochemical signatures seen during early childhood development and parental bonding, particularly those seen during breast feeding (which reduces *the* feelings of pain*).*

Brain Health

Neuroscientific effects of moderate physical exercise are proving its major contribution to brain health. "Neurogenesis," or the production of new nerve cells in the human brain is a relatively recently added term to the lexicon of science. The circuitous pathway from moderate physical exercise to the creation of new brain cells and new connections between brain cells is one of the most compelling reasons why physical exercise must be encouraged throughout the lifespan. In fact, scientists who study positive brain aging now refer to some of the activity-induced exercise factors that promote neurogenesis during aging as *gerokines*, key promoters of emotional and cognitive health during aging. You do not have to know the intricacies of just how the miracle of physical activity favors your brain to enjoy its benefits.

B

DEDICATION

Drs. Brown and Phillips dedicate this book to all people who are clinically depressed, to all those who have ever been depressed, and to their families and loved ones. The authors also wish to acknowledge with heart-felt gratitude all those who have committed their professional lives to the research and treatment of clinical depression.

Much more needs to be done to help relieve the suffering caused by depression. Far too many people caught in its grasp have suffered unbearable pain to the extent that it became terminal. Suicide will continue unabated until depression is conquered.

We salute depressed people who seek treatment and the many researchers and therapists who stand ready and prepared to treat them.

Those who experience depression now have ample reason for hope. The unprecedented magnitude, extent, and pace of depression research today is breathtaking and assuring. Indeed, there is nothing like the encouragement that scientists, clinicians, and collaborating depressed patients are understanding at this time in the medical history of the treatment of depression. We believe that the discovery of brain derived neurotropic factor (BDNF), a growth hormone released by moderate physical activity to convert stem cells in the brain into new brain cells is as scientifically important as the antibacterial effects of penicillin discovered and first used in World War II. Thus, we join the excitement of fellow scientists and clinicians in the deeply held belief that ultimately major depression will be swept away.

C

HEALING DEPRESSION

Sal's Pizza

Last night, my daughter, Nancy, a recently early-retired reading teacher turned librarian, asked how my book on depression was progressing. "It's taking much longer than I imagined," I replied. "I've spent most of the summer, for example, working on the spiritual dimensions of clinical depression. At most, the subject occupies no more than two or three of my intended 20 chapters. It's frustrating. This book is taking much longer than the four I've written about treating combat posttraumatic stress disorder."

We were celebrating Nancy's birthday at Sal's Pizza in Crozet, a small community near

Charlottesville. My wife has a heart for the depressed and a deep understanding of my undertaking. She was my secretary and office manager for most of the four decades I practiced psychiatry. She interjected, "No wonder it's taking so long to write about depression; it's the biggest challenge facing us. Depression is worldwide. It strikes all ages, men and women. Neither you nor anyone else has found the cure for depression, but you have some ideas about depression that you need to share. I know you have important contributions that depressed people will find helpful. You are retired, but unlike most retirees, you want to write about your lifelong interests. You are finding that writing is hard work. I admire you for sticking to it. I also like the idea of *healing*. That's why it's more demanding than you imagined."

Dottie stated her unsolicited opinion in a matter-of-fact-manner. I had not seen the forest. I was lost in the trees. Strangely, but plainly, her words of wisdom lifted a heavy burden from my shoulders. "Yes, that's it," I said to myself. I'm not writing to sell books about a fad or pop topic, and I don't have to enter my study thinking I'm a heroic figure who has discovered the cure for humanity's worst disease. I'm here to tell the stories of depressed people who found a reason for hope. Yes, that's it, but it is still hard work, and I have always known that good things require hard work. I like challenges. Her insight gave me new energy.

If there is a thread woven through my philosophy of how to live a flourishing life, it is the appreciation of the importance of fitness. Sensible regular exercise improves the brain; it even helps generate new brain cells to replace those that were damaged or destroyed by toxic depression. The mind and the human spirit are also powerfully influenced by fitness. This book is about the reasons I have come to believe the evidence supporting these truths.

University of Virginia's Mental Health Course

I taught Mental Health at the University of Virginia for four decades. I wanted my students to reflect on the ancient prayer for a healthy mind in a healthy body. I also wanted my students to experience the sense of well-being that I felt after a workout. It may surprise you, but I gave academic credit in this course for physical exercise. Later, I will discuss the Mental Health course in greater detail.

I had been athletic in high school and for a brief time in college. I let other things in my life crowd out the time I had previously earnestly devoted to exercise. My employment was sedentary— and inattention to what I ate had caused moderate obesity. Though these changes in my lifestyle were profound, they seemed to have occurred outside my awareness.

Fortunately, a wake-up call shocked my sensibility. As a medical student, I participated in the autopsies of three young men killed in a car crash. Their deaths were caused by closed head injuries, but what impressed me and my fellow students was the large amount of glistening yellow fat that lined their blood vessels.

Holding up the large aorta removed from the body of one of three young men killed in the accident, the pathologist said, "Look at the evidence of their unhealthy lifestyles. These fat deposits would have hardened over time, impaired their circulation, and a stroke or heart attack would soon have followed."

Suddenly, I understood just how irresponsible for my health and well-being I had become. In an ideal universal health system, every individual assumes responsibility for his or her health-enhancing behavior. My health-enhancing behavior had been irresponsible for a decade. It was almost too late: I was 32 years old, married with three children, and a second-year medical student with a fourth child on the way. Time was scarce.

Someone told me about a book entitled *Royal Canadian Airforce Exercise Plans for Physical Fitness.* The exercises it recommended required no equipment, little space, and not more than a few minutes of daily running in place, push-ups, prone leg lifts, sit-ups, and trunk bending. After several weeks of this manual-driven exercise, I rediscovered the sense of well-being I had not known since I was a physically fit high school athlete. I've tried to follow some form of regular daily exercise for the last 55 years.

The Influence of Exercise on My Career

I practiced psychiatry until I was 85. In all those years, I treated many depressed patients, but **I never treated a physically fit depressed person**. Intuitively, I knew there was an essential relationship between physical exercise and depression. The physical activity, I reasoned, must cause just as many positive changes in the brain as it does in the heart, and maybe more. It is a known fact that the left frontal lobe of many patients with major depression is less metabolically active, which is problematic given that this region of the brain contributes to logic and linear thinking. Fortunately, studies now show that there is a surge in brain activity in the left frontal cortex following aerobic exercise. The increased blood flow to the left frontal cortex is important because it may promote the growth of new blood vessels and bring along factors that provide resilience to the brain in the presence of stress.

The Cause of Depression

Despite several competing theories of depression, the actual cause of depression has not been fully elucidated. Rather, decades of research now reveal that biological, psychological, and environmental factors converge in those with a genetically vulnerable background to alter brain and mind activity and give rise to the symptoms of depression. Even more importantly, convergent evidence shows that regular physical exercise lowers the risk for depression (Schuch et al., 2018) and attenuates depressive symptoms by optimizing brain health. This startling discovery is found to be true across all geographical regions, for all ages, all races, and both genders. I hope those who read this book will join me in the enthusiasm and gratitude for the extraordinary evidence that virtually all depressed people can MOVE from despair to a joyful appreciation of a flourishing life.

Dr. Fred H. Gage

Dr. Fred Gage, President of the Salk Institute and Adler Chair for Research on Age-Related Neurodegenerative Disease in the Genetics Laboratory, demonstrated that exercise may relieve the depressed brain by inducing the release of brain-derived neurotropic factor

(BDNF), a protein in the brain that promotes the maturation, maintenance, and differentiation of neurons. Another key function of BDNF is the formation and maintenance of synapses, the actual site of communication between neurons. Significantly, evidence shows that physical exercise potently induces the release of BDNF from neurons in an activity-dependent manner, an effect that is vitally important for the production of synapses, neuronal health, and the birth of new neurons in key brain areas.

Unitl the 1960's, it was thought that the brain was static. According to that view, damaged neurons in the brain could not be repaired or replaced once they were injured. However, later work showed the static view of the brain was inaccurate. Rather, it is now known that brain is plastic, or changeable in an experience-dependent manner. One key way the brain changes throughout the lifetimes is by incorporation of new neurons into key brain circuits in a BDNF-dependent process called neurogenesis. Knowledge of neurogenesis suggests an avenue for the prevention and treatment of depression. Thankfully, exciting research in this area is ongoing. For now, let us reveal a snapshot of these findings that shows that regular exercise of moderate intensity promotes neuronal health in key areas of the brain affected by depression and, thereby, may help repair depression-injured brains.

Life Is Movement

What is it that all human life has in common? The answer is movement. Scientists refer to this phenomenon as *irritability*, not in the emotional sense, but motion in response to stimulation. Problematically, much of the movement in our life can be reflexive in nature. Conscious goal-directed movement, the kind that is uniquely human and that makes life worth living, takes far greater awareness and discipline. Failing to develop the awareness and discipline of our conscious movement invites physical and psychological illness.

More and more things are done to us or for us. For example, the recent epidemic of online shopping and next-day home delivery saves time, but to what end? History suggests that we save time in one area only to resume a frenetic pace in other areas of life. Speaking to this thoughtless way of life, Kierkegaard wrote:

> "Surrounded by hordes of people, busy with all sorts of secular matters, more and more shrewd about the ways of the world—such a person forgets himself, forgets his name divinely understood, does not dare to believe in himself, finds it too risky to be himself, far easier and safer to be like the others, to become a copy, a number, part of the crowd" (Kierkegaard, 1941).

Why might people enmesh themselves with all the secular distractions? According to Ernest Becker, in his 1973 book *The Denial of Death*, humans suffer from a debilitating anxiety when considering their own mortality. Drawing upon the prior works of Kierkegaard, Becker suggests that we tranquilize ourselves with the trivial to avoid having to deal with an awareness of our mortal nature (p. 81). While doing so, we quell our anxieties.

Because there is power in numbers, conforming to secular standards can be comfortable, until it isn't. At our lowest, tensions and crisis may prompt us to search for the greater meaning in life. Perhaps during those times, it is best to stop using distractions and confront our situation straight away.

> "This is the terror: to have emerged from nothing, to have a name, consciousness of self, deep inner feelings, and excruciating inner yearning for life and self-expression- and with all this yet to die. It seems like a hoax ... What kind of deity would create such complex and fancy worm food?" (p. 87, Becker, 1973).

Failing to consider our mortality places us at risk of blindly marching alongside our neighbors without ever asking what is in store for us should we keep to the current path, an unthinking pattern of behavior that may leave more casualties in its path than the American and French Revolutions.

Think about the morbidity and mortality associated with our Digital Revolution, one that dangerously seats us much of the day and night in front of computer and television screens, sanctuaries in which mindlessness carves us into unthinking, nonmoving forms. Then consider whether an awareness of our own mortality can help us to undertake our search for meaning, life-giving relationships, and health-protecting practices like regular physical activity. While contemplating these possibilities, lace up your exercise shoes while considering purposeful movement in the form of physical activity.

Mental Health and the Exercise Option

I taught Mental Health at the University Medical Center in the old Medical School Auditorium or the McLeod School of Nursing Auditorium for nearly four decades. I was a clinical professor of psychiatry as well as a professor of education, both adjunct professorships, and for most of that time I taught Mental Health.

I tried to promote the notion of purposeful movement and physical activity by presenting the exercise option in my Mental Health course. The exercise option appealed to the majority of the Mental Health enrollment. It is described in a chapter to follow. Suffice it here to say that it was *pledged* work. Each student kept an exercise journal, recording mood and exercise data. The goal was to get students into the habit of regularly exercising and also noticing the mood elevating effects of exercise.

Initially, the Mental Health course started with 14 students. Quickly, the enrollment increased to 800 scholars, too large at that time for any University of Virginia classroom. As a temporary solution, I rented the University Baptist Church to accommodate the large class, filling its sanctuary and balcony. Despite a favorable review by members of a faculty committee appointed to visit and evaluate each weekly lesson, the University restricted enrollment to 500 students, where it remained for nearly the next four decades. Students appreciated the dedicated time to invest in their health.

Equally appealing as the exercise option were the clinical case presentations. Patients came to class and shared their stories of how mental illness and treatment had affected their lives. Patients who were interviewed in Mental Health gave their fully informed consent before coming to the class to tell their story and answer students' questions.

Having patients share their stories proved fruitful for both patients and students.

What Students Learned

Large numbers of University students took Mental Health over many years. Chance meetings with former students provide a unique pleasure. I usually ask my former students, "After all these years, what do you remember most about our Mental Health class?" Without exception, the reply is the same: "I'll always remember your statement that you have never treated a physically fit depressed person." Often, they will add something more, such as, "Just the other day, I quoted you to one of my children who is under much stress in college. I told him or her to get back into exercise. It helps; it helped me."

I'm writing this preface after the book is mostly complete. I'm discovering just how much I am modeling the book after my University of Virginia Mental Health course and just how much I did the same with my psychiatric practice. As you read this text consider me your private tutor, a teacher who spent his life trying to reach people who want to renounce unhealthy lifestyles and enjoy health and fitness of their body, mind, and spirit, each of equal value to health.

The Never-Exercisers

If you never loved to exercise, please do not stop reading. You are one of the most important readers I want to reach.

In the beginning, no one loves to exercise. As you become fit, you will like how exercise makes you feel and look. I'm not encouraging you to run a marathon. I'm just urging you to walk your dog, work in your garden, or physically exert yourself just a little more, conscious of its necessity for your health.

A little exercise is better than none, but too much activity is irresponsible.

You *know* your capabilities. At this time, you may only have the strength to barely squeeze a tennis ball. Do what you can do. Keep a record of it and watch your strength and stamina surge.

After hesitating too long, I joined an exercise class for those my age. Rick Moore, a physical therapist, leads the exercise class. He laughs at my jokes, and the social component is a bonus. Within the context of group exercise, it's easy to remember that movement is life-affirming. I hope you too will find an arena to MOVE your depression and despair to real joy. No one can do it for you. Yet even those who cannot move independently can experience the joy of fitness with assistance. Passive movement of the limbs of the disabled by a trusted person can help, particularly when under the guidance of trained professionals in rehabilitative medicine.

Considering Daily Physical Activity

In the final analysis, is there a valid or legitimate excuse for a sedentary lifestyle, other than illness or impairment? Who can honestly say, knowing that daily physical exercise can prevent and successfully treat depression, "It's not for me?" Can a thoughtful person reject light or moderate activities, such as walking 30 minutes daily, five days a week? Regular physical exercise works wonders when it becomes a habit, particularly when it's something you do as regularly as brushing your teeth. It's worth the time and effort. Make it an essential part of your daily schedule.

For most of my adult life, I've exercised at noon; only the weather changed my place of exercise. During the hot Virginia summer months, I walked on a treadmill in an air-conditioned gym. In the cold of winter, I exercised indoors, but most of the time I walked briskly on a track at the University of Virginia, or similar locations if I was traveling.

Healing Depression by Degrees of Fitness

In this book, we will discover how you and others can heal depression gradually by improving physical, mental, and spiritual fitness. We begin our story with a personal account of one man's struggle against depression, a section that is followed by research that elucidates what happens in the depressed brain and how effective treatments can be used to mitigate those issues. Along the way, we will explore the stories of other people who have suffered with depression, and consider the various ways that they used to deal more or less so effectively with their illness. In doing so, we will come to recognize the symptoms of major depression, the mental disorder of clinical depression this book addresses throughout. While presenting each case, every reasonable effort was undertaken to protect each patients' identity. Later, we gradually build our understanding and knowledge about mental, spiritual, and physical fitness in the hopes that we can leverage that information and knowledge as we embark on our journey of attempting to lead a flourishing life.

Dr. Cristy Philips

I invited Dr. Cristy Philips, associate professor at Arkansas State University, a scholar and skilled physical therapist, to join me as co-author. The invitation was based solely upon her academic achievements and publications in the field of neuroscience, a field in which she has excelled. Dr. Fred Gage, a pioneer in brain neurogenesis, predicted in 2004 an increasingly important future role for physical therapists in the prevention and treatment of neurological and psychiatric disorders. Our collaboration, a psychiatrist and a physical therapist, seemed fitting for this project of providing encouragement and proven science ready for use in healing depression.

References

Becker, E. (1973). *The Denial of Death*. New York, NY: Free Press.

Brown, R., Synder, D.M., Peterson, D.W. (2002). *Textbook for Mental Health: A Narrative Approach*. Boston, MA: Pearson Publishing.

Gage, F. H. (2004). Structural plasticity of the adult brain. Dialogues CNeurosci, 6(2), 135-141.

Kierkegaard, S. (1941) *The Sickness Unto Death*. Princeton, NJ: Princeton University Press.

Royal Canadian Air Force. (1962). *Royal Canadian Airforce Exercise Plans for Physical Fitness*. New York, NY: Pocket Books.

Schuch, F. B., Vancampfort, D., Firth, J., Rosenbaum, S., Ward, P. B., Silva, E. S., . . . Stubbs, B. (2018). Physical activity and incident depression: a meta-analysis of prospective cohort studies. *Am J Psychiatry, 175*(7), 631-648.

CHAPTER 1

JOHN'S INTUITIVE TREATMENT OF DEPRESSION

John, a 50-year-old, divorced, senior business executive said, "Doctor, I'm very depressed." It was his first visit to a psychiatrist, something he had angrily resisted when his family doctor urgently recommended it. John refused to come for several months after antidepressant medications failed to help.

With graying, uncombed hair, a somewhat unkempt appearance, and a sad face, this man looked at least 10 to 15 years older than his age. It was hardly the appearance of a successful business executive. The trembling of both hands and voice worsened as he persistently stopped and restarted wringing his hands tightly together, all the time restlessly moving around in his chair.

"Things have not gone well for me socially or at work for the past year. To be honest, I think of myself as an utter failure, and I feel as if I have always been a failure. Right now, I don't count on my future being any better.

"I have no appetite for food or much of anything else. I can't concentrate. I think I'm losing it, Doc. I've lost my motivation to do anything. Everything seems like a big deal; more than I can handle. I fall asleep at night alright, but no matter what, I wake up in the middle of the night every night, and I can't go back to sleep.

"I believe I'm losing my memory. It scares the hell out of me, and I wonder if I'm getting Alzheimer's disease. The worst part of all this is my terrible anxiety. I stay extremely nervous. I can't stand it. I get up and pace."

Cloaked in shame, he spoke as if confessing, "I must pace six miles a day, or night; whatever you want to call it." Sounding thoroughly disgusted with himself, he was shouting his guilt!

The reference to pacing was the only encouraging thing he had said. "Pace 12 miles daily and you will feel better and sleep better," were my first spoken words to John. I modulated my tone trying to sound kindhearted, understanding, and not too harsh. That's not the way my new patient took what I said.

He was shocked by my recommendation to double his pacing, and he was annoyed by it.

"Doctor, I'm so desperate that I'm seriously considering taking my life, and you are joking with me."

Angrily, he shouted, "Damn it, what kind of doctor are you?"

"I have never been more serious," I said. "Intuitively, you are doing the right thing. We have nothing more robust for depression than regular physical exercise. You are doing the right thing, but you disregard its value. It is not wrong. Exercise is right for depression."

"You mean I was doing the right thing for depression and complaining about it?"

"You were making yourself feel bad about doing something that your intuition and I am telling you is the right thing to do.

"Yes," I continued. "Keep pacing, but let's see if we can rename it. I think you have associated pacing with something pejorative. I would call it brisk walking. Brisk walking is an important treatment for depression. Charles Dickens, one of the greatest authors of the Victorian era, was a prodigious walker. One night amidst nervous tensions in his London home, he decided to undertake a 30-mile trek to his home in Kent. Another literary giant, William Wordsworth, also shared a penchant for mulling over things in motion. Wordsworth, subject to severe episodes of depression beginning at 32, was walking with Dorothy, his sister, when he saw the golden daffodils dancing in the breeze, a sight he remembered for us with his 'inward eye.'

Silence and a form of reverence filled the space between John and me. He knew the poem. We could both see the daffodils, and suddenly we were in that 'vacant or pensive mood.' He was experiencing a particular closeness to

Wordsworth, previously unknown by him: Though separated by 200 years, they were bound together by depression. He was gently nodding his head in the affirmative, as if saying, "Yes, Wordsworth and we dealt with depression the best way we could."

Finally, he broke the silence which we both relished, with a question, "Doc, when I double my exercise, should I stop my antidepressant medication?" It was the first hint he gave me that he wanted to cooperate.

I detected a lilt in his voice, a sense of relief barely emerging now that he understood that he had followed his instinct to briskly walk and had learned that it was a good treatment for depression.

"No, continue your medication, and I will help you manage it. Antidepressant medication has a modest effect on depression. Combined with exercise, medication may be even more effective."

"Sit quietly with your eyes closed for 15 or 20 minutes after you exercise and stretch. It's a good time to meditate or pray. During that period of relaxation, breathe deeply and slowly, saying to yourself, "I am safe. I am healthy. I am happy, and I live with ease." [I learned this relaxation method from Rick Moore, my physical therapist in Charlottesville. Rick voluntarily leads a weekly exercise group. All of us in the group join together saying these four simple statements at the end of each class as we relax together. As a bonus, Rick walks around the group giving each of us a soothing neck massage. Maybe you have a friend who will provide a similar reward for you in the future.]

I continued, "I will review your medical records, and we can discuss them at your next session. What else will we need to review at your next meeting?"

John replied, "My exercise and meditation or prayer sessions will be on my agenda when I return. I see from the booklet you just gave me, *Lifestyle Accountability and Measures of Commitment to Health,* that you want me to exercise at least 150 minutes every week."

"Yes," I said. "That's a minimum, but you can start low and go slow. If you get tired or bored with brisk walking, there are many other exercises you can try. You can ride a stationary bicycle, play tennis, or swim. You name it. You choose the one most appealing to you, do it faithfully, and record it. Bring your record to each session, and we will review it."

"Doctor, I know I should probably pray every day."

The patient was quietly reflecting. I chose not to interrupt. With the facial expression of a man determined to 'start over' as he said, he expressed himself as follows: "You might have trouble believing this, because I do, but years ago I read scripture and prayed daily. I want to get back to that practice. I felt right with God. I know God is not pleased with me now."

"God loves you no more and no less now than when He breathed the breath of life into your nostrils," I said reassuringly. "Spiritual health is no less vital to your total fitness than exercise and sensible nutrition."

George Herbert, a 16th-century Church of England priest and insightful poet, put it plainly in his poem "The Pulley." God gives us everything but contentment. That's His end of the pulley; God pulls us toward him because He is the only source of meaningful, authentic peace.

"You are and have been listening, John. It encourages me to be very hopeful about you."

Dr. Herbert Benson, former Director and founder of the Institute for Mind Body Medicine, Harvard Medical School, author of *The Relaxation Response* (1975), made an interesting observation. While teaching heart patients to relax, some patients reported they prayed while relaxing. Patients of faith who prayed while relaxing experienced fewer complications than those who did not pray. Moreover, they enjoyed an earlier recovery from adverse coronary events than those that did not pray.

"John, you are a man of faith who understands and knows the value of prayer and relaxation. Had you not been a man of faith, would you understand why I'm assigning relaxation or specific quiet times?"

"I suspect it's another kind of treatment for my anxiety."

"I'm aware of nothing better for anxiety. Holy scriptures often describe ways to calm our nerves and tell us how to improve sleep. "In peace I will lie down and sleep, for you alone, Lord, make me dwell in safety" (Psalms 4:8 NIV). "Sleep in peace" may be interpreted to mean sleep without anxiety.

Another long period of silence followed. I cannot imagine what John was thinking, but if feelings and thoughts of hope are ever communicated by one's facial expression and general demeanor, they are what I observed. These are infrequent, precious, even sacred moments every counselor is privileged to share.

We both sat in a peaceful silence, neither of us wishing to abbreviate it.

I waited for a clue from John that he was ready to move on to the next topic. It came when he opened his eyes. I then asked the next question.

"Have you ever had racing thoughts or marked irritability for most of the day, nearly every day, for a week or longer?"

"No."

"Have you ever been told you talk too much, that you cannot be interrupted, or have you felt the need to keep talking no matter what?"

"No."

"Have you ever felt the decreased need for sleep, been on shopping sprees, or did things that had a great risk of harmful consequences?"

"Doc, why are you asking me questions like these? Before you answer, let me guess."

"Go right ahead. What do think I'm looking for in your answer to these questions?"

"Are you making sure I do not have a bipolar disorder?

"Yes, you are correct. How do you know?"

"I have a bipolar friend. I've seen him do just about everything you asked me. At first, it was fun to be with him, but after several months of his friendship, I found I wanted to avoid him because no one could convince him to stay on his medicine. When he took it, he was fine. He told me he prefers feeling 'high,' he called it, to the medication effects. He was a poor judge of the benefits of the medication."

Bipolar disorders will not be the subject of our attention in this book, except for noting that some people are mistakenly treated for depression only to learn later their condition is a bipolar disorder, a condition that requires a different approach.

After a comprehensive suicide-risk assessment, I judged John competent to give and withhold information about suicide and found him to be, at the time of evaluation, at low risk to harm himself or others. We worked out a safety plan, including how he could reach me any time his suicidal thoughts recurred.

He agreed to increase his brisk walking followed by a 15-minute post-exercise "quiet time," as he called it, and to return in three weeks. I preferred a sooner follow-up visit, but he was going to be "on the road." John's family physician assured me that his patient's general state of physical health permitted him to exercise as much and as often as he wished.

When John returned three weeks later, unlike at his initial session, he was relaxed and looked younger and healthier, more like a successful executive. His agitated depression had lost its discomforting sharp edges. He had not completely healed, but he had improved by significant degrees. He no longer referred to himself as a "failure" in the past, present, or future. He was making necessary lifestyle changes, all for the best.

John's Progress

We worked together for several months, gradually increasing the time intervals between sessions. John discovered the physical and mental health benefits of daily exercise. He also realized that his thoughts determined what he did and how he felt. He learned how to monitor his thoughts. John learned these lessons from cognitive therapy, explained more fully later. He successfully used thought records as described in Greenberger and Padesky's *Mind Over Mood: Change How You Feel by Changing the Way You Think.* He enjoyed reading, so I recommended Aaron Beck's *Cognitive Therapy of Depression*. He found Dr. Beck's book helpful. "It made more sense than other books about depression."

When I last heard from John and about him from his family physician, he had continued to do well. Dottie said, "I ran into John at Costco. He looked so much better. I did not recognize him and would have walked right past him had he not stopped me to say 'hello.'" His sustained progress encouraged me as I recalled what John was like when I first met him and learned about his wonderful *pacing*. It is just amazing how much better we can do when we start and continue to take care of ourselves. Knowing John's life is better makes me feel happy. It gives special meaning to my daily profession.

References

Beck, A.T., Rush, A.J., Shaw, B.E., Emergy, G. (1979). *Cognitive Therapy of Depression*. New York, NY: The Guilford Press.

Becker, E. (1973). *The Denial of Death*. New York, NY: Free Press.

Benson, H. (2001). *The Relaxation Response.* New York, NY: Harper Collins.

Greenberger, D., & Padesky, C. A. (2016). *Mind Over Mood: Change How You Feel by Changing the Way You Think (2nd ed.).* New York, NY: The Guilford Press.

Wall, J.N. (1981). *George Herbert: The Country Parson and the Temple.* Mahwah, NJ: Paulist Press.

CHAPTER 2

DISCLAIMING AND EXPLAINING

Education Versus Treatment

Healing Depression by Degrees of Fitness is intended for educational purposes, not for diagnosing or treating mental or physical disorders. Let me encourage you to seek professional help in your community when it is needed. If expert assistance is unavailable nearby, ask your family doctor for a referral. Please do not perceive that I am a substitute or replacement for your therapist. Let me be one of your teachers. The term "doctor" is derived from a Latin word that means "teacher." Sir William Osler said, "One of the first duties of a physician is to educate the masses not to take medicine." We will keep Sir Osler in mind, but we will judge for ourselves.

Listed at the end of this chapter are several helpful referral agencies available to assist those seeking professional treatment for depression.

Learning

Learning is a change in behavior as a result of experience. I want to help you learn about depression so you can eventually control your behavior in ways that help conquer it.

Instead of attempting to treat you, a person I have not been privileged to know, which is an unethical practice, I want to teach you what I learned about depression. I also want to help you learn how to understand and master anxiety. Anxiety is closely related to depression. Some clinicians say that anxiety and depression are "first cousins." Dr. Aaron Beck, the founder of cognitive behavioral therapy (CBT), provides us with the best statement about anxiety. Dr. Beck said that anxiety is the result of overestimating danger and underestimating your ability to cope with it (Clark & Beck, 2010).

Armed with the benefits of knowledge of depression and anxiety, you may learn how some patients described in this book heal naturally. Your contribution to healing may be unrecognized, but it is enormous, and that is what this text is about.

Principles of Living a Flourishing Life

Begin now asking yourself, "How can I help myself heal from depression, and how can I protect myself from experiencing another one of its episodes?" Keep these questions in mind as you read how other depressed people found these principles helpful when they applied them to their troubled lives. There are three pure, but critical, principles. I will list them here and explain them in the remaining chapters.

1. Some daily physical activity is essential.
2. Learn to identify and correct the errors in your thoughts.
3. Humbly and reverently regard yourself as made in the image and likeness of God and behave accordingly.

We Already Have What We Need

Do you remember the Tin Man in the *Wizard of OZ*? It is still a most enjoyable 1939 hit. The Tin Man asked the Wizard for a heart. This scene caught the attention of song writers. Meaningful to me is America's 1974 version of "Tin Man," in which a particular lyric from the song is relevant background humming music for the beginning of our journey of learning to heal:

> "But Oz never did give nothing to the Tin Man
> Nothing he didn't, didn't already have."

I lack suitable qualifications to interpret the remainder of the lyrics of this song; it's the two lines quoted above that most appeal to me. I find them encouraging. The composer is saying we already have within us most of what we need to solve problems. He assumes we have the components of success within us, but we do not recognize our potential, and we give up. I believe he also thinks we have the right conditions around us, enabling success.

Remembering the Pleasant From the Past

Watching the *Wizard of Oz* brings back pleasant childhood memories to me. I first saw it as a child, then with my children, and later with my grandchildren. My wife frequently uses an amended form of one of its lines, referring to me after I've said something preposterous: "Pay no attention to that man behind the screen!"

If you have pleasant associations with children's movies or books, by all means, find copies and get back into them. I'm serious. Depression blocks out pleasant memories. Depression marches sad, despairing memories alongside regretful images across our screen of awareness, a capacity that is painfully unique to the condition and difficult to remove—until you revisit a place fondly remembered from childhood or see old movies you once loved as a kid.

When you recall a past pleasant memory, write it in a private journal. Let me encourage you to keep a written record of our journey. Lewis and Clark kept such journals as they bravely crossed the unexplored West, a trip like ours, requiring both courage and records. In-so-far as possible, briefly describe facts as you observe them on your journey.

David wrote in the Old Testament Book of Psalms (139:14 NIV), written approximately 1000 years before the birth of Jesus, "I praise you because I am fearfully and wonderfully made." Does the lyric selected above from "Tin Man" convey the same thing? Are we created with all we need to succeed under the right circumstances? I believe we are cognitively, physically, and spiritually matchlessly endowed with the capacity to flourish. These endowments come with requirements to develop our gifts by discipline, integrity, and unwavering faith.

The Human Body as the "Temple of the Holy Spirit"

Too many Christians are openly defiant to strong statements in the Holy Bible that their God emphasizes the fitness of the human body. Christians who are not working on improving their physical fitness are ignoring the importance of the human body and the Holy Spirit. For example, Saint Paul wrote frankly on this too frequently overlooked but important subject: "Do you not know that your bodies are temples of the Holy Spirit, who is in you, whom you have received from God? You are not your own; you were bought at a price. Therefore, honor God with your bodies" (1 Corinthians 6:19-20 NIV).

So, must we maintain our bodily temples to find and maintain favor with God? The prophet Micah answered the question of how we are to please God: "He has showed you, O mortal, what is good. And what does the Lord require of you? To act justly, and to love mercy and to walk humbly with your God" (Micah 6:8 NIV). In simple summary, the only requirement that God has for us is to trust, obey, and live in faith.

While humbly walking with God, we depend upon our understanding of scripture to strive for physical and spiritual fitness, all the while realizing that following God's word does not ensure that hard times will never come, a crippling notion insinuated in the ancient expression that "God helps those who help themselves." Rather, scripture tells us that Jesus died for us while we were still sinners. Jesus helped us when we could not help ourselves, the very definition of grace. He helped us because we were his chosen treasure.

Thus, we say no to worldly passions and live self-controlled upright lives in the present age because to do so is virtuous (Titus 2: 11-12 NIV). We choose to obey his commandments and respect our bodies because we trust God's good intent for our life and want to keep His commandments (John 14: 15-21 NIV). Espousing a similar notion in Ancient Greece, Hippolytus (428 B.C.) reminded us "Try first thyself, and after call in God; For the worker God himself lends aid."

Death and Depression

Perhaps you are too depressed at this time to concentrate on reading about depression, a natural state for severe depression. Worse, you may be too depressed to want to do anything, including taking up the work to get well. Everything may seem overwhelming, magnifying your state of extreme anxiety and unrest. The anxiety associated with depression is exceptionally all-encompassing. It is the first consideration in every decision. Silently you think, "Where to go, what to do, what to eat? If it increases my anxiety, I must avoid it. I hate change."

If anxiety results from overestimating danger, then depression occurs from emphasizing the negative. In 1944, a favorite song by Bing Crosby and The Andrews Sisters offered sound advice on this topic. It went like this: "You've got to accentuate the positive, eliminate the negative, latch on to the affirmative, don't mess with Mister In-between. You've got to spread joy up to the maximum, bring gloom down to the minimum, have faith or pandemonium, liable to walk upon the scene."

"Don't mess with Mister In-Between" nearly perfectly describes ambivalence. When ambivalence is extreme, so commonly the case in depression, it is a miserable state to experience.

Misunderstood Depression

Those around you who are unfamiliar with depression may think you are "lazy." They will accuse you of chronic procrastination. You may wonder if you "lack character because you don't try." This kind of thinking piles guilt on your fragile frame. You may feel this way yourself although it may not be said aloud.

After a while, you may believe your critics or your negative thoughts and start hating yourself. Misinformed by misinformation and by misinformers, your psychological pain mounts. This pain has been called "the pain of pain." It is exhausting to bear. The search for relief becomes all-consuming for some, overriding reason and sound judgment. Amidst the unremitting pain a person may contemplate suicide. People in such a desperate state do not want to die. They still love their loved ones. They only want to stop the excruciating pain. Every family who loses a loved one to suicide needs to hear this message.

These thoughts are critical for families trying to heal from the incomparable emotional pangs of grief caused by the suicide of a family member.

Eventually, they may get used to it, but the family never gets over it.

In my role as a forensic psychiatrist, I studied suicide notes. Nearly without exception, suicide notes written before people end their life reveal just how irrationally their mind was functioning at the fatal moment. The notes are laced with tones of isolation, anger, self-blame, and hopelessness. The contemplator believes they do not belong and views suicide as a mercy act to end suffering. As a result, suicide notes often convey more concern about personal psychological pain and less about the effect on others. While these notes may acknowledge the hurt to family, the contemplator counters this knowledge with the rationalization that he or she was a burden and that the inflicted pain will cancel out over time. Consequently, a person in this mental state contemplates hiring their own firing squad to execute an innocent critically ill person, a grim and sad set of circumstances for all who have suffered through this situation with a cherished family member.

I do not wish to overly burden you with facts and theories about suicide, but the relationship between death and depression is significant because most people who commit suicide are deeply depressed. I bring up this fact early and openly to alert you to the potential gravity of depression.

Of course, not all depressed people commit suicide. Suicide is the 20th most common form of death around the globe, making it a relatively rare event. The average number of deaths by suicide for all ages in the U.S. each year is about 13 per 100,000 people, with older men accounting for considerably more suicide deaths than older women, or an estimated suicide rate of 50 per 100,000 in those who are 75 years or older. Established risk factors for suicide include significant suicidal ideation, prior suicide attempt, severity of depression, substance abuse, recent stressful life events, functional impairment, and physical illness.

For young adults, suicide is the second leading cause of death, second only to automobile accidents. Studies show that young adults with severe depressive symptoms, a personal or parental history of suicide attempts, and childhood abuse were relative factors for increased risk. Other known factors include access to firearms, bullying, and acute social rejection.

As a behavioral health scientist, I say we are not yet able to prevent suicide, but we can assess the different types and degrees of suicidal ideation while assessing risk for suicide. Later, we will return to this vital subject.

How to Read This Book to Enhance the Healing of Depression

Some people are too depressed to read *Healing Depression by Degrees of Fitness*. Trouble concentrating, a common symptom of depression, makes the book difficult to understand. In fact, the mind of a depressed person may become so severely cognitively impaired that it can be confused with that of a demented person. If this sounds disheartening, I hope it motivates you to promise yourself that you will try earnestly to learn how to master your depression in part by becoming patient with yourself during the challenging process.

In medical jargon, a "pearl" is a helpful fact to keep in mind. Pearls come from centuries of medical experience. Two pearls come to mind. The good news about depression is that it will improve and go away on its own, even without treatment. The bad news about depression is that it will return when not treated adequately. Keep your sense of hope alive. Hope motivates change. The remainder of this book provides confidence and knowledge-building facts to help you heal from depression, find a sense of security and lead a flourishing life.

There are several ways for you to effectively access this book. If it is just too much for you to read and understand, consider having someone slowly read the material aloud to you and patiently answer your questions. Alternatively, you can read this book, if necessary, just a little at a time. Finally, you can listen to the audible version of *Healing Depression by Degrees of Fitness* at your own pace and as often as desired. Get used to the idea of "by degrees." I want you to apply the concept to your cognition, self-regulation of mood, and as a way of learning to return to a fully functioning life. Along the way, remember each day to feel and think like King David of the Old Testament who said, "This is the day the Lord has made; we will rejoice and be glad in it" (Psalm 118:24 NIV).

Two Important Questions About Depression

If you are depressed, then you are the person I'm trying to reach. If you accept the fact that depression is your diagnosis, two questions require answers. How did you learn you are depressed? What caused your depression? Often, for complicated reasons, these questions are puzzling and not quickly answered.

No one wants to be depressed. The stigma of a mental disorder causes irrational shame, disgrace, and humiliation. Many consider depression a moral weakness, a failure of character, or worse. Too many of us, even patients anguished with depression, view depression today just as we understood alcoholism seven decades ago: "If they just tried harder, they would not be down like this." There is a place for trying harder in every condition, but effort alone is seldom, if ever, the answer to depression.

Another pearl comes to mind as we try to understand depression: "A person who is depressed may be the last one to know it." Six years ago, I needed a new aortic valve, an essential part of the heart through which it pumps blood to the body. The procedure required open-heart surgery. Thankfully, the operation was successful, and there appeared to be no obvious complications.

Once home, I slowly recovered. While I had no physical discomfort or pain after the surgery, things changed. I was anxious, jumpy, perplexed, cranky, needy, and entirely self-possessed. Nothing tasted good. I accused my wife of changing brands of food I once enjoyed. Her shopping habits, however, remained unchanged. "I can't stand this new brand of orange juice you are now buying," I had said grouchily. "It's the same Simply Orange I've bought for years," Dottie had replied. I have to shop for it early because the University students buy it up fast." I had remained unconvinced. I drank and ate only because I knew I should, but still lost 20 pounds. Nothing else seemed to interest me. Previously entertaining television shows lost their appeal. I delayed following my surgeon's advice to start cardiac rehab. I slept poorly.

"Dad," said Bob, Jr., my oldest son, also a physician, "I think you would feel better on a low dose of an antidepressant; enough to help you over this dip in mood." I tried to disguise it, but I was offended. Depression is the subject of my scholarly interests, I've treated hundreds of depressed patients, and I'm a psychiatrist. How could I be depressed? I wondered why my son would think that I was depressed. I was not crying or unduly discouraged.

Physicians are generally bad patients; I was no exception. In retrospect, I denied that I was depressed, too proud to fall victim to such an awful disease. Now I understand what my son saw. My sleep, appetite, interests, energy, and sense of well-being were no longer typical of me. The weight loss alone was loudly signaling a problem. I refused medication. I muddled through it with the help of my wife, children, and friends, started cardiac rehab, and fully recovered, but it took three months before I was able to return to work, not three weeks as my surgeon had predicted.

Knowing You Are Depressed

In the case described above, I did not *know* that I was depressed and no convincing from anyone was going to change my mind. After all, how could a psychiatrist, I foolishly asked myself, become depressed? This mental mechanism, which I was consciously unaware at the time, protected me. Denial was merciful in this situation because it allowed me to focus my attention and energy on getting back my physical health. Admittedly, I was afraid at some level that I was depressed, but I did not want to confront the facts. Thankfully, not all denial is harmful.

I believe I would have felt profoundly demoralized if I knew and acknowledged that I also suffered from major depression. Notwithstanding, my refusal to acknowledge depression meant that I refused medication. Recovery took longer, but I was in a position to spare the time, and it precisely followed the course of my participation in cardiac rehab, a combination of exercise and social interaction with fellow patients having the same or similar health issues. As I look back and write about it, I must confess that I was depressed.

It can be baffling to find a simple definition of depression, one that helps a person decide if he or she is depressed because depression involves an array of symptoms. Yet uncertainty is not always the case. All involved parties may agree on the diagnosis in the case of severe depression. Hamlet, acutely grieved over his father's murder, was emotionally paralyzed by ambivalence. As a result, he suffered from chronic indecision and uttered one of the clearest descriptions of depression:

> "I have of late— but wherefore I know not — lost all my mirth, forgone all custom of exercises; and indeed, it goes so heavily with my disposition that this goodly frame, the earth, seems to me a sterile promontory; this most excellent canopy, the air, look you, this brave o'erhanging firmament, this majestical roof fretted with golden fire— Why, it appeareth nothing to me but a foul and

pestilent congregation of vapors. What a piece of work is a man! How noble in his reason, how infinite in faculty! In form and moving how express and admirable! In action how like an angel, in apprehension how like a god! The beauty of the world. The paragon of animals. And yet, to me, what is this quintessence of dust? Man delights not me. No, nor woman neither…"

It is clear, as Hamlet continues in his soliloquy, that neither the world nor human beings, "this quintessence of dust," have any meaning for him. His life is devoid of meaning.

It is hard to imagine a depressed person who is mirthful, exercising, or leading an exciting life. Note that Hamlet's depression robbed him not only of mirth, but also it made him wholly ambivalent, a person no longer with the strength of mind to make decisions.

Other definitions and diagnostic criteria for depression will be delineated as we proceed.

Referral Resources

Ordinarily, it is useful from the beginning to discuss the treatment of depression with your primary care physician and your minister, priest, or rabbi. Other referral resources include your local mental health association, county medical society, health department, or university medical center.

The Beck Institute, located in Philadelphia, PA (or you may connect with them online at http://www.beckinstitute.org) maintains a current list of names and addresses of professionals qualified to treat patients with CBT.

References

Clark, D.A., & Beck, A.T. (2010). *Cognitive Therapy of Anxiety Disorders, Science and Practice*. New York, NY: Guilford Press.

CHAPTER 3

PERSONAL IDENTITY AND DEPRESSION

Achieving a Sense of Identity

In this chapter we discuss how the psychological birth of the infant is accomplished and how the infant develops the sense of his or her self as a fully individualized person. It is about how you were given a name and how you were given an identity. This chapter is relevant to our topic of healing depression because depression uniquely disturbs one's identity. Repairing or recovering identity is part of the healing process in depression. As described below, the first sense of our self as a person is the sense of our body. Physical activity that gradually achieves physical fitness is one of the ways to strengthen identity.

Psychological birth is no less real than biological birth, and it normally takes about three times as long as gestation, the period from conception to birth. We also examine in this chapter how the mind matures, and how the mind and body interact to achieve a flourishing life. Spiritual birth and development are reviewed later.

We view this chapter as being particularly important to those who are depressed and to those whose loved ones are depressed. It is about how you acquired your identity as a person and how you must maintain it, never forgetting who you are. Depression infamously hacks your identity, engulfing your sense of self. As one of my respected friends said, "Depression is a great liar. It will lie to you about your past, present, and future. Its biggest lie is about who you are as a person."

John Locke

We introduce this chapter with John Locke, 1632-1704, an English physician and philosopher who was educated at Oxford University. His writings influenced the Age of Reason, the term applied to the 18th century, and contributed to an entirely new view of the rights of humanity. It is said that his simple concept of the tabula rasa, or the position that at birth the mind is a "blank slate," led to both the American and French Revolutions.

Locke rejected the universally accepted Divine Right of Kings by arguing that it was supported neither by scripture nor reason. He believed that all humans have absolute natural rights. He emphasized the role of experience, holding that at birth everyone is born with a blank slate and that what is written on that slate by experience will determine what that individual will become. The old idea that kings begat kings and common folk begat common folk was turned on its head.

Great Britain and several other nations continue to accept a constitutional monarchy with parliaments that are elected by the people and a prime minister that is appointed by the monarch. For most of western civilization, however, those who govern serve entirely at the pleasure of those governed, a practice that can be traced to Locke.

I find it interesting that psychological theory and practice in the 21st century, if understood in the broadest sense, adhere to Locke's tabula rasa concept. It is appreciated, of course, that no child is born with an entirely blank slate, but comes into the world with genetically influenced materials. What the infant experiences from its first breath and its interaction with its mother in the first three years or so will significantly influences its life trajectory.

Your Sense of Self

The first sense of one's self is the sense of one's body.

The good mother, attentive to her infant's needs, lovingly caresses her infant's body. The integument, or covering of the body, is comprised of skin, hair, and nails. It is the largest organ of the human body. Embedded in the skin and its underlying muscles are nerve endings transmitting to the brain important messages in response to being held and touched. Growth hormone is released by the infant's brain, for example, when the mother holds the infant in her arms, singing to and talking to the child, communicating warmth and acceptance, positively nurturing the infant. Truly, it is a kind of romantic relationship that may be replicated over and over into and through adulthood.

Tragically, many orphans of World War II were fed and their physical needs met, but they were seldom picked up and held or touched by a mothering person. Without stimulation by a mothering person, they remained infantile at six years of age, forming deep, permanent impressions in the tiny mattresses upon which they enduringly rested, unable to walk.

The mother or mothering person (the person consistently occupying the mothering role) to the infant can be described as the *master sculptor*. Through meeting the infant's needs for nurture, protection, survival, and chiefly for compassion, the mother loves the infant into a person who is eventually separate and apart from her, a unique individual.

Melanie Klein (1882-1960) and Anna Freud (1895-1982), Sigmund Freud's daughter, are considered the founders of psychoanalytic child psychology. Strongly influenced by Sigmund Freud (1856-1939), the father of psychoanalysis, they analyzed and interpreted the child's play in much the same way that Sigmund Freud interpreted an adult's dreams (Freud, 1900). We are indebted to these two women, and to Margaret Mahler, for our understanding of how children form healthy personalities beginning in the very earliest stages of life.

Psychological Birth

Margaret Mahler (1897-1985) observed that infants appeared to be in a twilight state during the first few weeks of life. She was strongly influenced by Sigmund Freud's statement that the very close early relationship between the mother and infant may form the foundation upon which all future relationships depend. Mahler later characterized this stage of development as normal symbiosis in which the mother and infant function as one psychological unit.

Mahler and her colleagues diligently focused on normal early childhood development and formulated object relations theory, a rational explanation of how an infant normally matures into early childhood. In 1975, Mahler published *The Psychological Birth of the Human Infant: Separation and Individuation*. In object relations theory, the object is a specific person. Accordingly, an infant is objectless at birth, bringing to mind John Locke's "tabula rasa," or the blank slate description of the mind. This stage lasts about five months. In object relations theory, the infant as an intrinsic part of the mother, without a separation between them.

The Smile of Recognition

The normal autism stage of the psychological birth of the infant is followed by normal symbiosis, during which the mother and infant are psychologically inseparable. This stage lasts until the infant is about five months old. "Crucial to the successful progression through the next stages are the availability and the ability of the mother to adapt successfully to the infant's needs." The symbiotic phase ends when the infant emits, primarily through its eyes, what Mahler refers to as the "smile of recognition," essentially acknowledging that the mother is first recognized as an individual, no longer an extension or part of the infant. Ideally, no one else must replace the mother during this critical phase of object constancy.

Separation and individuation are the final phases of psychological birth according to Mahler. Both these stages have sub-stages, but for our purposes it is enough to summarize the principal stages. During the separation phase of psychological birth, the infant realistically learns boundaries and discovers the mother as a separate entity, apart from himself or herself, and no longer always available. Melanie Klein said that the infant's first awareness of reality occurs when he or she distinguishes between the "good breast," the one always present, and the "bad breast," the one not present when the infant is hungry.

Object Constancy

During the separation and individuation phases, the infant develops an internalized mental model of the mother, which unconsciously supports the child during physical separation. This substage, referred to as object constancy, is similar to Jean Piaget's term *object permanence*, progresses. During this stage, the infant internalizes a mental image of the mother. The internalized mental image of the mother "provides the child with an image that helps supply an unconscious level of guiding comfort from their mothers."

The chief and most desirable goal of the separation and individuation phases, thought to last from five to twenty-four months of age, is the derivation of a meaningful mental representation of the mother that can be activated to reduce stress when the mother is not physically present. The internalized mental image of the mother becomes a template or model and a scaffold that may influence all future relationships.

The two extreme undesirable outcomes of separation and individuation are learned: fear of abandonment and enmeshment or overdependence. The failure to maintain a healthy sense of identity in adulthood may result from disturbances in the separation and individuation phases of psychological birth. Based on my experience of treating people who are depressed, their disturbed sense of identity may often have its origin in a terrible childhood. Thus, during therapy I was often perceived as a mothering person.

Internalization of Traumatic Images

When I treated soldiers and Marines who were severely traumatized during combat in our war against terrorism (2005-2016), I observed that many of these patients successfully formed mental images of me that were reported as helpful. Some of these patients said that they often "heard" my voice or experienced images of my presence that were reassuring. Not infrequently, some of these patients would call me on the phone to say, "Sir, I just needed to hear your voice. Thank you. I'm okay now." These patients had internalized a mental image of me that proved helpful.

Internalization of important mental images must be a lifelong process, refined with maturity. In posttraumatic stress disorders, for example, upsetting trauma images are often internalized and resistant to change. The challenge for the therapist in these cases is to help the patient uncover the meaning of the internalized traumatic mental images. The meaning of these mental images to the patient must be accurately determined. The uncovering procedure is successful when the therapist is perceived as consistently trustworthy, competent, and caring. Succinctly stated, the successful therapist is one who is described as a "good enough" mothering person. The patient's inaccurate meanings drive the persistently disturbing internalized trauma images, keeping them resistant to change. Often, it is a combination of depression, irrational guilt, and pathological grief that both distort the true meaning of the internalized trauma images and contribute to their cause.

Individuation Through the Lifespan

In my opinion, the individuation process follows an ongoing, lifelong course. It is influenced by education, religious institutions, marriage, military experience, combat experience, trauma experience, and a host of other powerful factors.

Furthermore, every romantic relationship is influenced by the infant's first relationship and replicates it. As an adult, for example, nearly endless numbers of people encounter others without a romantic impact. Then there is the smile of recognition that ushers in a new relationship. You and your new relationship function as one symbiotic unit. There is even "baby talk" by adults falling in love within the symbiotic entity during this phase of the relationship; and frequent, nearly constant, communication is essential. Gradually, there is a separation and individuation stage of the relationship. If the relationship lasts, it is because the couple survives this phase and can truly love each other on the most mature level. Based on a cursory review of relationship types described on Facebook entries, few relationships successfully survive the separation and individuation phase today.

Natalie

When I was a first-year psychiatric resident at the University of Virginia, the chief nurse informed me that a newly admitted patient was being assigned to me. I had to interview the patient, conduct a physical examination, order indicated laboratory tests, make a diagnosis based on my findings and available medical records, and present her case to the attending psychiatrist the next morning. This clinical case goes back more than five decades, but I remember it as if it were yesterday.

Natalie's depression was so severe that it met the diagnostic criteria for major depression with psychotic features. She had formerly won beauty contests in the community and had recently married a man who wanted to understand her depression but had helplessly grown impatient with it.

Her family was warm and supportive. She was close to her father, who visited often and stayed as long as visiting hours permitted. Tears flowed down her face when Natalie told me her father was "dead." I replied, "Natalie, your father is standing outside your door now. I do not believe he is dead. How can you say that he is dead?"

Natalie's piercing gaze into my eyes communicated to me that her father, as an important internalized object, was actually dead to her. She had regressed to an objectless state. It must have been a terrible living nightmare for Natalie. While she knew cognitively that her father was alive and standing less than 10 feet away, in her miserable state of depression he was dead. She was losing her sense of identity.

Thankfully, her depression was successfully treated during her month-long hospitalization, her sense of identity was fully restored, and she recovered from that depressive episode. Other episodes of depression followed for which she was treated by other therapists.

Skip

Skip's mother sought information about her son, three-and-a-half years of age. "He was premature at birth and is a little behind on the normal growth curve chart for his age," she said. "He is our only child. Both my husband and I are employed. Skip spends the day in a preschool daycare center. We thought he was doing well until his teacher called and demanded that my husband or I come to school and take him home because was behaving defiantly ... he would not return to the school building after recess. The teacher said that Skip was kicking, crying, and would not obey her."

"Have there been any recent changes in Skip's life?" I asked.

His mother said, "Skip was born during the month of September, so he is either the biggest child in his class or the smallest child in the next higher-class level. I thought he was bored in the lower or younger class. I asked his teachers to move him up to the next level."

I asked what Skip had been told about the new class he was going to.

"I'm afraid that I made the new class sound like it was better than the class he was attending."

I asked how Skip replied to learning he was being moved to another class.

"At first, Skip seemed excited about the move, but I told him about it in January and the change did not occur until three months later. For a long time, his teacher did not respond to my request. As I think about it now, Skip had probably forgotten about the move. When the move was finally made, it may have come as a surprise."

"What changes in Skip's behavior did you first observe?" I asked.

"He was just recently moved to the upper level. We had been letting his hair grow until one day he came home from the upper level and said, 'I want a big boy's haircut.' He also said, 'The other children will not play with me.' Also, Skip started getting out of his bed in the middle of the night and coming to our room and trying to get into bed with us. We take him back to his bed, reassure him, and he seems okay after that. I am very concerned about Skip. What should my husband and I do?"

"What do you want to do?" I asked.

"I want my son to be happy, but I don't know what to do," she replied.

"Let me see if I can help you understand what is happening to Skip. First, his situation is a common one and does not suggest to me that he has a major psychiatric illness. Do you agree with me?"

"Yes."

"Skip, as you said, was premature at birth. It takes a preemie a little longer to develop physically and emotionally. Your son is not expected to have verbal skills that are sufficiently developed to communicate his thoughts and feelings," I said.

"He is showing you and his teachers that he is unhappy with the recent changes in his life. It is like a pantomime. Yet some of his verbal skills are rather remarkable for his age. With no uncertainty, Skip told you he wanted to have a haircut. He wanted to look like the other 'big boys' in his class.

"In situations like this one, our job as parents and teachers is to help Skip know that he is connecting with us and that we are understanding him. We can connect with Skip by telling him we know that his change to a new class at school is not easy. Change can be difficult for anyone. We may understand that several recent events are causing Skip to feel angry, disappointed, and even rejected. It is unlikely that Skip understands the causal relationship between changes in school and his feelings.

"When we validate Skip's feelings with him, it is ordinarily best to approach the topic in a nonjudgmental manner, framing it in the form of an inquiry. If you agree with me, perhaps we can role-play this approach. I will assume the role of Skip. You nodded to me your willingness to role-play. You just assume your role as mother, keeping mind that we are simply practicing a way to assist Skip to identify his thoughts and feelings by using a Socratic or inquiry method."

Role-Playing

Skip: "I want a big boy's haircut."

Mother: "Your dad took you to the barber shop a week ago and the barber cut your hair, Skip. It still looks good to me. Why do you want another haircut so soon?"

Skip: "I thought it would make the other kids play with me. They still don't want to play with me."

Mother: "Does it make you feel sad when they won't play with you?"

Skip: "Yes, but when we go outside for recess, sometimes they let me play with them and sometimes they won't."

Mother: "Does it make you happy when the other children let you play with them?"

Skip: "Yes."

Mother: "Is that why you like to play outside?"

Skip: "Yes."

Mother: "Is that why you don't like to come inside when the teacher wants all the children to come back inside the school building after recess?

Skip: "Yes."

Mother: "Skip, do you miss the children in the class you left?"

Skip: "Yes."

Mother: "Do you want to go back to the class where you had friends, Skip?"

Skip: "I don't know."

Mother: "Shall I ask your teacher to put you back in the class you left?"

Skip: "No."

The Role-Playing Stopped

"After role-playing, do you see how to approach the issues troubling Skip?" I asked.

"Yes," said Skip's mother, "but I am still confused. Why did Skip say he did not want to go back to his friendlier class?"

"I sense strength in this little boy with 'a big boy's haircut.' Skip knows that you understand what is happening to him. This is helpful. He is still in the process of what child psychoanalysts call the very early phase of the 'individuation stage' of psychological birth. I believe he's going to work through this temporary detour."

"You said that Skip's dad drops him off at school each morning and you pick him up at the end of the day. How long is Skip's day at the daycare center?"

"Twelve hours. The children take a two-hour nap in the middle of the day," replied his mother.

"That's a long day for a three-and-a-half-year-old, but he enters school without clinging or tears and he is happy, you said, when you pick him up at the end of the day?"

"Yes," said Skip's mother.

"You told me that several months ago Skip said, 'Jesus loves me.' Does religion play an important role in family?"

"I am sorry that religion has not been important to us as a family ... not for the past few years. My husband and I are employed full-time. We are exhausted by the weekends and we need to rest. I am a Christian and was baptized as a child. My mother was raised in a Christian home, and my grandparents are people of faith. I smiled when Skip said that Jesus loves him, but I was surprised and I have no idea where he got that."

"Do you believe it would be important to find a church with good Sunday school teachers for your family?"

"Yes."

I replied, "I believe it may be helpful for your family."

I concluded the session with several recommendations for Skip's mother.

"First," I said, "I believe you and Skip's dad are doing the right thing by taking Skip back to his bed when he tries to crawl into your bed in the middle of the night; reassurance is very helpful when that occurs. Skip is undergoing a lot of stress. Like all children, his development is uneven, but it must proceed at its own pace. You can't push a river faster than it wants to flow."

"Second, I want to see Skip with you next week. Please have him bring a favorite toy. By the way, would Skip's dad be willing to go into his school each morning and stay there for a few minutes as an interested parent?"

Skip's mother said, "I know his dad will accompany Skip into his class every morning, if you think it may help him."

"Good," I said. "The boy with a little boy's haircut temporarily needs a show of force and strength, a firmer individual identification. If the daycare center would not object, the presence of Skip's dad, even if he was there no longer than a few minutes as an observer, may prove helpful to the youngster's developing sense of his self as a person."

Skip's is an ongoing clinical case that is now managed by another professional; thus, his long-term follow-up is unavailable, but I believe his prognosis is favorable. I made a phone call check-up several days after my consultation with his mother, and I learned from her: "Skip is complaining less about school. His grandmother gave him books suitable for his age on how dinosaurs get angry and how they manage it successfully. His dad is taking him into class and staying awhile, and we are picking him up together at the end of the day. One day, Skip had dirt on his face. When we asked about him the about the dirt, he said another boy was picking on him. We don't know if we should report this to the teacher."

Being picked on, now called "bullying," is a significant problem in all grades, apparently even for three-year-old children. Bullying is not our primary topic in Healing Depression by Degrees of Fitness, but it must not be swept aside hastily. In Skip's case, I urged his parents to report the bullying immediately to the daycare/school authorities.

The "Good-Enough Mother"

Donald Winnicott (1896-1971) was a British pediatrician and psychoanalyst who contributed significantly to the object relations theory of psychological birth. He introduced the important concept in 1953 of the *good enough mother*. Winnicott said that the mother need not be perfect. "Babies and children actually benefit when their mothers fail them in manageable ways." He is not endorsing neglect or abuse, but merely advocating for children's need to learn on their own when they are ready to learn by managing challenges. Infants require the mother's full attention during their first months of life, but as they mature physically and are capable of waiting and of resolving manageable challenges, their earliest steps toward identity are achieved.

Good-Enough Parents and Teachers

Thus far, we have been concentrating on psychological birth, a process that Margaret Mahler called "hatching." The concept of the *good-enough mother* applies equally well to parents and teachers as the child continues to develop. A good enough teacher, for example, sees and knows what is going on in class but chooses not to comment on it. Perhaps the greatest teacher is failure. I believe failure has taught me much more than success. More precisely, learning how to optimally respond to failure is the biggest lesson to be learned.

The Toolbox Is in the Woodshed

My childhood spanned the 1930s and 1940s, a period defined by the Great Depression and World War II. Like many around us, we were poor. Looking back, my sister Edith would say, "We were poor but proud." Ironically, the Brown economy brightened with the war, but we remained weary throughout because my brother Randolph served in the U.S. Navy and was in 14 major battles in the Pacific.

In 1943, I was 12-year-old youngster who wanted to build a basketball goal in the field behind our house. An iron pipe caught my attention. I had noticed it lying uselessly on the ground under our house. I thought it would make an ideal post to hold the basketball goal. I picked up the pipe and tugged at it with some force.

Suddenly I heard the gushing sound of water pouring out from under the house. I had unknowingly broken off the pipe from the water main. My heart pounded with fear that I might soon flood the neighborhood. I ran inside our house with the news. My mother and father were in the kitchen. Upon hearing what I had done, my mother, addressing her remarks to my dad, said, "George, go fix the pipe."

My dad usually submitted to all my mother's wishes, but on the occasion of my emergency flooding of the Lamberts Point section of Norfolk, Virginia, he replied, not to my mother, but to me: "The toolbox is in the woodshed ... get the Stillson."

If a person can have a panic attack while already having a panic attack, it happened to me. I found a wrench in the woodshed. To this day, seven-and-a-half decades later, I still do not know what a Stillson wrench looks like. Nonetheless, armed with a wrench, I crawled under the house into its dark crawl space. Fighting off spider webs, and maybe even crying as well, I reached the torrential cold water. Somehow the wrench fit the broken pipe control valve. Suddenly, the blinding water stopped as I turned off the flow with the wrench that was clutched tightly in my two hands.

My dad, prepared by no formal education, unable to read or write, and blinded in his right eye from battery acid while working on a tug-boat when he was 12 years old, proved to be both a wise and *good enough* dad. He knew that his son had to learn to fix the problems he created. My dad's practical intelligence was admirable. As a child, I watched him disassemble his car's engine, wash each component in a cleaning fluid, and reassemble it without flaw. He had the combined skills of a plumber, auto mechanic, and finish carpenter. Without question, my dad could have immediately repaired the broken pipe just as he was told to do by my mother.

My dad chose to step out of his submissive role and gave me the opportunity to learn that I had the skills to successfully manage a task. This seminal experience for me was one of the most valuable lessons I needed to learn. It became part of my personal identity. Over and over, I failed, sometimes in very deeply disturbing ways, but success, by one means or another, followed. If being tried in front of a jury and asked by the prosecutor what I had learned from a long life of failures, I would reply with the words of Winston Churchill, "Never give in. Never give in. Never, never, never, never—in nothing great or small, large or petty—never give in, except to convictions of honor and good sense. Never yield to force. Never yield to the apparently overwhelming might of the enemy."

When the Master Sculptor Is Depressed

As we have been discussing, the mother is the *master sculptor* whose loving attention to the needs of the infant, whose holding, caressing, cooing, singing, and speaking to her infant "sculpts" him or her into a person. The mother need only be good enough for the successful psychological birth of her infant. But what if the mother is depressed? What if the depression is severe and long-term, as in postpartum depression?

Those with experience know that attending to the needs of a newborn is physically and emotionally exhausting, often associated with sleep deprivation and complete disarray of routines and lifestyle. Imagine what it is like for a depressed mother of a newborn. Without major assistance from others, the infant will come up short. In addition to the likelihood of neglect, the psychological birth of the infant will be impeded, at least in part, by the internalization of the mental image of the depressed mother, incapable to meet its basic needs. The impact of the depressed mother may have lasting effects.

Fisher and colleagues (2019) designed and published the results of a study of women who became depressed after the birth of a child. They were looking for a way to predict those women who were most likely to become depressed after delivery in order to help identify these women early for the treatment of depression. To do so, they developed a predictive model of women most likely to become depressed during the postpartum period. The "four key characteristics found to predict inclusion in the chronic severe group were less education, higher parity, more severe depressive symptoms and worse global functioning."

How Common is Depression After Childbirth?

Postpartum depression, classified in DSM 5 as Major Depression with onset in the peripartum period (during pregnancy or in the 4 weeks following delivery). This form of depression affects 15–20 percent of childbearing women each year, or 600,000–800,000 women annually (Guile, Newman, Fryml, Lifton, Epperson, 2013).

The condition has potentially negative consequences for mothers and their families, with an elevated risk for self-harm Metz, Rovner, Hoffman, Allsouse, Beckwith, & Binswanger, 2016.

Particularly relevant to our concern are the effects of depressed mothering on the development of infants. Studies show that maternal depression is associated with impairments in the development of stress regulatory, cognitive, and behavioral systems (Beck, 1998, PMID: 9489170; Campbell, Matestic, von Stauffenberg, Mohan, Kirchner, 2007; Gump et al., 2009), with the timing and level of maternal symptoms moderating cognitive and behavioral effects (Campbell, Matestic, von Stauffenberg, Mohan, Kirchner, 2007; Gump et al., 2009).

Valarie

I saw Valarie, a 27-seven-year-old married woman, two months after the birth of her first child, a healthy baby girl. Valarie, feeling very depressed, was extremely anxious, the cause of which she did not wish to reveal during our first session. Valarie's mother lived in another city many miles away. She had come to be with Valarie during the week before and after delivery, but Valarie called her mother and asked her to return to help manage the baby because, "it is far more demanding than I can handle."

After several therapy sessions, Valarie revealed that she was nearly obsessed with unwanted and dreadful thoughts of injuring or killing her infant. "I did not tell my mother," Valarie, crying and trembling said, "but that is the reason I asked my mother to return. I'm afraid to be alone with my child." Other than depression, I detected no evidence that Valarie had lost contact with reality. Sometimes, however, depression is so severe it is associated with psychotic thinking.

Valarie's husband joined her therapy sessions. He was very supportive, related well to his mother-in-law, and happily welcomed her help with caring for their baby. Valarie could not bring herself to reveal her secret thoughts of wanting to harm their daughter, Missy. Valarie was breast-feeding and did not want to take medication, but she responded well to CBT and agreed to walk briskly for 30 minutes daily. She was improved in 30 days and fully functioning as a mother and wife in 90 days. Psychoeducation about the potential severity of postpartum depression proved to be very beneficial to Valarie.

Major Depression, Peripartum Onset

Peripartum depression is a common and potentially life-threating disorder. It may affect the privileged, such as Lady Diana, or the average woman, such as Valarie described above, but may exert especially deleterious effects on those with limited support and resources. Its severity ranges from mild to severe. Not only is the mother disturbed by depression during pregnancy and following child birth; her infant may also be affected by postpartum depression.

When I contacted the publisher of an excellent review of peripartum depression and requested consent to include the publication in *Healing Depression by Degrees of Fitness,* I received the following reply: "The National Institute of Mental Health (NIMH) and the National Institutes of Health (NIH) conducts and supports research on the brain and disorders of mental health ... NIMH encourages you to reproduce them and use them in your efforts to improve public mental health." This is precisely our purpose in *Healing Depression by Degrees of Fitness.*

Below is the postpartum information provided by the NIH.

(Major Depression, Peripartum Onset, DSM 5)

The NIMH's

Postpartum Depression Facts

With postpartum depression, feelings of sadness and anxiety can be extreme and might interfere with a woman's ability to care for herself or her family.

What is Postpartum Depression?

Postpartum depression is a mood disorder that can affect women after childbirth. Mothers with postpartum depression experience feelings of extreme sadness, anxiety, and exhaustion that may make it difficult for them to complete daily care activities for themselves or for others.

What Causes Postpartum Depression?

Postpartum depression does not have a single cause, but likely results from a combination of physical and emotional factors. Postpartum depression does not occur because of something a mother does or does not do.

After childbirth, the levels of hormones (estrogen and progesterone) in a woman's body quickly drop. This leads to chemical changes in her brain that may trigger mood swings. In addition, many mothers are unable to get the rest they need to fully recover from giving birth. Constant sleep deprivation can lead to physical discomfort and exhaustion, which can contribute to the symptoms of postpartum depression.

What Are the Symptoms of Postpartum Depression?

Some of the more common symptoms a woman may experience include:

- Feeling sad, hopeless, empty, or overwhelmed
- Crying more often than usual or for no apparent reason
- Worrying or feeling overly anxious
- Feeling moody, irritable, or restless
- Oversleeping, or being unable to sleep even when her baby is asleep
- Having trouble concentrating, remembering details, and making decisions
- Experiencing anger or rage
- Losing interest in activities that are usually enjoyable
- Suffering from physical aches and pains, including frequent headaches, stomach problems, and muscle pain

- Eating too little or too much
- Withdrawing from or avoiding friends and family
- Having trouble bonding or forming an emotional attachment with her baby
- Persistently doubting her ability to care for her baby
- Thinking about harming herself or her baby.

How Can a Woman Tell if She Has Postpartum Depression?

Only a health care provider can diagnose a woman with postpartum depression. Because symptoms of this condition are broad and may vary between women, a health care provider can help a woman figure out whether the symptoms she is feeling are due to postpartum depression or something else. A woman who experiences any of these symptoms should see a health care provider right away.

How is Postpartum Depression Different from the "Baby Blues"?

The "baby blues" is a term used to describe the feelings of worry, unhappiness, and fatigue that many women experience after having a baby. Babies require a lot of care, so it's normal for mothers to be worried about, or tired from, providing that care. Baby blues, which affects up to 80 percent of mothers, includes feelings that are somewhat mild, last a week or two, and go away on their own.

With postpartum depression, feelings of sadness and anxiety can be extreme and might interfere with a woman's ability to care for herself or her family. Because of the severity of the symptoms, postpartum depression usually requires treatment. The condition, which occurs in nearly 15 percent of births, may begin shortly before or any time after childbirth, but commonly begins between a week and a month after delivery.

Are Some Women More Likely to Experience Postpartum Depression?

Some women are at greater risk for developing postpartum depression because they have one or more risk factors, such as:

- Symptoms of depression during or after a previous pregnancy
- Previous experience with depression or bipolar disorder at another time in her life
- A family member who has been diagnosed with depression or other mental illness
- A stressful life event during pregnancy or shortly after giving birth, such as job loss, death of a loved one, domestic violence, or personal illness
- Medical complications during childbirth, including premature delivery or having a baby with medical problems
- Mixed feelings about the pregnancy, whether it was planned or unplanned
- A lack of strong emotional support from her spouse, partner, family, or friends
- Alcohol or other drug abuse problems.

Postpartum depression can affect any woman regardless of age, race, ethnicity, or economic status.

How is Postpartum Depression Treated?

There are effective treatments for postpartum depression. A woman's health care provider can help her choose the best treatment, which may include:

- Counseling/Talk Therapy: This treatment involves talking one-on-one with a mental health professional (a counselor, therapist, psychologist, psychiatrist, or social worker). Two types of counseling shown to be particularly effective in treating postpartum depression are:
    - CBT, which helps people recognize and change their negative thoughts and behaviors; and
    - Interpersonal therapy (IPT), which helps people understand and work through problematic personal relationships.

- Medication: Antidepressant medications act on the brain chemicals that are involved in mood regulation. Many antidepressants take a few weeks to be most effective. While these medications are generally considered safe to use during breastfeeding, a woman should talk to her health care provider about the risks and benefits to both herself and her baby.

These treatment methods can be used alone or together.

What Can Happen if Postpartum Depression is Left Untreated?

Without treatment, postpartum depression can last for months or years. In addition to affecting the mother's health, it can interfere with her ability to connect with and care for her baby and may cause the baby to have problems with sleeping, eating, and behavior as he or she grows.

How Can Family and Friends Help?

Family members and friends may be the first to recognize symptoms of postpartum depression in a new mother. They can encourage her to talk with a health care provider, offer emotional support, and assist with daily tasks such as caring for the baby or the home.

Where Can I Find More Information?

For more information on conditions that affect mental health, resources, and research, go to MentalHealth.gov at http://www.mentalhealth.gov, or the NIMH website at http://www.nimh.nih.gov. In addition, the National Library of Medicine's MedlinePlus service has information on a wide variety of health topics, including conditions that affect mental health.

National Institute of Mental Health
Office of Science Policy, Planning, and Communications
Science Writing, Press, and Dissemination Branch
6001 Executive Boulevard
Room 6200, MSC 9663
Bethesda, MD 20892–9663
Phone: 301-443-4513 or 1-866-615-NIMH (6464)

TTY: 301-443-8431 or 1-866-415-8051 toll-free
Fax: 301-443-4279
Email: nimhinfo@nih.gov
Website: http://www.nimh.nih.gov

U.S. Department of Health and Human Services
National Institutes of Health
NIH Publication No. 13-8000

References

Campbell S.B., Matestic P., von Stauffenberg C., Mohan, R., Kirchner, T. (2007). Trajectories of maternal depressive symptoms, maternal sensitivity, and children's functioning at school entry. *Dev Psychol, 43*(5):1202-1215.

Fisher S.D., Sit D.K., Yang, A., Ciolino, J.D., Gollan, J.K., Wisner, K.L. (2019). Four maternal characteristics determine the 12-month course of chronic severe postpartum depressive symptoms. *Depress Anxiety, 36*(4): 375-383.

Freud, S. (2004). *The Interpretation of Dreams*. Place of publication not identified: Kessinger Publishing.

Guile, C., Newman, R., Fryml, L.D., Lifton, C.K., Epperson, C.N. (2013). Management of postpartum depression. J Midwifery Woman's Health 58(6): 643-653.

Gump, B.B., Reihman, J., Stewart, P., Lonky, E., Darvill, T., Granger, D.A., Mathews, K.A. (2009). Trajectories of maternal depressive symptoms over her child's life span: Relation to adrenocortical, cardiovascular, and emotional functioning in children. *Dev Pscyopathol, 21(1): 207-225.*

Mahler, M. (1975). The Psychological Birth of the Human Infant: Separation and Individuation. New York, NY: Basic Books.

Metz, T.D., Rovner, P., Hoffman, M.C., Allsouse, A.A., Beckwith, K.M., Binswanger, I.A. (2016). Maternal deaths from suicide and overdose in Colorado, 2004-2012. (2016). *Obstet Gynecol, 128*(6): 1233-1240.

CHAPTER 4

THE NORMAL ADULT HUMAN BRAIN

To be one of the most complex objects in the universe, the brain that resides within our skull doesn't seem like much to look at; yet this pinkish-colored three-pound mass is comprised of an astonishing 100 billion nerve cells, called *neurons*, that work together. Throughout our lives, experience helps to create and strengthen pathways and connections between all the neurons in the brain. These pathways increase in complexity as we age. The resultant anatomical and physiological complexity helps us to coordinate the patterns of activity that turn air to breath, pulsating blood flow to passion, and mere proteins to immune warriors.

At the experiential level, our brain is the source of pleasure, joy, and laughter, as well as pain, grief, and sorrow. Functionally speaking, our brain prompts us to eat and sleep and stores the memories that form the essence of "self." Perhaps one of the most inspiring aspects of the brain is its ability to enhance performance by responding to our efforts to take care of it. Learning about the brain offers a tremendous opportunity to improve our brain function and, in turn, our quality of life.

Thanks to centuries of investigation, along with technological innovation, we increasingly have come to understand how the brain works in conditions of health and disease. We also have learned how the brain contributes to our abilities to think and to reflect on how we know things, a state referred to as *consciousness*. Admittedly, the task of studying the human brain has proved to be difficult throughout history. As a result, many scientists in the past had to rely on studying the outcomes of persons with brain injuries.

Today, we know a lot about the brain because of advances that allowed sophisticated studies at different levels of scale. Because the brain controls behavior, researchers study human and animal behavior using behavioral tests like those that mimic states of depression. To better understand the workings of the brain, scientists use imaging devices. Functional magnetic resonance imaging, or fMRI, is a commonly used imaging device. fMRI measures changes in the brain as they are happening in real time. For example, if a person is imagining something that makes him or her happy, then fMRI machines detect activity in the regions of the brain that are associated with happiness.

Studies of the brain using fMRI are important because they help determine the parts of the brain that are responsible for certain kinds of activities and functions as well as which regions often work together. Scientists also use microscopes and advanced staining methods to study neurons, the building blocks of the brain. While doing so, scientists often compare the anatomy and function of neurons in healthy people to those in people affected by disorders like depression. Their aim is to figure out the mechanisms that are implicated in disorders so that they can derive more effective treatments.

Nerve Cells

Underlying the brain's complex functions are two fundamental types of laboring nerve cells: neurons and neuroglia. Glimpses of the structure of neurons first became evident in the late 1800s when the Spanish neuroscientist Santiago Ramón y Cajal used a specialized staining method to sneak a direct peak at neuronal anatomy. Prior to his work, there was no definitive proof that cells in the brain and spinal cord were separate, a finding that awaited better tissue preparation techniques, microscopes, and staining methods. Bolstered by these advancements, Cajal was ideally positioned to harden blocks of nervous tissue in potassium bichromate and submerse them in silver nitrate to create tissue preparations for microscopic examination.

By staining only an estimated one in a hundred neurons, Cajal's histological preparations removed enough of the forest to see the trees. In fact, the cleared background showed black threadlets emanating from small dense spots: silhouettes of neurons. Awestruck and empowered, Cajal continued his studies of neuronal anatomy. With a clearer grasp of the anatomy in hand, Cajal later proposed the *neuronal doctrine*. By definition, the neuronal doctrine states that the brain and spinal cord are made up of individual neurons along with their supporting structures. Central to the neuronal doctrine is the conjecture that neurons do not fuse together; rather, they conduct business via an intervening space between them called the *synapse*.

Also, we now know that each neuron can be divided into three parts: a dendrite, axon, and body. All three parts of a neuron are utilized as each one communicates to other nearby neurons via electrical and chemical signals. An array of dendrites called an *arborization* conveys incoming information to the cell body of the neuron. The dendritic arborization increases the surface area of a neuron and functions like a veritable receptor. In this capacity, dendrites increase the sensitivity of the neuron to electrical signals to their neighbors, which can induce neuronal firing patterns called *action potentials* when summed to a sufficient strength.

At the other end of the cell body are axons, which vary in length, from a fraction of an inch to meters long. Numerous branches at the axon terminal spread out and interdigitate with the dendrites of other neurons. Every axonal branch has a terminal called a *synaptic knob*. When an electrical impulse of sufficient intensity reaches the synaptic knobs, it communicates across the synaptic gap by release of a neurotransmitter. Many axons connect with other neurons, but some neurons have different connections and responsibilities. Sensory neurons receive environmental stimuli from receptors embedded in sensory structures like the eyes and ears and then convert the stimuli to electrical impulses before conveying the information to the brain for processing. Motor neurons carry information to muscles and glands.

Juxtaposed alongside neurons are cells called *neuroglia*, whose function is to promote and monitor the health of neurons as well as remove injured or dead neurons. Underscoring the importance of neuroglia in the healthy brain is the fact that they outnumber neurons fivefold. Astrocytes, a special type of neuroglia, regulate glucose metabolism, neurotransmitter uptake, and synaptic development and maintenance. Studies show that astrocytes are pathologically altered in depression.

Neurotransmitters and Hormones

Neurons communicate with each other by exchanging chemicals called *neurotransmitters*. The exchange of neurotransmitters occurs at synapses. Neurotransmitters bridge the gap between neurons in less than a thousandth of a second to carry the electrochemical message from the pre-synaptic neuron to the post-synaptic neuron.

The process of neurotransmission can be likened to a game of pinball. In this metaphor, neurotransmitters pop up from a presynaptic neuron to make a play in a manner similar to a steel pinball. Once in motion, the post-synaptic neuron becomes the target of the neurotransmitter. The neurotransmitter obtains a high score by making sure it hits and attaches to a post synaptic target at specialized receptors, a process that increases or decreases the chances for neuronal activation. Once the postsynaptic neuronal receptor has been activated by the neurotransmitter, propagating communication again takes the form of an electrical impulse which travels to the synapse to start the process over again. After the neurotransmitter has done its job at the post-synaptic neuron, it is absorbed by the pre-synaptic neuron and recycled for future use.

While there are dozens of neurotransmitters, there are four that are vitally important for mood: serotonin, norepinephrine, dopamine, and glutamate. These neurotransmitters communicate to the brain in different ways. In the brain, serotonin activity tends to generate signals about eating, sleeping, learning, and feeling good. Dopamine tends to generate signals about motor function, reward learning, and motivation. Together, serotonin and dopamine communicate about well-being. Norepinephrine communicates about pervasive threat and the need to fight or flee.

Neurotransmitters play vital roles in the functioning of neurons. In conditions of health, neurotransmitters interact sufficiently with the postsynaptic neuron so that proper synaptic connection and function is maintained. In conditions of mental illness, imbalances in neurotransmitter level and function often occur. The actions of many psychoactive drugs alter the balance of neurotransmitters in the brain. Fortunately, aberrant levels and function of neurotransmitters can also be mitigated with psychotherapy, antidepressants, and lifestyle changes.

Notably, the endocrine system works in tandem with the nervous system to maintain stable states within the body. When challenged, the brain uses electrochemical means to trigger the release of hormones from endocrine glands. The hormones are the primary messengers in the endocrine system.

The targets of hormones are often a considerable distance from their source. For example, the brain releases hormones in response to stress, and some of those particular hormones target the adrenal glands, which sit upon the kidneys. After receiving messages of threat from the brain, the adrenal glands secrete cortisol. In turn, stress hormones control basic behavioral activities such as emotion, metabolism, energy use, growth, sex, and reproduction.

In the brain, hormones alter synaptic neurotransmission and affect the structure of brain cells. As a result of stress hormone release in the brain and body, the circuitry of the brain and its capacity for neurotransmission are changed over a course of hours to days following stress. While stress hormones are important for protection and adaptation in the short-term, they are damaging to the brain in the long-term.

How Do Neurons in the Brain Fit Together for Function?

According to the concept of localization of function, neurons in different parts of the brain and spinal cord serve different functions. For example, it is now known that the outermost cerebral portion of the brain, which is called the *cortex*, has regions that are responsible for thinking, language, creative thought, and movement. Originally the concept of localization was pioneered by Franz Gall (1758-1828) in a movement called *phrenology*, a term that translated to the "study of the mind." Gall thought that the bumpy features of a person's skull revealed their intellectual and moral faculties. To bolster his notion, he visited schools, prisons, and hospitals to locate persons with various talents and disabilities. He then associated these features with skull characteristics. His assumption was that the skull was an actual window to the brain. This notion was eventually deemed a form of quackery, a reassuring conclusion for Napoleon Bonaparte, who was quite miffed to hear that his skull lacked the expected qualities that were indicative of a noble brain.

Over 100 years later, Paul MacLean (1960s) extended the notion of localization of function by suggesting the brain could be divided into three nesting regions: the brain stem region (involved in learned motor patterns or reflexes), the limbic region (involved in emotions that guide self-preservation), and the prefrontal cortex region (involved in thinking and regulation of emotions)

(MacLean, 1985). Although the model is a bit simplistic, it does provide a good foundation from which we can explore the parts of the brain that work together to create a unified experience, with synergy resulting from the firing of billions of neurons that together give rise to automatic behaviors, emotions, thinking, and learning, a process which we will discuss below.

The Brain Stem

The brain stem sits above the spinal cord and comprises the most primitive portion of the brain. Included among its structures are the hypothalamus and thalamus. The brain stem receives sensory information from the peripheral nerves and spinal cord, which transmit information about the body and environment. That information is passed to the thalamus, a structure that serves as a gate-keeper and relay station for nearly all incoming sensory information that enters the brain. The brain stem region contains control regions for integrating unconscious processes like sleeping and waking, heart rate, balance, temperature regulation, and instinctual behaviors (e.g., feeding, sexuality, dominance, and aggression).

Various components of the brain then identify the sensory information in our environment as familiar or unfamiliar. Familiar things are generally tagged as safe, whereas unfamiliar things are tagged as suspicious until proven otherwise by input from other brain regions. During the process, the hypothalamus releases hormones to coordinate the activity of the autonomic nervous system, which is in charge of involuntary reactions to elicit automatic feelings of acceptance or rejection of scenarios, situations, objects, or people.

The Limbic System

Layered atop the more primitive region is the limbic system. The limbic system is regarded as the emotional and motivational brain. It plays a key role in learning, simple memory, social bonding, fear, and anger. When a stress response is triggered after viewing an object or event, the limbic system is activated and contributes to reactions of intense feelings. Among the key structures that comprise the limbic system are the amygdala, hippocampus, and frontal cortex.

Positioned laterally on each side of the brain is an almond-shaped amygdala. The two amygdalae control instantaneous emotional responses and, thereby, contribute to feelings of safe or unsafe, good or bad, and friend or foe. To do so, the amygdala couples a sensory stimulus (e.g., a man hiding in a dark corner) to an adaptive response (fight or flight). The amygdala facilitates an emotional response by activating a sympathetic response. The effects of damage to the amygdala were made clear by a case study of a woman with bilateral disease in the amygdala who exhibited an inability to recognize fear expression in a human face. Parallel studies in animals revealed that destruction of the amygdala negates the fear response, an alteration that has disastrous consequences for safety awareness. In contrast, studies in humans show increased activation of the amygdala in persons with depression and anxiety.

Positioned just a bit behind the amygdala is a seahorse-shaped structure called the hippocampus. While the amygdala is best known for its role in fear and alarm in the presence of threat, the hippocampus is best known for memory. The hippocampus regulates inward flow of information prior to its distribution to the rest of the brain. Within this context, the hippocampus helps to collect memories, stories, experiences, and information about our self and our environment. These details form the foundation of identity and self-esteem. Thereby, the hippocampus plays a vital role in determining how we feel about ourselves and the stories we tell ourselves and others about who we are.

During conditions of health, the hippocampus creates a context for memories and supports a narrative of what is and is not really dangerous. Working in this capacity, the hippocampus serves as a brake to the stress-response system, which is crucial for termination of cortisol secretion and keeping the amygdala regulated so that it is active only when appropriate. Neuroimaging studies reveal that the hippocampus is larger in people with greater aerobic fitness and higher levels of self-esteem, suggesting it may play a role in overall health.

By contrast, chronic stress can damage the hippocampus and reduce its overall size. Hippocampal damage impairs our ability to remain in touch, to varying degrees, with that which gives meaning to our lives; our very self is reduced. Meaninglessness prevails. What's worse, the balance sheet of good and bad memories is altered so that nothing keeps out the bad memories anymore. During the process, physical health suffers. Abundant research shows that size of the hippocampus is smaller in persons with Type 2 diabetes, hypertension, chronic jet lag, inflammation, Alzheimer's disease, and depression.

The Cerebral Cortex

The third region is the cerebral cortex. This uniquely human region comprises around 75% of brain mass and helps us problem solve to get things done, regulate emotion, and utilize language. A specific portion, the frontal cortex, inhibits behavior in a variety of social settings, such as when we choose to return insults with a blessing. While performing its functions, the frontal cortex can store short-term information for approximately one minute at a time while communicating with the hippocampus and amygdala to determine the relationship of the information with the stress response. Thereby, the frontal cortex contributes to emotional regulation, reasoning, planning, problem solving, creativity, judgment, and awareness of self.

MacLean (1985) suggests that the three major parts of the brain do not always work well together even in states of health, a result of the fact that each region processes information in a characteristic manner according to unique priorities. For example, the brain stem primarily controls instincts, yet lacks the capacity for self-awareness. As a result, the rationale for our behaviors is not always apparent to us or others, a situation that can give rise to internal conflicts and emotional distress. Compounding the problem of conflicting priorities are variations in brain development and influences of culture.

Branches of the Autonomic Nervous System

Like yin and yang, the autonomic nervous system has two integrated halves: the sympathetic nervous system (SNS) and the parasympathetic nervous system (PNS). Under typical conditions, the SNS branch facilitates wakefulness and the work that is required for self-preservation. Under conditions of threat, the SNS sounds the alarm to trigger processes in the body that are necessary for a quick energy surge. In times of both health and threat, the PNS is the branch that is in charge of calming and promoting well-being via the relaxation response. It lowers breathing rate, heartbeat, and blood pressure. Following extreme conditions, the PNS sounds the "all clear" signal.

Both branches of the ANS help to maintain the body's dynamic balance by inducing hormone release from the endocrine organs (adrenal glands, pancreas, thymus, parathyroids, pineal, pituitary, pancreas, and ovaries). Working as the master controller of the autonomic nervous system, the hypothalamus ensures that many of the body's core functions run on autopilot. Our food is digested. Our sleep cycles occur on cue. Our core temperature adjusts alongside changes in the ambient environment. When balanced, this self-regulating system helps to keep the body stable and healthy.

Homeostasis

The ability of the body to remain stable within a changing internal and external environment is referred to as *homeostasis*—a term coined by the American physiologist Walter Cannon. In keeping with its Greek root, homeostasis acknowledges that our body and brain require an optimal range of factors to maintain healthy functioning. For example, some feedback mechanisms either suppress or enhance functions in the brain and body. A lack of appropriate neurotransmitter level and function in the brain can deleteriously alter homeostasis to the degree that emotion regulation and cognition are impaired, a situation that occurs in depression and Alzheimer's disease. In the case of migraines, increased impulses in nerve cells cause the blood vessels in the head to constrict and then dilate, triggering the release of serotonin, prostaglandins, and inflammatory chemicals—changes that collectively reify as pain.

The importance of homeostasis to brain health cannot be overstated. Many neurons and neuroglia in the brain work throughout the life of the individual and are not replaced like other cells in the body. Thus, damage to neurons results in a permanent loss of function. The exception to this rule is the hippocampus, where new neurons grow from stem cells throughout the lifespan in states of health, but are deleteriously altered in stress-related conditions like depression.

Fascinatingly, a bevy of research shows that physical activity can be used to coax the birth of newly born neurons in the hippocampus, a process that is vitally important for healing from depression and re-regulating the stress response.

The Stress Response

The stress response is triggered by a perception of emergency in the mind or body. Its function is to keep you safe and maintain homeostasis. Triggers of the stress response system, called *stressors*, include physical agents as well as thoughts in response to a variety of situations.

The stress-response system handles challenges via coordinated activity of neurotransmitters and hormones. Within seconds of the hypothalamus receiving a message of a threat, it triggers the sympathetic nervous system to release noradrenaline and adrenaline. Within minutes of encountering a stressor or thinking a stressful thought, the initial surge of noradrenaline in the body will wane, and a warning signal will then be transmitted to the hypothalamic-pituitary-adrenal axis. In response, the hypothalamus initiates the production of corticotropin-releasing hormone (CRH) and sends it to the pituitary gland to induce the release of adrenocorticotropin-releasing hormone (ACTH). Once released in the bloodstream, ACTH travels to the adrenal medulla to trigger release of the stress hormone cortisol. Together, the sympathetic nervous system hormones noradrenaline and adrenaline work alongside cortisol to coordinate the stress response.

Under conditions of health, our body and brain experience only fleeting glimpses of stress hormones. Once challenges pass, cortisol levels fall, and the PNS then dampens the stress response. The rapid return of cortisol to basal levels is essential because persistent exposure causes our tissues to become used to stress hormones, a situation that damages the feedback mechanisms designed to shut off the stress response system. Our hippocampus— which is important for short-term memory —shrinks. Shrinkage of the hippocampus damages the feedback mechanisms that are important for breaking the stress response system. Shrinkage of the hippocampus also alters short-term memory and weakens our experience of self.

Our amygdala—the part of the brain that detects threat and makes us feel fear—grows in size and begins to communicate too much to other brain regions. Brain communication or "brain talk" changes as a result of chemical changes in the brain. Negative brain talk dominates, causing us to increasingly sit around and worry about the hassles of life. In turn, our attention increasingly focuses on attending to and processing negative events in a vicious recurrent cycle, changes that go undetected in the affected individual and that result in automatic, maladaptive behaviors. Thus, temporal and sequential regulation of stress response is paramount lest the allostatic mechanisms that are designed to protect against stress go awry and cause excess wear and tear on brain health and disrupt mental functioning.

References

Dranovsky, A., & Leonardo, E. D. (2012). Is there a role for young hippocampal neurons in adaptation to stress? *Behav Brain Res, 227*(2): 371-375.

Dranovsky, A., Picchini, A. M., Moadel, T., Sisti, A. C., Yamada, A., Kimura, S., Hen, R. (2011). Experience dictates stem cell fate in the adult hippocampus. *Neuron, 70*(5): 908-923.

Elmquist, J. K., Coppari, R., Balthasar, N., Ichinose, M., & Lowell, B. B. (2005). Identifying hypothalamic pathways controlling food intake, body weight, and glucose homeostasis. *J Comp Neurol, 493*(1): 63-71.

Haleem, D. J., Kennett, G., Curzon, G. (1988). Adaptation of female rats to stress: shift to male pattern by inhibition of corticosterone synthesis. *Brain Res, 458*(2): 339-347.

King, J. A., Abend, S., Edwards, E. (2001). Genetic predisposition and the development of posttraumatic stress disorder in an animal model. *Biol Psychiatry, 50*(4): 231-237.

MacLean, P. D. (1985). Evolutionary psychiatry and the triune brain. *Psychol Med, 15*(2): 219-221.

Namburi, P., Beyeler, A., Yorozu, S., Calhoon, G. G., Halbert, S. A., Wichmann, R., Tye, K. M. (2015). A circuit mechanism for differentiating positive and negative associations. *Nature, 520*(7549): 675-678.

Pacak, K., & Palkovits, M. (2001). Stressor specificity of central neuroendocrine responses: implications for stress-related disorders. *Endocr Rev, 22*(4): 502-548.

Sapolsky, R.M. (2004). Why Zebras Don't Get Ulcers. New York, NY: Holt Paperbacks.

Surget, A., Tanti, A., Leonardo, E. D., Laugeray, A., Rainer, Q., Touma, C., Belzung, C. (2011). Antidepressants recruit new neurons to improve stress response regulation. *Mol Psychiatry, 16*(12): 1177-1188.

Woods, S. C. (2009). The control of food intake: Behavioral versus molecular perspectives. *Cell Metab, 9*(6): 489-498.

Woollett, K., & Maguire, E. A. (2011). Acquiring "the Knowledge" of London's layout drives structural brain changes. *Curr Biol, 21*(24): 2109-2114.

CHAPTER 5

THE DEPRESSED HUMAN BRAIN

Leo Tolstoy

While riding on the waves of public acclaim for some of his greatest literary works, Leo Tolstoy (1828-1910) inched deeper and deeper into a depression soon after turning 50. Plagued by dark moods, gripping fear, and worsening anxiety, he desperately inquired, "Why should I live, wish for anything, or do anything?" Tolstoy's confusion led him to seek answers in science; yet to his dismay, science surreptitiously sidestepped the harder questions of life by reducing the infinite questions of existence to those that were investigable, a limitation that prompted him to return to the wisdom of philosophical and spiritual traditions.

The Depressed Bain

And yet slowly over time, disciplined scientific questioning, along with serendipitous findings in the 1950s showed that pharmacological cocktails could alter mood. The foundations for more efficacious treatments of major depressive disorder were established. As a result, we now know that a depressed brain is one that is genetically vulnerable, chronically stressed, and struggling to adapt to ongoing challenges. We know that short-lived exposure to excess cortisol negatively alters the structure and function of key limbic structures at best and that chronic exposure to excess cortisol levels causes death of neurons at worst. We know that imbalances in the limbic versus cortical portion of the depressed brain occur, as do imbalances between the left versus right cortex, changes that collectively induce feelings of numbness and emptiness. To sum it up, **the depressed brain is one that is structurally and functionally different than the healthy brain**.

To better understand these issues, we necessarily turn to neurochemical, neuroanatomical, and immunological correlates of depression. We then wrestle with the effects of chronic stress on each of the correlates as well as their downstream effects on the mind. **Finally, we consider how homeostatic mechanisms in the brain utilize brain-derived neurotropic factor (BDNF) to initiate regenerative processes in the hippocampus and help reverse the symptoms of depression.**

Nature Versus Nurture

Whether aspects of behavior are a product of inherited or learned influences has fueled scientific debate for hundreds of years. Yet slowly, this nature versus nurture debate has revealed that heritability contributes to nearly 40 percent of depression risk, whereas the remaining 60 percent of risk is attributed to environmental factors. This fact means that having a relative with depression increases the risk that others in the family will develop the disorder.

In fact, having a parent or sibling with depression increases the risk for the disorder three to five times as compared to those without a family history; yet no single gene is thought to confer depression risk. Rather, a host of genes serve as underlying triggers that, when turned on or off by environmental triggers, increase the risk for depression. The silver lining in these findings is that the majority of depression risk is conferred by the environment, meaning that there is ample room to discover how to treat and prevent major depressive disorder.

Neurochemistry of Depression

Research suggests that depression arises from imbalances in neurotransmitters. Neurons in the depressed brain appear to release too little neurotransmitter into the synapse, or neurons may remove it from the synapse too quickly for it to have an effect. Alternatively, receptors may be oversensitive or undersensitive to a neurotransmitter, causing their response to the chemical messenger to be too high or too low. All of these situations are problematic because brain regions responsible for interpreting and regulating stress are highly influenced by neurotransmitter level and function. Ultimately, fluctuations in levels, function, and ratios of neurotransmitters alter neuronal communication and induce problems with mood.

Interestingly, the link of neurotransmitters to depression was discovered by chance. In 1930, Indian researchers noticed that reserpine, a drug used to treat persons with high blood pressure, was associated with depressive symptoms. Later it was determined that reserpine reduced the level of norepinephrine and serotonin in the brain stem to alter mood. In the 1950s, doctors recognized that the drug iproniazid created a sense of euphoria and energy in patients undergoing treatment for tuberculosis, prompting interest in its application for depression. Still later, imipramine, mistakenly thought to be an antipsychotic, was found to have antidepressant effects. Together, these findings led to the suggestion that depression is caused by low levels of norepinephrine or serotonin, prompting the development of early antidepressant medications.

How Prozac Works

Many drugs for depression attempt to restore neurotransmitter balance to restore normal moods. For example, a selective serotonin reuptake inhibitor (SSRI) is a commonly prescribed category of antidepressant medication. Prozac— the brand name for fluoxetine—was one of the first SSRIs to be developed and approved by the U.S. Food and Drug Administration on December 29, 1987.

Prozac's main job is to conserve the limited amount of serotonin at the brain synapses of clinically depressed patients. It purportedly blocks the reuptake of serotonin and allows the neurotransmitter more time to deliver its electrochemical message, strengthen brain circuits, and keep mood from down-trending.

While this mechanistic view made sense intuitively and provided an explanation for depression, proponents soon realized that serotonin deficiency did not always lead to depression and that medications did not work for everyone. For those that find relief, the drugs can be life changing; yet nearly 30 percent of persons who are prescribed SSRIs fail to get significant relief. For those that do benefit, the onset takes four to eight weeks.

"Why the delay in response to treatment?" It is now known that a key mechanism of action involves normalization of plasticity in the depressed brain. Plasticity refers to the ability of the adult brain to change its structure and function in response to internal or external activity in an attempt to adapt to changing circumstances. Those who respond positively to antidepressants show a reversal in plasticity deficits in the brain.

What is on the horizon for the nonresponders to current antidepressants?

Science has gradually revealed a more nuanced picture of depression, and one wherein big data and genetic testing may offer psychiatrists options for precision prescription. In a recent meta-analytic study, data from 246,263 persons with depression were compared to 561,190 controls. Findings from the study implicated that 269 genes, 15 gene sets, and 102 genetic variants appear to contribute to neurotransmission and plasticity deficits in depression. Also, the work identified novel drug targets and current medications that could be repurposed to treat depression (Howard et al., 2019). Long-term, the hope is that genetic tests can inform doctors of a person's genetic makeup, information that can be used to prevent unwanted side-effects.

In keeping with the latter notion, a 2018 presentation at the American Psychiatric Association detailed how the genetic test called *GeneSight* guided medication selection for patients with moderate-to-very-severe depression. Results showed a 50% greater chance of remission among prior non-responders after just eight weeks. While the genetic test cannot guide doctors to the right drug, it may help them avoid drugs that induce troublesome side-effects (Greden, 2018).

Admittedly, some stakeholders claim that a bias towards pharmacological management overemphasizes aberrant biological processes in the depressed brain, an approach that divorces itself from the inner workings of the mind and propagates false narratives by neglecting key social factors (e.g., early childhood experiences, family issues, poverty, unemployment, isolation, trauma, and discrimination). Moreover, the biological approach downplays the ability of social and environmental factors to alter gene expression, an approach that divorces itself from a holistic view of scientific understanding.

Structural and Functional Changes in the Depressed Limbic Brain

Brain structure and function is abnormal in depression. Among the structures affected consistently by stress-related depression are the limbic structures, including the hypothalamus, hippocampus, prefrontal cortex, and amygdala.

Hypothalamus

Several layers of evidence link depression with the hypothalamus and a dysregulated stress axis. Postmortem tissue from persons with a lifelong history of depression exhibits an increased number of cells in the hypothalamus that produce CRH, a biological marker of stress. Other work shows that injection of CRH into the animal brain activates hypothalamic neurons and induces depressive-like symptoms such as fearfulness, decreased appetite, psychomotor retardation, sleep changes, and loss of libido. Clinical work shows that persons with a history of childhood traumatic stress and abuse exhibit an amplified stress response in adulthood as compared to those with no such history.

Hippocampus

Shrinkage of the hippocampus occurs during depression, which is not surprising given that the structure has high levels of receptors for stress hormones and that excess stress hormone exposure is toxic to neurons. During states of health, the stress- response system is held in check by the hippocampus; yet the excess cortisol state that is endemic to depression causes death in hippocampal cells. Excess cortisol also adversely affects neuronal support cells like astrocytes and the neurogenic processes that enable adaptation and learning in a changing environment.

Over time, excess cortisol reduces other factors that are meant to repair damaged neurons, particularly BDNF. As a result, shrinkage and disconnection of hippocampal neurons functionally impair its ability to act as a brake on the stress response system. Changes in brain functioning worsen as changes in the hippocampus disrupt communication patterns within and between other brain regions. Increasingly, the ability to remember wanes, and with that loss comes changes in identity.

Interestingly, people who respond to antidepressants and physical activity show improvements in hippocampal structure and function, an effect that requires around four weeks to occur. The four-week time range reflects the time necessary for stem cells in the hippocampus to divide, differentiate, and fully incorporate into the hippocampal circuit — changes that are associated with decreases in depressive-like behaviors in rodents and an improved self-appraisal in humans.

Frontal Cortex

Another area of the depressed brain that is greatly affected is the frontal cortex. The frontal cortex area is exquisitely sensitive to stress and plays a critical role in the pathophysiology of depression. Imbalances in the level and function of glutamate contribute to widespread changes in other key neurotransmitters; as a result, overexcitation of neurons occurs, along with damage and death. Activity in the left frontal cortex declines, which is problematic because this region plays a crucial role in positive moods.

During the process, the frontal lobe neurons can retract dendritic processes, a change that reduces connectivity in the prefrontal area that controls emotion and cognition. The altered connectivity impairs the ability of the cortex to integrate information from the hippocampus and to direct the amygdala to alter its perception of threat. As a result, a positive feedback loop is created wherein increased levels of stress activate right prefrontal cortical activity, a region associated with negative emotion. These changes make it difficult for a person to automatically calm down. With time, pervasive negative emotions increasingly override normal circuit function — which explains the difficulty with problem-solving and inhibition of fear memories that result.

Further underscoring the importance of the frontal cortex in depression is the therapeutic efficacy of treatments on prefrontal cortex function. Neuroimaging studies show that taking

Prozac results in more balanced brain activity between the cortical and limbic regions. Other studies show that deep brain stimulation of the ventromedial prefrontal cortex reduces the symptoms of treatment-resistant depression. The rapidly acting antidepressant effects of ketamine hydrochloride, a drug under investigation but not approved for widespread clinical use, directly stimulates excitatory activity in the prefrontal cortex to powerfully impinge upon plasticity cascades for a period of 24 hours to seven days, fueling increased research interest in the psychedelic, particularly given its anti-suicidal effects.

Amygdala

In the amygdala, repeated stress initially accelerates activity to the degree that it becomes enlarged and overactive in depression. The resultant overactivity causes it to sidestep the frontal cortex and hijack the brain by repetitively triggering the stress-response system. An amygdala from a depressed brain exhibits more intense (up to 70% greater reactivity) and longer (up to three times) reactions compared to a healthy brain, a response that can occur often in a natural environment. For example, the processing of sad faces results in increased activation of the left amygdala in the depressed brain, a situation that continues in the absence of stimuli.

Left unchecked, the overactive amygdala induces widespread hormonal and neurotransmitter changes that disrupt repair mechanisms, sleep, and self-care activities. As a result, affected persons find it increasingly difficult to focus strategically on stress management and self-care techniques, resulting in poor psychological well-being. Eventually, the amygdala succumbs to excess cortisol exposure and atrophies with disease progression.

Anxiolytics act by dampening activity of the amygdala and preventing adverse brain effects when administered from the onset of stress-induced symptoms. Unlike antidepressants, anxiolytics do not reverse stress-induced symptoms after the symptoms are well established. Interestingly, the practice of putting emotions into words during talk therapy or journaling has been shown to have therapeutic effects by decreasing the activity of the amygdala and tamping down the fear response.

Endocrinology of Depression

Abundant evidence suggests that depression results in alterations in the axis of the brain that deals with stress hormones: the endocrine axis. Drugs that block endocrine stress hormones prevent depressive-like symptoms in animals following stress exposure. Removal of the adrenal glands, which are the organs that synthesize stress hormones, prevents depressive-like symptoms in animals. Conversely, physiological and behavioral correlates of depression can be induced by chronic administration of stress hormones to animals, showing that stress is necessary and sufficient to induce depressive pathology.

The problem with a state of chronic stress in the brain is that it causes excessive wear and tear on parts and processes while simultaneously limiting repair mechanisms that would heal the brain under normal circumstances. As a result, brain function becomes increasingly impaired, and increased mental suffering ensues.

Various explanations exist to explain how psychological and physical stress contribute to depression. According to psychological theories, the depressed brain requires effort to divert attention from negative stimuli. The brain's focus on negative stimuli is problematic because it contributes to ongoing internal conflict and a triggering of the stress-response system.

Biological theories show that both psychological and physical stressors (such as ongoing inflammation, obesity, or traumatic injury) elicit measurable changes in the release of the stress hormone cortisol, a change that adversely affects depressed brain structure and function; as a result of long-term stress exposure, circuits in the brain that regulate mood operate in a less efficient manner.

Importantly, both types of theory suggest that the depressed brain can recover from excess stress-induced cortisol exposure over time. The deployment of psychotherapy, antidepressant medications, and lifestyle changes can be used to reduce stress-induced cortisol exposure and jump-start repair mechanisms.

Inflammation and Depression

Recently, new links between inflammation and stress-related depression have been uncovered. It is known that inflammation is associated with stress-induced depressive behaviors and that persons with depression frequently exhibit inflammation. Such is not surprising given that depressed patients exhibit elevated cortisol levels and a dysfunctional stress response system, changes that alter immune cell function. One recent study showed that persons with depression were more likely to suffer a higher rate of inflammation in their brains, and persons with long-lived depression (longer than 10 years) showed 30 percent more inflammation than controls (Setiawan, 2018).

Chronic inflammation is problematic because it damages neurons by generating chemically reactive molecules that alter metabolism and DNA. These changes induce inflammation. In turn, inflammation alters neurotransmitter level and function, neuroplasticity, and hippocampal size.

Moreover, long-lived inflammation changes the gene activity of immune cells and causes them to be active in the absence of infection, creating a positive immune-stress feedback loop. Together, these inflammation-related changes lead to dysfunctions in learning, memory, and mood in persons who reach a threshold or inflammatory "tipping point."

Why the Link with Inflammation and Depression is Important?

The immune system permits crosstalk between the brain and body. For example, inflammation in the body acts as a stressor that causes tryptophan depletion. Tryptophan is used to make serotonin. We get tryptophan from foods that we eat. In the blood, levels of tryptophan are low in comparison to other amino acids. Tryptophan circulates in blood and plasma by attaching itself to a transport protein called *albumin*.

As tryptophan approaches the body-brain interface, it has to compete with other amino acids as it struggles to cross over into the brain. Eventually, about 10 to 20 percent of tryptophan in the body reaches the brain, with rates varying according to levels of metabolic and stress challenges. Once in the brain, tryptophan is converted into serotonin.

The pro-inflammatory state that often co-occurs in depression is responsible for tryptophan depletion in a process called *serotonin shunting*. In fact, the shunting of tryptophan toward the kynurenine pathway is associated with both the diagnosis and severity of depression. Notably, the kynurenine pathway appears to be linked to depression and other medical conditions such as Alzheimer's, Parkinson's, cancer, pain syndromes, and cardiovascular disease.

Kynurenine produces a variety of substances that are active in the brain, including quinolinic acid and kynurenic acid. During times of health, most kynurenine in the brain is converted by astrocytes to kynurenic acid, which is a substance that protects the brain. This conversion is of critical import since kynurenic acid inhibits neuron activity and, thereby, prevents excess excitability in neurons. Notwithstanding, astrocytic number and function are altered in the depressed frontal cortex and hippocampus. As a result, kynurenine is increasingly converted to quinolinic acid, a change that causes excess neuronal excitability, chemically reactive molecules, and neuronal dysfunction and death.

Brain-Derived Neurotrophic Factor (BDNF)

Researchers think that the stress-induced structural changes that occur in the depressed limbic brain are a direct result of changes in the level and function of BDNF. This notion is premised on evidence that BDNF plays pivotal roles in the formation and plasticity of neuronal networks that contribute to better communication between neurons in cognitive and emotional circuits.

Additionally, BDNF is important for repair following stress or damage. Problematically, persons with depression exhibit region-specific alterations in BDNF. Upregulation of BDNF occurs in the amygdala, which facilitates increased fear learning. Downregulation of BDNF occurs in the hippocampus and medial prefrontal cortex, which inhibits stress-response braking and future adaptation. In turn, BDNF abnormalities contribute to dysfunction of astrocytes in depression circuits, which further undermines structural integrity and function of the brain. Responders to antidepressant therapy and to physical exercise exhibit an optimization of BDNF levels in a regionally specific manner, a change that facilitates synaptic plasticity and remodeling and mitigates depressive symptoms.

Summary

In this chapter, we have discussed how long-lived or extreme stress can disrupt multiple brain systems to induce maladaptive changes in the depressed brain. Left untreated, these changes deleteriously alter neurotransmitter level and function, limbic brain structures, immune factors, and kynurenine production. As a result, the depressed brain enters a cycle wherein it becomes difficult to return to normal circuit function, even following the abatement of stressful situations (either psychological or physical in nature). This difficulty is partly a product of reduced plasticity. The disconnection and loss of brain function that occur secondary to synaptic decrements in the hippocampus and frontal cortex leave the stress response overactive, inflexible to changing circumstances, and incapable of fully activating homeostatic mechanisms.

Fortunately, many stressors are self-limiting, by either spurring coping mechanisms or spontaneously resolving over time. Notwithstanding, interventions can be implemented to hasten repair mechanisms and healing. In addition to cognitive behavioral therapy (CBT) and pharmacotherapy, lifestyle interventions like physical activity can be used to jump-start homeostatic mechanisms. In fact, physical activity's relatively low-risk profile, ease of implementation, and absence of side effects have led to its incorporation into basic clinical management protocols for depression, a notion that we discuss further, given that hope cannot come fast enough for those suffering with the disorder.

References

Autry, A. E., & Monteggia, L. M. (2012). Brain-derived neurotrophic factor and neuropsychiatric disorders. *Pharmacol Rev, 64*(2): 238-258.

Capuron, L., Hauser, P., Hinze-Selch, D., Miller, A. H., Neveu, P. J. (2002). Treatment of cytokine-induced depression. *Brain Behav Immun, 16*(5): 575-580.

Chen, J., Wang, Z. Z., Zuo, W., Zhang, S., Chu, S. F., Chen, N. H. (2016). Effects of chronic mild stress on behavioral and neurobiological parameters. Role of glucocorticoid. *Horm Behav, 78*: 150-159.

Disner, S. G., Beevers, C. G., Haigh, E. A., Beck, A. T. (2011). Neural mechanisms of the cognitive model of depression. *Nat Rev Neurosci, 12*(8): 467-477.

Drevets, W. C. (2001). Neuroimaging and neuropathological studies of depression: implications for the cognitive-emotional features of mood disorders. *Curr Opin Neurobiol, 11*(2): 240-249.

Duman, R. S. (2009). Neuronal damage and protection in the pathophysiology and treatment of psychiatric illness: stress and depression. *Dialogues Clin Neurosci, 11*(3): 239-255.

Duman, R. S., Heninger, G. R., Nestler, E. J. (1997). A molecular and cellular theory of depression. *Arch Gen Psychiatry, 54*(7): 597-606.

Duman, R. S., & Monteggia, L. M. (2006). A neurotrophic model for stress-related mood disorders. *Biol Psychiatry, 59*(12): 1116-1127.

Greden, J. (2018, May). *Combinatorial pharmacogenomics significantly improves response and remission for major depressive disorder: A double-blind, randomized control trial.* Paper presented at the meeting of American Psychiatric Association, New York.

Hamon, M., & Blier, P. (2013). Monoamine neurocircuitry in depression and strategies for new treatments. *Prog Neuropsychopharmacol Biol Psychiatry, 45*: 54-63.

Herman, J. P., McKlveen, J. M., Solomon, M. B., Carvalho-Netto, E., Myers, B. (2012). Neural regulation of the stress response: glucocorticoid feedback mechanisms. *Braz J Med Biol Res, 45*(4): 292-298.

Hill, A. S., Sahay, A., Hen, R. (2015). Increasing adult hippocampal neurogenesis is sufficient to reduce anxiety and depression-like behaviors. *Neuropsychopharmacology, 40*(10): 2368-2378.

Howard, D.M., Adams, M.J., Clarke, T.K., Hafferty, J.D., Gibson, J., … McIntosh, A.M. (2019). Genome-wide meta-analysis of depression identifies 102 independent variants and highlights the importance of prefrontal brain regions. *Nature, 22*(3): 343-352.

Jacobson, L., & Sapolsky, R. (1991). The role of the hippocampus in feedback regulation of the hypothalamic-pituitary-adrenocortical axis. *Endocr Rev, 12*(2): 118-134.

Krishnan, V., & Nestler, E. J. (2008). The molecular neurobiology of depression. *Nature, 455*(7215): 894-902.

Malykhin, N. V., Carter, R., Seres, P., Coupland, N. J. (2010). Structural changes in the hippocampus in major depressive disorder: contributions of disease and treatment. *J Psychiatry Neurosci, 35*(5): 337-343.

McEwen, B. S., Bowles, N. P., Gray, J. D., Hill, M. N., Hunter, R. G., Karatsoreos, I. N., Nasca, C. (2015). Mechanisms of stress in the brain. *Nat Neurosci, 18*(10): 1353-1363.

Phillips, C. (2017a). Brain-derived neurotrophic factor, depression, and physical activity: making the neuroplastic connection. *Neural Plast, 2017*, 7260130.

Phillips, C. (2017b). Physical activity modulates common neuroplasticity substrates in major depressive and bipolar disorder. *Neural Plast, 2017*, 7014146.

Phillips, C., & Fahimi, A. (2018). Immune and neuroprotective effects of physical activity on the brain in depression. *Front Neurosci, 12,* 498.

Setiawan, E., Attwells, S., Wilson, A.A., Mizrahi, R., Rusjan, P.M., Miller, L., ... Meyer, J.H. (2018). Association of translocator protein total distribution volume with duration of untreated major depressive disorder: a cross-sectional study. *Lancet Psychiatry, 5*(4): 339-347.

CHAPTER 6

EXERCISE FOR THE DEPRESSED HUMAN BRAIN

You may be reading this chapter right now because you are depressed. You may have decided to read because you are thinking about making regular physical activity a part of your lifestyle. On the other hand, you may have chosen to read this chapter because you are curious about how physical activity can protect you or a loved one against mental illness in the future. Regardless of the reason, you will soon learn that **physical activity is one of the most powerful methods for improving brain, mind, and body health.**

The connection between physical activity and health has long been conjectured. Ancient Greeks espoused the concept of "a healthy mind in a healthy body." In fact, health promotion practices in ancient Greece included physical activity as an integral part of medical care. Positing a physical component to mental illness, the Greek physician Hippocrates once said that "walking is the best medicine." Extending this notion further, he conjectured that the best way to health is to partake of the proper amount of nourishment and exercise.

Today, the processes that link physical activity to brain and mind health are well established. Physical activity initiates a biological cascade that results in many health benefits. It boosts our heart function, respiration, and metabolism. It induces the release of pain-killing molecules called *endorphins* to dull the strain of physical activity. It desensitizes the body to mental stress and reduces inflammation. It induces neuroplasticity processes that are critical for healing the brain, processes that not only calm the mind but also serve as a preventive or therapeutic for the depressed brain. These benefits make sense when we consider that our body, brain, and mind developed alongside movement.

In the case of depression, scientists have shown that physical activity reverses stress-induced alterations in homeostasis while simultaneously exerting brain-boosting effects. Physical activity increases our biochemical resilience by optimizing the level and function of endorphins, neurotransmitters, BDNF, astrocytes, and inflammation. It facilitates the growth and integration of new brain cells, bolstering hippocampal function and a positive sense of identity. It offsets genetic risk by altering gene function through epigenetic mechanisms.

Fortuitously, many people find physical activity to be practical, enjoyable, safe, and affordable. Together, this evidence provides a powerful message for those with depression that physical activity can be used to mitigate symptoms as well as lower the risk of future relapse. These facts establish a warrant for an increased understanding of the effects of physical activity on the brain, an endeavor that we undertake herein.

Humans Developed for Movement

The concept that our bodies were wired for movement becomes more apparent when we remember that a brain is only necessary for things that move. Plants lack a brain and the ability to move about on their own power; rather, their location in the environment is constrained by the whims of the wind. In contrast, sea squirt larvae use their simple brain-like structure to search for places to attach and filter food from warm sea water. Once secured in their new spot, they digest most of their 300 neurons, making it impossible for them to move in the future. These examples reinforce the idea that the brain developed for movement.

"But what does all that have to do with the mind?"

Movement can be thought of as a mind-brain state that is informed by sensory input. When we work outside in the summer and become hot and sweaty, we wipe our brow. When we are cold in the winter while shoveling snow, we rub our hands together. When we see a snake in the garden, our heart lunges back and forth inside our chest. When we stand in front of an imposing crowd, our stomachs flutter to and fro. When we gaze into the eyes of our lover, the warmth of his or her embrace draws us closer. Can you recognize how sensorimotor experience affects the mind and predicts future movement? If so, then you catch a glimpse of mind pulling us toward action.

Mind and Movement

"How did mind and movement become so strongly linked together?" The mind and brain further advanced two million years ago to facilitate goal-oriented movements in an increasingly complex environment. Our hunter-gatherer ancestors used sensorimotor mental images to access and make predictions about their environment as they foraged. While doing so, they traversed 4 to 9 miles a day on uneven ground, a task that required 300-800 kcals above basal metabolic rate—an excess energy expenditure level that exceeds what many contemporary Americans accrue in a week.

Part of the hunter-gatherer's high energy expenditure derived from the fact that foraging required intermittent bursts of moderate-to-high-intensity aerobic exercise in addition to strong capabilities for memory and complex problem solving. Undoubtedly, this challenge required physiological adaptations to accommodate it. As a consequence, every organ in the body down to the molecular level adapted to the active way of life.

At the brain level, the joint physical and mental challenges of hunter-gatherers initiated a massive expansion of the brain. To facilitate the process, physical activity became tied to the release of endorphins, which some identify as the source of the runner's high, and BDNF, which promotes neurogenesis and brain growth. Neurotransmitter adaptations also occurred that optimized neuroplasticity substrates in an activity-dependent manner. Metabolic switches evolved that paired metabolic rate with physical activity levels. Immune system effectiveness came under the regulation of physical activity. As a result of these collective changes, survival increasingly favored people who functioned at peak performance under intermittent conditions of dietary restriction and vigorous energy expenditure, given that these characteristics facilitated escape from imminent threat.

In addition to adapting to novel sources of stress and mapping troublesome environments, hunter-gatherers had to remember the locations of dangers so that they could be avoided in the future. To accomplish this, consolidation of memory became dependent upon seven hours of sleep per night. In the process, the brain became responsible for contextual memory, which is memory that is linked with details of time, place, emotion, and people.

Problematically, this blueprint for survival has been radically compromised over the last 100 years as sedentary, high-stress lifestyles have become the norm. Physical activity is no longer usually required for foraging or survival. Underscoring this point, a recent investigation using smartphone data from 111 countries showed that people now walk only 2.5 miles per day on average.

In America, 78 percent of adults fail to participate in light-to-moderate leisure-time physical activity five times per week, and 89 percent of adults fail to get any consistent vigorous leisure-time physical activity. Not surprisingly, this person-to-environmental mismatch has caused a spike in adverse health events. Nearly five million people a year die from causes related to decreased physical activity, and millions of others suffer from stress-related illnesses like depression.

Moving Muscles Trigger the Stress Response

"Why do our brain and mind function better when we move regularly?" In the moment, physical activity acts as a mild, intermittent stressor that modulates a bevy of neuroplasticity substrates. In doing so, physical activity helps the nervous and immune systems to better respond to threat by acting as a practice drill to hone the response in a low-risk situation, a process that partially de-sensitizes the brain to future stressors.

Soon after our muscles begin to work, they cause mechanical and metabolic stress. In fact, vigorously moving muscles induce a 10- to 20-fold uptick in energy requirements, a modification that initiates a host of physiological changes. The respiratory and circulatory systems work increasingly hard to maximize oxygen uptake and deliver it to mitochondria (the energy-producing structures in cells) so that oxygen can be converted to usable forms of cellular energy, an alteration that produces a significant amount of heat. Nerves in the body then detect both the rising heat levels and biochemical byproducts and convey that information to the hypothalamus, leading to a cascade of changes.

Within seconds of receiving the information, the stress-response axis and sympathetic nervous system alter neurotransmitter levels in the brain and body to restore homeostasis. At the same time, skeletal muscles begin to release natural substances that inactivate toxic stress metabolites, move glucose out of the blood stream into working cells, lower insulin levels, boost energy, and reduce inflammation. During the process, working muscles burn off excess stress hormones and enhance vim and vigor by altering the ratios and levels of neurotransmitters in the brain.

The intermittent stress response induced by physical activity helps the brain and body to optimize the level and function of neuroplasticity substrates that are responsible for the growth and survival of new neurons, support cells, and blood vessels. Over time, these short-lived practice drills expand a person's range of tolerance to stress, a change that is particularly important for reversing aberrant stress-hormone signaling. Just as muscles can get stronger with regular, intermittent physical activity, so too can the body's stress-response system get stronger alongside exercising muscles.

Physical Activity Improves Neurochemistry in the Depressed Brain

Regular physical activity boosts mood by improving circulation, and the level, and function of neurotransmitters, effects that are similar to those triggered by antidepressants. In the serotonergic system, physical activity restores depleted neurotransmitter levels in the limbic brain. In the noradrenergic system, physical activity lowers noradrenaline release from neurons in the brain stem and converts active forms of stress hormones to inactive forms to lower stress reactivity. In the dopaminergic system, physical activity optimizes dopamine release to enhance the function of motivation circuits. In the glutamatergic system, physical activity optimizes the turnover of glutamate to reduce the risk of overexcitation and neuronal damage. Together, these physical activity-induced changes allow neurotransmitters to orchestrate complementary functional effects in the cognitive and emotional circuits, optimizing overlapping yet unique aspects of brain communication and function.

Physical Activity Improves Limbic Structure and Function in the Depressed Brain

Another aspect of the antidepressant effect of physical activity relates to its ability to elicit the production of BDNF, a change that endures for two weeks following activity cessation. Physical activity increases the level of BDNF in the hippocampus, a change that helps neurons extend their axons and dendrites to make more synaptic connections, increase the efficiency of neurotransmitter signaling by lowering the threshold for neuronal firing, and induce a state of readiness for learning. These BDNF-associated changes in plasticity are associated with gains in hippocampal size and are thought to optimize emotional and cognitive circuit function.

Optimized BDNF levels in the hippocampus also increases the rate of neurogenesis. The process of neurogenesis preserves the hippocampal ratios of old, middle-aged, and young hippocampal neurons. Maintaining the ratio of the hippocampal population is important because neurons of different ages possess different characteristics. The contrast in function is particularly apparent in older versus younger hippocampal neurons. On the one hand older hippocampal neurons are more resistant to experience-induced changes; therefore, they are ideally positioned to serve as a source of historical memory and the sense of self. On the other hand, newly born neurons possess unique characteristics that predispose them to new learning and memory consolidation; therefore, they are ideally positioned to serve as change agents that reflect new learning experiences. Thus, a physical activity-induced bias toward younger neurons promotes opportunity for emotional and cognitive learning, a state that helps to reverse rumination tendencies that predominate in depression.

The ability of physical activity to influence BDNF levels and hippocampal health implicates gene-environment interactions. At the interface between genes and the environment are epigenetic changes—alterations in gene expression that occur through modulation of DNA folding around proteins called histones. That is, physical activity produces metabolic byproducts that are placed on DNA, a process that affects DNA folding and increases the production of BDNF in the hippocampus. Via these mechanisms, physical activity stimulates BDNF production to counteract genetic susceptibilities for depression, a change that can dramatically improve neuronal health in the hippocampus.

By converting active forms of stress hormones to inactive ones, regular aerobic exercise dampens the ill effects on the hippocampus. Simultaneously, the anterior part of the hippocampus receives sensory signals which induce growth in the very portions that interact with brain structures to regulate autonomic function. These changes mitigate stress-induced damage and enable the hippocampus to quieten signals down from the amygdala and simultaneously regain braking function over the stress response.

How frequently does one have to participate in aerobic exercise to Optimize Limbic function?

Research suggests that aerobic activity at moderate intensity three to four times a week is sufficient to increase BDNF levels and mitigate the effects of stress. These effects are particularly important for persons with depression. Interestingly, the increases in BDNF levels can be recovered rapidly in those who are fit and temporarily stop exercising, as long as the break is constrained to a two-week period.

Physical Activity Increases Astrocyte Number and Function in the Depressed Brain

Further supporting the link between physical activity-induced improvements in brain structure and function is evidence of activity-dependent astrocyte changes. The depressed brain exhibits a reduction in astrocyte number, function, and connections, a change that reduces its ability to regulate overexcitability following stress-induced glutamate excess. Interestingly, physical activity increases BDNF levels. The increase in BDNF helps to reverse stress-induced reductions in the hippocampus and frontal cortex by mechanisms that involve glutamate clearance from the synapse. By clearing excess glutamate, astrocytes limit the stress-induced neuronal damage that occurs from overexcitability in depression.

Physical Activity Reduces Inflammation in the Depressed Brain

When our body and brain are threatened by infection, they release chemical messengers called pro-inflammatory cytokines to increase inflammation levels. Similarly, when we experience chronic mental stress, we often have higher levels of pro-inflammatory cytokines within regions of the brain that are affected by depression. Left unmitigated, the persistent presence of pro-inflammatory cytokines in the brain can cause imbalances of neurotransmitters and hormones, changes that adversely affect mood and cognition.

Admittedly, not everyone with inflammation will develop depression, and not everyone with depression will exhibit increased levels of inflammation. Rather, the manifestation of depression is the result of a complex interplay between genes, biology, environment, emotional support, and lifestyle choices.

For persons with depression, regular physical activity decreases inflammation in the brain and body. Evidence suggests that physical activity provides a transient stress to the immune system to trigger the production of anti-inflammatory cytokines that normalize immune function in the long-term. Moreover, regular physical activity increases tissue sensitivity to stress hormones, a change that also elevates the levels of anti-inflammatory proteins. Once inflammation is reduced, neurotransmitters and hormones will approximate normal levels and decrease the risk and effects of depression.

Clinical Evidence for Physical Activity as a Treatment for Depression

The literature for the benefits of physical activity for depression is extensive, with numerous reviews and randomized controlled trials touting its benefits. In seminal work, Blumenthal and colleagues (1999) studied the effects of antidepressants, physical activity, or both on 156 men and women diagnosed with depression. After 16 weeks of treatment, all three groups showed equal reductions in depressive symptoms, but relapse rates were lowest in those who were in the physical activity group. In a follow-up study (2007), they studied the effects of supervised exercise, unsupervised exercise, medication, or placebo. They noted that persons who participated in supervised exercise exhibited a greater reduction in depressive symptoms than those who were unsupervised and achieved similar remission rates as those taking antidepressants.

Other work shows that physical activity is effective for persons with depression. Recently, a Swedish study by Hallgren and colleagues (2015) examined the effects of physical activity, internet-based cognitive-behavioral therapy, and treatment as usual. People in all three groups showed a reduction in depressive symptoms, but effects were larger for the exercise and internet-based cognitive therapy group.

Parallel work showed that people on antidepressants who participate in regular physical activity require a lower dosage for symptom relief. In a 2016 meta-analytic review, a team of researchers examined 25 of the most robust studies on physical activity and depression and determined that moderate to vigorous aerobic physical activity is a powerful treatment for depression.

Physical activity is also advantageous protecting mental health in those who are healthy. It has been estimated that active people have a 45 percent lower risk for depression than those who are sedentary. By extension, it was recently shown that forced sedentary behavior is sufficient to induce a bad mood and depressive symptoms. Because of the aforementioned work, exercise is now regarded as an evidence-based medicine for maintaining mental health and for relieving or preventing depressive symptoms.

References

Agudelo, L. Z., Femenia, T., Orhan, F., Porsmyr-Palmertz, M., Goiny, M., Martinez-Redondo, V., . . . Ruas, J. L. (2014). Skeletal muscle PGC-1alpha1 modulates kynurenine metabolism and mediates resilience to stress-induced depression. *Cell, 159*(1): 33-45.

Althoff, T., Sosic, R., Hicks, J. L., King, A. C., Delp, S. L., Leskovec, J. (2017). Large-scale physical activity data reveal worldwide activity inequality. *Nature, 547*(7663): 336-339.

American Medical Association. (2013). *Study details which exercises fight depression*. Retrieved from https://amednews.com/article/20130527/health/130529959/6/.

Blumenthal, J. A., Babyak, M. A., Doraiswamy, P. M., Watkins, L., Hoffman, B. M., Barbour, K. A., . . . Sherwood, A. (2007). Exercise and pharmacotherapy in the treatment of major depressive disorder. *Psychosom Med, 69*(7): 587-596.

Centers for Disease, Control, & Prevention. (2008). Prevalence of self-reported physically active adults--United States, 2007. *MMWR Morb Mortal Wkly Rep, 57*(48): 1297-1300.

Cloney, R.A. (1982). Ascidian larvae and the events of metamorphosis *Integrative and Comparative Biology, 22*(4): 817-826.

Meeusen, R., & De Meirleir, K. (1995). Exercise and brain neurotransmission. *Sports Med, 20*(3): 160-188.

Nabkasorn, C., Miyai, N., Sootmongkol, A., Junprasert, S., Yamamoto, H., Arita, M., Miyashita, K. (2006). Effects of physical exercise on depression, neuroendocrine stress hormones and physiological fitness in adolescent females with depressive symptoms. *Eur J Public Health, 16*(2): 179-184.

Neeper, S. A., Gomez-Pinilla, F., Choi, J., Cotman, C. (1995). Exercise and brain neurotrophins. *Nature, 373*(6510): 109.

Noakes, T., & Spedding, M. (2012). Olympics: Run for your life. *Nature, 487*(7407): 295-296.

Phillips, C. (2017a). Brain-derived neurotrophic factor, depression, and physical activity: making the neuroplastic connection. *Neural Plast,* 2017: 7260130.

Phillips, C. (2017b). Physical activity modulates common neuroplasticity substrates in major depressive and bipolar disorder. *Neural Plast,* 2017*:* 7014146.

Phillips, C., & Fahimi, A. (2018). Immune and neuroprotective effects of physical activity on the brain in depression. *Front Neurosci,* 12*:* 498.

Phillips, C., & Salehi, A. (2016). A Special Regenerative Rehabilitation and Genomics Letter: Is There a "Hope" Molecule? *Phys Ther, 96*(4): 581-583.

van Praag, H., Shubert, T., Zhao, C., Gage, F. H. (2005). Exercise enhances learning and hippocampal neurogenesis in aged mice. *J Neurosci, 25*(38): 8680-8685.

Vaynman, S., & Gomez-Pinilla, F. (2006). Revenge of the "sit": How lifestyle impacts neuronal and cognitive health through molecular systems that interface energy metabolism with neuronal plasticity. *J Neurosci Res, 84*(4): 699-715.

CHAPTER 7

HOW PROFESSIONALS DIAGNOSE DEPRESSION

The Diagnostic and Statistical Manual of Mental Disorders (DSM)

The *DSM* is the authoritative guide used by many researchers and clinicians in the United States. It contains descriptions, symptoms, and other criteria for diagnosing depression. By providing a common language, the *DSM* helps clinicians, payers, and researchers to communicate effectively with one another. Health insurance companies will not pay for the treatment unless it is consistent with the condition as described in *DSM-5* or a compatible system like the World Health Organization's International Classification of Disease (ICD). The DSM and ICD are readily discoverable on Google; thus, the information contained within the systems are not really proprietary anymore.

When I was a psychiatric resident at the University of Virginia, 1968-71, the   second edition of the *Diagnostic and Statistical Manual of the American Psychiatric Association (DSM-2)* contained the hallmark symptoms of all psychiatric diagnoses; it was 139 pages long. Today, the most recent edition of this manual, the Fifth Edition (*DSM-5*), is 947 pages long. While some diagnoses have been removed from *DSM-2*, many others have been added.

Depressive Disorders

The *DSM-5* delineates the diagnostic criteria for unipolar and bipolar depression. Earlier editions of the *DSM* combined the two conditions into a single chapter entitled "Mood Disorders." In the latest version of the *DSM-5*, separate chapters have been dedicated for "Depressive Disorders" and "Bipolar and Related Disorders."

A total of seven different kinds of depression comprise the chapter on unipolar depression, which includes the diagnostic criteria for major depressive disorder, premenstrual dysphoric disorder, dysthymic disorder, substance/medication-induced depressive disorder, depressive disorder due to another medical condition, other specified depressive disorder, and unspecified depressive disorder. For our purposes, major depressive disorder (or clinical depression) is the most important type of unipolar depression. Depending upon the number and severity of the symptoms, depression may be specified as mild, moderate, or severe.

Major depression is the focus of our attention. "The symptoms of major depression cause clinically significant distress or impairment in social, occupational, or other important areas of functioning" (The American Psychiatric Association, 2013, p. 161).

An in-depth discussion of bipolar and related disorders is beyond the scope of this text except for several medical pearls. Previously, bipolar disorders were referred to as *manic depression*, a confusing term that, according to its French and Greek roots, referred to periods of frenetic activity and rage that alternated with depressive episodes. The opening line of Homer's *Iliad*, for example, talks about Achilles' "manie" or enduring rage. Today it is known that many patients with bipolar disorder experience significant shifts in mood, anger or irritable temperament, along with excess energy and activity levels—characteristics that can make day-to-day social and professional functioning problematic.

Notably, depression and bipolar disorder can look similar, but they are different and respond differently to medication. A single episode of mania or hypomania is sufficient to mark the distinction between the two conditions. During a manic or hypomanic episode, patients may engage in conduct that is not typical of their usual or customary behavior. For example, patients with bipolar disorder may engage in unrestrained buying sprees, sexual indiscretions, or foolish business investments (American Psychiatric Association, 2013). Forensic psychiatrists are useful in explaining to the court how an offender's bipolar disorder is an important mitigating factor in litigation. The detection of illness dependent crime—such as that found in psychotic distortions of manic thought disorder— may constitute the rationale for an insanity defense, particularly if the disorder was severe enough to render a person's ordinary capacity to appreciate wrongfulness ineffective."

It is also important for families of bipolar patients to understand that the condition may cause misconduct. It is a disease for which we do not yet have enough comprehension. The embarrassing misconduct is not necessarily a character flaw or personal weakness. I have seen several sad cases involving devoutly religious people who, after falling prey to the disease, behaved shamefully and embarrassingly to their faith.

How a Professional Uses the *DSM*

A mental health professional, as you may imagine, must be very familiar with the *DSM-5*. Familiarity aids recognition of the signs and symptoms of mental disorders. While taking a patient's history, a mental health professional considers these criteria as they use targeted questioning to reduce, eliminate, or confirm diagnostic clues. For example, some severely depressed people with major depression may exhibit abnormal perceptions that include delusions (i.e., a deeply held belief without regard to logical reasoning proving the belief is false) and hallucinations (i.e., a perception without a relevant stimulus), a condition called psychotic depression. While psychosis can look like schizophrenia, a person with schizophrenia experiences delusions and hallucinations irrespective of depressive symptoms. The *DSM* provides a framework that is useful in disentangling this and other diagnostic nuances, helping the clinician to establish a valid diagnosis.

Major Depression

Critics of the *DSM-5* say it is like reading a "Chinese menu." This notion derives from the fact that the *DSM* provides a list of diagnostic criteria from which a clinician selects a threshold number of symptoms to make a diagnosis (American Psychiatric Association, 2013, pp. 160-161). An abbreviated list of criteria follows:

1. Depressed mood (feeling sad, empty, or hopeless) most of the day, nearly every day or observations made by others.
2. Markedly reduced interests.
3. Significant weight loss when not dieting, or weight gain.
4. Insomnia or hypersomnia.
5. Agitation or retardation in psychomotor activity.
6. Fatigue or loss of energy.
7. Feelings of worthlessness or excessive or inappropriate guilt.
8. Diminished ability to think or concentrate or indecisiveness.
9. Recurrent thoughts of death and thoughts and/or plans for committing suicide.

To make a diagnosis of major depressive disorder, criteria require that five symptoms from the list of nine are present for the same 2-week period and represent a change from previous functioning; at least one of the symptoms must be a depressed mood or loss of interest or pleasure.

An understanding of the various nuances of depression subcategories is important in helping the mental health professional derive an accurate treatment plan. Understanding the importance of diagnosis by a skilled professional, Sir William Osler said, "A physician who treats himself has a fool for a patient." Thus, if you think you may be depressed but are uncertain, you would be well advised to begin the discussion with an honest friend, a trusted religious leader, or your family doctor. Should you have the means, go to a psychiatrist who is accredited by the American Board of Psychiatry and Neurology. You can find their names in your telephone directory. Alternatively, you may call the American Psychiatric Association and ask for their list of board-certified psychiatrists who practice in your location. Community mental health clinics offer professional assistance.

Clinical Case History of Major Depression

Beverly Green saw her family doctor. She complained to him that over the past two months, she had lost 20 pounds without dieting. She denied feeling depressed, and she convincingly said she had no plans to commit suicide. He examined Beverly, and when she returned in a week, he reported that she was physically well and a battery of blood tests was normal. Her doctor asked about stress in her life. She told him she divorced her husband a year ago, describing it as a "good thing to do and I should have done it years ago." She also had to put down her dog, saying "it was hard to do ... much harder than my divorce ... but I'm dealing with it." Despite her denial, Beverly's doctor suspected depression.

He reassured her. "Weight loss is common for some people like you in their 60s," he said. "If your depression has a physical cause, it is not apparent yet. I would feel more comfortable if you agreed to see one of my colleagues who can spend more time with you reviewing the important issues in your life." Smiling and placing his hand on her shoulder, Beverly's doctor asked, "Will you do that for me?"

Beverly felt his more profound concern, the one he had not said to her. She thought, "My doctor cares for me." The thought brought with it a good feeling of reassurance.

"The colleague you have in mind, doctor, I suspect is a psychiatrist. Of course, I will see your colleague. Thank you."

I used the *DSM-5* to make Beverly's diagnosis. I have the *DSM-5* in the back of my mind each time I meet with a patient. Beverly had dropped out of her bridge club and no longer attended church. She had stopped watching TV shows she once enjoyed. She no longer found much of anything interesting. Markedly reduced loss of interests is a *DSM-5* criterion for major depressive disorder.

Beverly had lost 20 pounds because she had lost her appetite. "I feel like I'm force-feeding myself, almost like a young anorexic woman who is strongly urged to eat." Weight loss without dieting or weight gain is a *DSM-5* criterion for major depressive disorder.

She said, "Time seems to pass so slowly during the day, and yet the weeks and months seem to fly past. Somehow, I feel good when time seems to speed up. My daughter lives in another town. On the phone, my daughter tells me I seem to have slowed down in many different ways. She said it is not easy to talk with me on the phone because I speak too slowly." Beverly's psychomotor retardation was unequivocal during her psychiatric session. Agitation or psychomotor retardation is a *DSM-5* criterion for major depressive disorder.

Sleep was a significant problem. Beverly said she could fall asleep fairly quickly, but every morning she woke up between 2:00 and 3:00 a.m. Then she tossed and turned, never returning to sleep. Troubling dreams were not present. Insomnia or excessive sleep is a *DSM-5* criterion for major depressive disorder.

Beverly's fatigue was profound. She barely had the energy necessary to dress and she spent most days in her bathrobe. Make-up unsuccessfully covered dark bags beneath her eyes. Fatigue or loss of energy is a *DSM-5* criterion for major depressive disorder.

Putting down her dog was a more significant problem for her than she had shared with her family doctor. Her guilt over this necessary act of mercy was excessive and inappropriate. She had Rosie buried in her backyard. "I can't bear to return to my yard under any circumstances since I put Rosie down almost a year ago," said Beverly. "I haven't been able to cry for her either." Inappropriate or excessive guilt is a *DSM-5* criterion for major depressive disorder.

"I used to complete my grocery shopping in less than an hour. Now it takes much longer because I cannot make simple decisions anymore. It makes no sense, but I spend a lot of time trying to decide between two brands. I'm not looking for the least expensive brand. I just can't decide. It's that way with other things as well. It's one of the reasons I don't get dressed every day. I can't decide what to put on. Sometimes I wonder about dementia. I canceled the newspapers because the ads made it even more troubling about what to buy." Decreased concentration or indecisiveness is a *DSM* criterion for major depression.

Beverly Green fully met the *DSM-5* criteria for major depressive disorder. We discussed treatment options. She signed a release for me to keep her family doctor informed about her response to treatment. Beverly made a follow-up appointment. I communicated my diagnosis to her family doctor, and he said, "Beverly was different than her usual self, and I had a feeling it was in your field of expertise, not mine alone, to help with."

I gave Beverly summary articles about the most critical research confirming that regular physical activity has as many beneficial effects on the brain as on the heart, and maybe even more. She promised to begin slowly walking one mile on level ground at least five days weekly.

We also started and completed a 12-week course of cognitive behavioral therapy (CBT) for depression.

I went with Beverly and her priest to Rosie's grave in her backyard. Beverly cried softly as her priest read a touching and meaningful prayer for the death of a pet. It was during the seventh week of her therapy. After the ceremony for Rosie, Beverly served her priest and me a lovely tea. I believe it was a turning point in her recovery.

After her 12th session, Beverly was physically fit, committed to daily exercise, and rid of her depression.

As promised, Beverly phoned me six months after her last appointment. "Doctor, I'm doing just fine," she said. "My appetite returned. I work out at our nearby senior center. It's actually fun now to be with friends and I like the way they complement me. I am committed to physical exercise. When I returned to church, our priest said, "You must have been on a much-needed vacation. You look relaxed, fit, healthy, and stunning. Welcome back."

References

American Psychiatric Association. (2013). *Diagnostic and Statistical Manual of Mental Disorders* (5th ed). Arlington, VA: American Psychiatric Association.

World Health Organization. (2018). *International Statistical Classification of Diseases and Related Health Problems* (11th Revision).

CHAPTER 8

SEARCHING FOR THE CAUSE OF DEPRESSION

Exit Events and Depression

Another pearl comes to mind: "The cause of depression is usually unknown to the affected, but it is worth the search to find its cause in the presence of a skilled person." Some very depressed people are perplexed over why they are depressed, saying, "I have a caring family, my finances are stable, and I have a good job, but I'm depressed. Why should I be depressed? I have no reason to be depressed, and that thought makes me more depressed."

It is often helpful to review the circumstances of your life when you first became depressed. *Exit events* is a term that identifies changing situations or losses of meaningful people, places, or positions that were once important to you but are no longer available. Losses, exit events, or their anniversaries may trigger a depressive episode. Losses, failures, and exit events come in many forms. Some people experience retirement as a loss. Some construe aging as a loss again. Loss of status may be incredibly depressing. The loss of a loved one, discussed below, may tumble some people from normal grief into severe depression, not an ordinary reaction to grief.

Competing theories of depression fill the pages of scientific literature as progress in our understanding of mechanisms continues to advance. We may be encouraged by research findings actively supporting physical activity to prevent and treat depression. A previous chapter discussed these findings.

The Importance of a Complete Medical Examination

The search for the cause of your depression begins with a complete physical examination. A comprehensive physical exam is a must-do assignment, and excuses for failing to obtain one are unacceptable. Try to accept the fact that any symptom of depression could have a correctable physical disorder as its cause. For example, hypothyroidism—which results from an under-functioning thyroid gland—can cause many symptoms that are identical to clinical depression. In this case, a single blood test can mean a lot. In most cases, treating the condition with medication for the under-active thyroid gland will resolve all the symptoms of depression. Antidepressant medicines will not help if an under-active thyroid gland is left uncorrected.

Medication-resistant depression is sometimes treated successfully by adding synthetic thyroid extract to the antidepressant medication. Estrogen supplementation, proven helpful in women whose antidepressant alone was ineffective, is used with more caution owing to its potential harmful side effects. In the few cases where I used estrogen supplementation, I did so in consultation with the patient's gynecologist.

Depression and Grief

Grief is not depression. Grief is a natural, necessary, and culturally acceptable response to the loss of a person, pet, or valued possession to which you were emotionally attached. It is characterized by a yearning and sadness of the deceased. Grief is the price we pay for the loss of someone or something we cherished.

For most people, the all-consuming intensity of grief abates over time as the loss becomes accepted and an optimistic sense of the future becomes imaginable, although the path to abatement may be erratic. Yet when the death is unexpected, traumatic, or the result of assaultive behavior such as military combat, murder, or suicide, grief may be extremely difficult and complicated. The complexity of the relationship with the deceased at the time of the loss may also increase the burden and prolong the grief.

No relationship is perfect. All have their ups and downs, positive and negative emotions, and firmly held disagreements. It is not uncommon to have unfinished business in the relationship at the time of the loss. Regrets, unspoken feelings, or failure to say goodbye haunt many people. Sometimes, the intensity and unfamiliarity of the feelings of grief alongside the sudden confrontation of mortality can fuel a sense of isolation.

Regardless of the circumstances surrounding the loss, grief is laudable and praiseworthy. It should be encouraged by those nearest the grieving person during the provision of reassurance and support. Admittedly, it is sometimes difficult to offer support to someone who is grieving. Well-meaning people fear that they will do or say the wrong thing in the midst of difficult times. Yet personal discomfort should not preclude a well-intentioned person from supporting those who are grieving. Rather, the well-intentioned need only to realize that being present and quietly doing what appears to be needed is productive. Undoubtedly, the latter strategy is more helpful than asking the griever, "How can I help?"

Ordinarily, psychotropic medication is not indicated, though it may be used sparingly and with caution if normal grief will not run its course otherwise. Failure of grief to run its course is problematic given that it can morph into depression, particularly when it is unremitting, interrupted, avoided, or delayed for any reason. The grieving person must be encouraged to seek professional help should they fail to find a resolution of symptoms, reconnect with love ones, or regain a sense of positive emotion about their self or world.

Healing

Please do not glibly scan or superficially speed read the word *healing*. I view healing as the most important word in my manuscript, not because I fully understand it, but because its importance and relevance are underappreciated. "We dress the wounds but God does the healing" is declared publically in large printed letters on the walls of some Catholic hospitals, a notion first espoused by Ambroise Parè (1510 – 1590), a French barber surgeon to the Royalty and considered one of the fathers of surgery. Underlying this saying is a belief that the human body, mind, and spirit play an active role in healing.

After the siege of Turin in 1537, Parè found himself simultaneously facing carnage and limited resources to heal the afflicted. In desperation, he utilized a cold mix of egg yolks, oil of roses, and turpentine in lieu of the conventional cauterizing oil, creating two test groups. To his amazement, patients who were not exposed to conventional treatment, the cauterizing oil, healed more quickly. Thereby he realized that keen observation of patients could teach him what esoteric theories could not.

Parè's ideological change was fueled by religious conviction. His coining of the phrase "I dressed the wound, but God healed him" was an intended reminder of where his abilities started and stopped. A similar notion is conveyed in Psalm 147:3, "He heals the brokenhearted and binds up their wounds."

Among its many attributes and synonyms, healing always restores something important that is missing or corrects something that is out of balance. Those with a broken heart have usually experienced the loss of something or someone. After being wounded—whether by physical injury or emotional rejection, abuse, or neglect—we can find ointment for the soul in scripture.
King David is a prime example of someone who found refuge after suffering from a broken heart time and again, only to recover stronger than before the injury. According to Psalm 34:4, "I sought the Lord, and He answered me; He

delivered me from all my fears." Thus, when we are overwhelmed with pain, we must recognize that authentic healing almost always involves our soul, which is the part of us through which we may choose to listen to, speak with, or have our most intimate of conversations. After all, the soul is the part of us that binds us to our most valued attachments.

My Best Friend

My best friend, someone I've known for seven decades, visited me recently after an absence of 16 years. He and his son had driven many hours to make the trip. I greeted them on my front porch. I hardly recognized my friend and would not have picked him out of a crowd. Stooped over by osteoporosis, he was five inches shorter than he had been. There was less of him physically, less hair, less weight, and less balance, but when I looked into his eyes, I saw the person I loved, admired, and respected. Without question, his eyes told me instantly that this was my friend. Confidently, I recognized the spirit of the person I was closest to in college and during my first year in medical school, my lab partner, my closest friend.

I believe it is the spirit of each person to which we respond, relate, become attached, and remember in their absence. We bury the bodies of our loved ones when they die, but they continue to "live" in our memory, spiritually real.

Depression and the Human Spirit

As we discuss our topic more thoroughly, what seems to be most impaired by depression is the person's spirit. I do not say that depression is wholly a disorder of the spirit, just that depression spares no part of a person. Dr. Aaron T. Beck, the father of cognitive behavioral therapy (CBT), states that the cause of depression is unknown, but it is kept alive by thinking depressing thoughts, along the lines of, "I am worthless. I've always been a failure, and I will always be a worthless failure." His emphasis is on the thinking mind of the depressed person. Fortunately, scripture supports those who have lost what is precious to them and, thereby, can help promote recovery of emotional and spiritual wounds.

As fellow travelers on this earth, we can support others on the journey of healing my extending a kind and loving hand. I have been privileged to know Dr. Aaron Beck, one of the twentieth century's greatest behavioral scientists. I have experienced his gentle kindness and human warmth, almost palpable evidence of his healing spirit. Dr. Beck is 97 years old. His mind and his spirit today are just as creative, competent, and compassionate as when I first met him nearly four decades ago. So touched by his presentation of cognitive therapy, I asked if his work was theologically based. He replied, "A lot of people ask me the same question. I did not intend it to be theological, but if there is a similarity between cognitive therapy and religion it is their common search for truth." Dr. Beck is a living example that the gifts of a sound Spirit are love, joy, peace, longsuffering, gentleness, goodness, faith, meekness, and temperance. Undoubtedly, he recognizes the tripartite of health (mind, body and spirit).

Depression and Guilt

During my childhood (in the 1930s and early 1940s), children who misbehaved were punished. Perhaps this notion stemmed from the idea of "spare the rod, spoil the child," the line coined by the 17th-century poet and satirist Samuel Butler. Fascinatingly, the biblical phrase that most closely aligns with this phrase derives from Proverbs 13:24, "Whoever spares the rod hates their children, but the one who loves their children is careful to discipline them." Despite maturity and sophistication, some still hold the view that illness is the result of misconduct or sin.

Frank, an intelligent businessman in his mid-70s, was home alone when he fell down a flight of stairs. When he was found at the bottom of the steps several days after falling, he could not move, was helpless, and in severe pain. Frank had broken his neck during the fall.

His accident left him as a person with quadraplegia whose pain was unyielding. Months after his fall, aware his condition would not improve, Frank asked his wife, "Do you think I'm being punished?" Frank wanted reassurance that his accident did not stem from misconduct.

The book of *Job*, written between the first and second centuries B.C., addresses the theodicy question, "Why does a just God permit the innocent to suffer?" Job was a thriving, healthy, morally upright man who lost his children, health, and possessions. "That which I feared has befallen me," Job lamented, but he did not curse God. Faced with this suffering, Job reasoned, "Shall we accept good from God and not trouble?" (Job 2:10 NIV). Rich in theological truths far beyond the purposes of our text, Job is a go-to resource for suffering humanity burdened by the unanswerable question, "Why has this befallen me?" Job teaches us that problems rain on the just and unjust. The latter statement is not made lightly; it reflects the belief that bad things happen to good people, but does not negate the fact that our thoughts and action sometimes contribute to our coping abilities.

Misconduct May Contribute to Illness

There is a dynamic relationship between behavior and disease, but that relationship is highly nuanced. *Lifestyle disease* is a recently coined phrase to describe the causal relationship between behavior and adverse health outcomes. Smoking is a prime example of how a behavior can contribute, but not cause, disease. Many otherwise intelligent people knowingly disregard cautions to avoid smoking, a risk factor that contributes to heart disease and cancer. Problematically, if you believe, for example, that smoking is morally wrong, and you are a smoker with a particular case of lung cancer that is positively associated with a smoking history, then you may believe you are being punished with cancer for committing a morally wrong act. In such a tragic case, excessive guilt may fester and feed the stress response to impair chances for recovery, despite the fact that causality is much more complex than once believed.

Particularly germane to the current conversation is a bevy of research that shows that many people who smoke have problems expressing their emotion and, therefore, partake of cigarettes in an effort to self-medicate. Overtime, nicotine addiction results and seriously complicates smoking cessation. Left unmitigated, the risk of cancer in male smokers who lack the ability to express their emotion is five times higher than those who express their emotion effectively. Given that 90% of lung cancer mortality is attributed to smoking, and that emotional stress contributed to the act in the first place, it seems imprudent to cling to Western orthodoxy that separates the body from the mind despite centuries of evidence to the contrary. Perhaps then we will be able to recognize that many disorders are modifiable or preventable by behavior change. The same principle applies to our emotional and spiritual disquiet, particularly when frenetic activity and seemingly benign neglect contribute.

More About Depression and Grief

The author acknowledges repetition here without apology. It is in the service of driving a point home in the way that Ryan Zimmerman drives a home run for the Washington Nationals. Sadness and depression are not the same. It may seem counterintuitive, but the diagnosis of depression does not require sadness. Forms of sorrow, such as good grief, are not depression. Grief is an expected emotional response to the death of someone or something you loved. Grief-stricken people who find no acceptable end to grieving may become depressed.

Informed doctors do not treat normal grief as depression. They encourage it. In most cases, those who are grieving need no antidepressant medication. One exception comes to mind, and there may be more. If death is unexpected and unusually tragic, severe anxiety may overtake a mourner. Severe stress may prolong sleep disturbance. In such cases, an antidepressant's soporific effects help.

For the most part, by and large, clinical depression is not caused by misconduct. Hold that thought firmly in your mind and retain it no matter how strongly you may feel that somehow you created your case of clinical depression.

At this point in our understanding of the history and science of mood disorders, it is clear that depression is something that happens to many people. It is also apparent that depression is a complex medical condition; its causes are unknown. These factual statements may appear straightforward, even unnecessary to one who has never experienced depression. Believe me they are neither simple nor apparent to those who are depressed. The depressed person feels that depression describes who they are. They don't say, "I have depression," as one might say I have a broken arm or a bad cold. They say, "I am depressed." That's who they believe they are, robbed as it were of their very sense of themselves as a person. This identity problem will be emphasized and explained later.

What's Your Age Got to Do with It?

Late-life depression affects about 6 million Americans ages 65 or older. Up to 5 percent of older adults living in the community suffer from the condition, a number that rises to 15 percent for those requiring hospitalization, home health, or long-term care. This suggests late-life depression commonly co-occurs alongside other chronic medical conditions, oftentimes in conjunction with cardiovascular or neurological changes, although these impairments are seldom sufficient to cause depression in isolation. In fact, research suggests that health impairments contribute to issues with negative self-evaluation and social engagement, issues that can be compounded by prolonged stressors such as role changes, relocation, or bereavement.

Problematically, health care practitioners and family members often mistake symptoms in older adults as an acceptable reaction to illness or life changes despite the fact that depression is not considered a normal part of aging. Partially contributing to the phenomenon of failed diagnosis in older adults is a difference in presentation: Older adults present with complaints of somatic issues, sleep disruptions, and loss of interest in activities, not sadness per se. Complicating their clinical course is the fact that older people seek treatment less frequently than younger individuals and, when they do present, are less likely to be treated aggressively. Unfortunately, missed diagnoses and ineffective treatment can have fatal consequences in suicide and nonsuicide mortality, with older white males having the highest suicide rate in the United States.

Given that the fastest growing sector of the population is comprised of those who are 65 years of age and beyond, more needs to be done to recognize the critical problem of late-life depression. Fortunately, it's never too late to learn how to manage depression. Consistent with my stated objectives for this book, I hold to the equal importance of fitness of the body, mind, and spirit. "Start low and go slow" is sound advice for anyone committing themselves to physical activity; it is particularly appropriate for our mature adults.

I emphasize non-exhaustive physical activity, rational nutrition, and refreshing sleep for the body. These are reasonable, achievable objectives for those who have healthy self-regard.

When older people experience prolonged psychological distress, it is important to ascertain recent changes in the social or physical environment as well as long-standing difficulties. To understand how we assign meaning to these changes, and how meaning affects the mind, I promote CBT, explained as we proceed. Fundamentally, CBT teaches us how to reduce the errors in our thinking so we can more accurately assign meaning to our experiences. In the case of aging, this type of therapy can help one rid the self of self-defeating thoughts regarding physical or medical impairments or change less productive ways of thinking in order to regain control over one's life.

What's Your Soul Got to Do with It?

I believe everyone has a soul, as addressed above, a topic that is nearly forbidden to discuss among a vastly expanding intolerant "intellectual" segment of society. Nonetheless, here it is, sans apology. There is a time in every person's life when virtually all that is left is the soul. While revising his book Denial of Death, Becker was dying of cancer. He was 49 years old, father of two children and married to a devoted wife. Perhaps this reality helped him to further realize that his life was much more valuable than that which would be realized in 2 score and 10. Therein he inquired, "What kind of deity would create such a complex and fancy worm food?"

Note that the terms *soul* and *psyche* stem from the same origin. In Ancient Greece, the word soul or psyche was associated with breath, the very essence of a living being. In contemporary times, psyche refers to the characteristic mental abilities of humans: feeling, memory, perception, and complex thought and reasoning—abilities that are inextricably melded with the body.

Few realize that Americans are among the top spenders for health care and yet neither our health span nor life expectancy is among the top twenty countries in the world. Even fewer realize that we now spend 75 percent of healthcare dollars on stress-related conditions that are preventable, spending that results in less than optimal results." Can we dislodge ourselves from entrenched behaviors that contribute to adverse health outcomes? Can we learn from our mistakes? The widespread emergence of mind-body medicine in the 20th century suggests the affirmative. The mind body approach regards fundamental the need to enhance each person's capacity for self-knowledge and self-care, and it emphasizes techniques that promote balance, internal harmony, and the elimination of stress.

Medical Approval to Exercise

It is unwise to begin an exercise regimen, no matter how modest, without first discussing it with your physician. Some guidelines say that persons who are middle age or less and that do not have comorbidities can proceed with moderate exercise without physician clearance. I do not concur with such guidelines and hope you will go to a physician. While there, ask the doctor how much and how often he or she exercises. You are looking for good role models. Assertively declare that you want to be competently treated by excellent physicians who begin by taking care of themselves. Take a moment to explain what you are learning about depression and the relationship between fitness, rational thinking, and the sense of well-being.

We are getting a little ahead of ourselves in this book, but it's healthy to have some fun. I'm going to presume that your doctors are busy, have little time for chit-chat, and may not have listened to or looked directly at you up to this brief period in your visit, preferring keyboards to people.

Now for fun (you need to have some fun every day), casually say, "Doctor, what can you tell me about BDNF?" If your physician does not stop in his or her tracks and gaze into your face with surprise, I'll be amazed!

Continue: "I hope you can tell me more about BDNF. I understand that physical exercise can raise my level of BDNF and help me feel better by creating new brain cells to replace those damaged by stress and depression." By the time you finish reading this book, you will know even more about the neurophysiology of depression than the average physician, and that's a shame for the doctor and a plus for you, my friend.

References

Becker, E. (1973). *The Denial of Death*. New York, NY: Free Press.

CHAPTER 9

EVIDENCE-BASED TREATMENT FOR DEPRESSION

**"The Prescription of Exercise for Depression,"
1978**

Four decades ago, I started writing this book. I thought I had discovered a safe and effective, even ideal, treatment for depression.

The foundation of my ideal treatment for depression is and was the concept of the critical importance of *fitness* of mind, body, and spirit, beginning with regular physical exercise. The editors of a prestigious psychiatric journal rejected the article I submitted for publication about the treatment in 1978. "If what you describe in your manuscript were true," said the editors, "it would revolutionize the practice of psychiatry, but we remain unconvinced by your data."

Regretfully, annoyed and disheartened, I crumpled the rejection letter from the editor of the psychiatric journal. The letter hastily found its home in my trash can. I kept no copy of the letter; only its memory remains. But it did not stop my enthusiasm for the role of fitness in treating major depression. It did not change my treatment approach, and it did not change my teaching of Mental Health at the University of Virginia. If it had a positive effect, and I believe it did, the rejection challenged me to continue motivating patients and students to discover the rewards of fitness.

The July 2018 issue of the *American Journal of Psychiatry* published an article by Schuch and colleagues, "Physical Activity and Incident Depression: A Meta-Analysis of Prospective Cohort Studies." This landmark study concluded that "Available evidence supports the notion that physical activity can confer protection against the emergence of depression regardless of age and geographical region." This remarkable study confirmed my original research. It appeared exactly 40 years after I published "The Prescription of Exercise for Depression," in *Physician and Sports Medicine,* 1978, and after *Time* magazine published an article about my work entitled "Jogging for the Mind," July 24, 1978.

Admittedly, my original research was barely minimal, unlike my enthusiasm. I have the highest praise and respect for the diligence and magnitude of Schuch and colleagues (2018) who reported their meta-analysis study in the *American Journal of Psychiatry.* At last, the evidence is in hand to "revolutionize the practice of psychiatry." I believe we can now hope that depression will finally yield to a very different approach, one beginning with physical exercise.

I had witnessed the beneficial effects of physical activity first hand in my practice since 1971. I encourage all who doubt the evidence that physical exercise prevents and serves a major role in treating clinical depression to read the laudable *American Journal of Psychiatry* by Schuch and his colleagues.

Psychotherapy

Cognitive behavioral therapy (CBT) developed by Aaron T. Beck (1979) is the leading approach to restore the fitness of the mind damaged by depression, and other disorders.

The fitness of the human spirit is the most challenging to achieve as has been shown by a series of major disappointments, beginning with the realization that mankind's imperfectability is immutable. Until the mid-1940s, it was widely believed that human beings could be perfected. We only lacked the right education, the best economy, or the right government. Nearly all hopes for humanity's perfectibility were dashed after we learned that the Nazis tried to eliminate the Jews, and the additional evil that made the use of atomic bombs on Hiroshima and Nagasaki, 1945, necessary to end World War II. The vital work of the three Abrahamic religions will not cease until the human spirit is at last at peace with its Maker and Redeemer, although the task is sometimes a faltering one.

Disappointingly, I put off the writing of this book until now. Nonetheless, I continued to treat depressed patients with the same treatment. I also taught psychiatric residents under my supervision the same methods that evolved from my observations of depressed patients. Some 30,000 students who enrolled in my Mental Health course at the University of Virginia from about 1965 to 2005 were encouraged to favorably consider the understanding and treatment of depression from the exercise perspective. I gave academic credit to students who participated in the exercise option, described earlier and more completely below.

"For goodness sake," you may ask, "What is this treatment for depression you propose?" Oddly, the answer is not a simple one. Depression is a challenging disorder to understand, and its treatment is equally tricky. Permit me to retrace the steps that led me to the position that occupies my thinking about depression and explain why I waited until now to finally set out to write about it, despite encouragement from others to come forward much earlier. Among other reasons, my depression book was slow seeing daylight because of a lack of time. Now, at last, I have the time this critical task deserves since I recently retired from the practice of psychiatry and from teaching.

Scholars whose careers are devoted to the treatment of depression will tell you that, at best, antidepressant medication has a "modest effect" on depression. Psychotherapy, at best, has a "modest effect" relieving depression, and exercise also has, at best, a "modest effect" on the treatment of depression. On the other hand, the most recent research demonstrates a more vigorous antidepressant effect of exercise than previously reported.

Why not combine the three approaches to the treatment of depression? The merit of a combinatorial approach seems plausible, but the practice is rare. Most psychiatrists prescribe antidepressant medication for depression. Most psychologists, unlicensed to prescribe antidepressant medication, treat depressed patients with psychotherapy. Most everyone believes physical exercise is probably a good thing to do, but few therapists begin treating depressed patients with physical activity. Keep this in your mind because I want to return to it.

In this book, I'm addressing people who struggle with depression and those who love them, but I also want scholars to nod approvingly towards its content. As we proceed, I will provide references that confirm my observations. Please be patient. Make no changes in your current treatment without first discussing it with your provider. Thoughtfully and skeptically, consider what I write and determine if it passes the logic test for you.

The History of an Idea

As the sixth child of a family caught up in the economic depression of the 1930s, I always felt loved and protected, but I was shy, sensitive, and easily frightened by the events swirling around me. Mounting tension between my visually impaired dad, and Randolph, my brother 10 years my senior, led to Randolph's early enlistment in the Navy, at age 17, precisely two years before the Japanese attack on Pearl Harbor on December 7, 1941.

Randolph survived World War II, but he was traumatized. Twice he went over the side when the ships on which he served were torpedoed in the North Atlantic and were sinking. He was never the same person after the war, held no job for any considerable length of time, never married, and died of colon cancer at 87, several years after my dad, with whom he lived following the death of my mother, died at age 93.

It was natural that education was not valued in my family because my dad never learned to read or write and signed his name with an "X." The highest grade in school my mother attended was the fourth. My parents were intelligent, and my siblings were bright, but none of them attempted to complete high school. There were no magazines or books in my home except the Holy Bible, but it gathered dust until my parents became Christians when I was a teenager. From then on, my mother, despite terrible lighting from a single high-hanging bulb in the ceiling and the worsening of her glaucoma, faithfully read the Good Book every night for what seemed to me to be hours.

My dad was a quiet man who was often at his workbench in our backyard. A smoking pipe dangled from his lips. He seldom lit his pipe, but Prince Albert tobacco packed its bowl. As a house painter, his employable hours were best suited to the good weather. On rainy days, altogether a common occurrence in Norfolk, Virginia, he assumed his lying-down position upon a daybed in our kitchen, a posture my mother hated. Far too frequently to forget, she cautioned me with a fearfully dreaded angry warning: "Bobby, never end up on your back like your father. Get an education!"

I was never encouraged to be like my dad, to fix things. This formally uneducated man had the combined and unique skills of a carpenter, electrician, plumber, automotive mechanic, painter, and general fixer-upper. He loved the sea, spent his youth on tugboats in the Elizabeth River, and always wanted to own a boat, but he never did. Instead of attending school, he was on a tugboat at 12 years of age when battery acid splashed into his face, blinding him in his right eye for the rest of his 93 years. As a hobby—you guessed it—he made sea-worthy small sailboats and rowboats. Today, one of his model rowboats, painted white with dark red trim, sits within my view on my window sill.

My mother was a strong, authoritarian woman. Neighbors came to her with many of their medical needs, to get their family members out of jail, or for counsel. She was the captain of our ship, one familiar with storms. I had three sisters, all married twice, with six brothers-in-law. Out of respect for, or perhaps fear of my mother, their ship sailed smoothly. There were periods when my sisters experienced physical spousal abuse and neglect, but it all seemed to work out well over the years. I was like an older brother to my nephews and niece who spent most of their childhood under the roof and care of my mother.

From the early years of my life, my mother's dream for me was to sing country music and learn to play the guitar. It simply did not happen, but our son, her third grandson, Clinton, fulfilled her dream for me to become a musician. His musical talents are abundant, surpassing all expectations, with a chosen genre that is consistent with the Beatles. Clinton can play and sing country music as well as anyone, but it is not his first choice.

My dreams were different. I always wanted to become a soldier and a physician. My mother died in 1971, within hours of receiving the announcement that I had finally completed my medical education. It was confirmation of the powerful contribution of her unfailing prayers for my family and me. My mother, endowed with wisdom, always encouraged me. She knew that I needed her prayers.

The Birth of an Idea

The birth of the notion most relevant to my approach to understand and treat depression occurred on the playground at James Madison Elementary School located on Hampton Boulevard in Norfolk, Virginia. I was in Ms. Gray'second grade class in the spring of 1938. The class ran the 50-yard dash. To everyone's surprise, I was the fastest runner in the second grade. Thin and speedy, I enjoyed learning something about myself that was previously unknown to me. It may have been the tiniest first step in the direction of self-confidence. It did not change my life, but it helped. For a long time, it seemed, I remained the last man chosen when teams selected players for pickup ball games.

Self-doubt still reigned five years later when W.P. Sullivan, the principal of James Madison Elementary School, asked me to play for the school basketball team. Yes, I was fast, even tall, but I was conscious of what I could not do. I turned him down, thinking I could not dribble, play defense, or shoot baskets well. To be factual, I had never played basketball. I later regretted that I permited my fear of failure and self-doubt to over-ride Mr. Sullivan's invitation.

The advantages of running fast were emerging slowly within my developing sense of awareness. Those who knew Norfolk in the late 1930s, 1940s, and early 1950s need no reminder that my neighborhood, Lamberts Point, competed with Atlantic City as the bluest of the blue-collar districts: high crime rates, low income, and limited opportunity except for those with athletic ability. I cannot honestly state that I fully appreciated at the time the ramifications of what I just wrote. Instead of an influence on my consciousness, I was only aware of the embarrassment I felt, exiting the bus at 38th Street, that others would discover I lived in a poor neighborhood.

I never liked telling people where I lived. I experienced the prejudice that was rampant towards the poor. In this way, I felt a kinship with Negroes, as these people were called during my childhood and young adulthood, because they were also treated prejudicially or, perhaps even worse, with indifference. I grew up within two city blocks of their neighborhood, but our interactions were extremely infrequent. I remember attending a Negro Baptist Church, struck by differences between my church services and theirs.

I was 15 years old when Coach Collings asked me to play football for the Lamberts Point Rangers in the Junior Football League, sponsored by the city of Norfolk's Department of Recreation. During the season, we lost every game and scored no points, but I learned that I enjoyed competitive sports, felt at home on the field, and loved the game. The following year we were undefeated, untied, and unscored upon. Our success came to the attention of Tony Saunders, Maury High School football coach. He came to one of our games and extended an invitation to play for the

Maury High School Commodores the following season.

There is still something special about the smell of freshly mown grass that renews the great memories of playing football at Maury High School. We practiced Monday through Thursday and played our opponents on Friday nights under the lights at Foreman Field, now the stadium for Old Dominion University. After 15 minutes of calisthenics at the beginning of football practice, we ran plays. I was a starting wingback on the single wing formation. I also played safety because in those days we all played both offense and defense. Maury had successful seasons. Until my junior year, we wore leather helmets.

Without knowing it, I was in good physical shape. I was physically fit, but I did not exercise for its own sake. I did things I loved, and most often they involved physical activity. I was not a body-builder or a weight-lifter, but my main daily chore at home was carrying two heavy buckets of coal from the backyard coal-bin to their place behind the coal stove in our kitchen, our only source of heat during cold weather. My dad banked the coal fire at night, and he accelerated its fire early each morning, skillfully employing the poker that hung beside the stove.

To every destination, I rode a Western Flyer gearless bicycle. It was my only means of transportation. Looking back on my life then, it was what cardiologists today would describe as ideal and rewarding. My mother prepared nutritious meals, I seldom overate, and I was never overweight at that time in my life. Each morning, I received a glass of freshly squeezed orange juice. My mother had removed the seeds. Attuned to the needs of her son, she continually nurtured and strengthened his character and self-confidence.

I spent the summers from 1949 to 1953 as a counselor at Camp Greenbrier in Alderson, West Virginia, stayed in good shape, and worked out with fellow athletes. Counseling at Camp Greenbrier opened a vista I would never have known had it not been for Kitty Garnett, who was one of my teachers at Maury High School. Her husband, Theodore Garnett, was a prince of a man. He co-owned the camp with two other principals, one being Bus Male who was a University of Virginia assistant football coach. Bus Male had been an outstanding athlete at Virginia years earlier. The other co-owner, Cooper Dawson, a Navy veteran of World War II, owned the Penn-Daw Hotel in Northern Virginia.

When I graduated from Maury High School, January 1950, Bus Male saw that I had a room in the Football House at 504 Rugby Road, Charlottesville, and an opportunity to join the University of Virginia football team during spring practice in 1950. I enrolled at the University in January 1950. Without excuses, I walked away from the opportunity to become a Virginia football player after a half-hearted attempt. It was a painful decision, one clouded with shame and regret, one I have never felt good about making, one I cannot fully and intelligently explain even to the man whose image is beheld in the mirror each morning when I shave.

Did I lose interest in football? No. Did I lose interest in physical exercise? No. Did I lose interest in my state of physical fitness? Not immediately, but over time. The occasional times

I climbed on the scales to weigh myself, I discovered the scales revealed a disappointing weight gain.

"Tempus fugit," as Virgil reminds us; that is, time flies! In 1964, in medical school for a second try after a 10-year hiatus, as already mentioned in the Preface, several of my classmates and I were observing post-mortem examinations of three young men killed in vehicular motor accidents. The pathologist directed our attention to the early evidence of the consequences of a "lifestyle disease," a term I had not heard previously.

"Observe the bright yellow streaks of fat throughout the lining of the aorta, the large vessel through which blood courses from the heart. Typical American diets and physical inactivity are already at work in damaging the essential vessels that carry life-giving blood. These young men were only 18 to 20 years old, and they were well on their way to morbidity and mortality simply by the way they lived. Soon these yellow streaks of fat would have hardened, calcified, and closed down the functional diameter of their blood vessels."

It was stunning, eye-opening news to me, a 32-two-year-old medical student, father of four children by then, with little or no life insurance, but already medically followed for the treatment of hypertension. A decade engulfed in pursuit of education and holding down two jobs had brought me back to medical school, but I had neglected my health.

The pathologist's message, holding up in his hands the aorta of one of the three young men whose lifestyles had already damaged their hearts, was a wake-up call for me! It must remain a wake-up call for me because I repeat it here.

Medical students have little time for exercise, but as I said earlier, I purchased the *Royal Canadian Air Force Exercise Plans for Physical Fitness*, followed it religiously, and got back into a good state of physical fitness. I re-discovered the sense of well-being I had known as a physically fit athlete. It was a delightful state of body and mind. The feeling of well-being was astounding. I hesitate to say that I felt more spiritually healthy in my restored state of physical fitness, but I believe there is a relationship between the two.

Trust me—I was getting a rare second chance to study medicine. For that alone, I was humbled and thankful. To an even higher degree, I was also in need of prayer. My mother, described best by one of my friends as a "prayer warrior," had steadily prayed for me. Whenever given the opportunity to make a prayer request, it was for "my son, Bobby, and his family."

Can People Change?

Can people change? We are continually changing, evolving creatures. At times, it is helpful to reflect on the changes one undergoes, examining the reasons for the favorable and unfavorable changes in our lives. A few pages earlier in this book, for example, I described changing from a threat-sensitive child to a physically fit athlete. I then described changing, pretty much outside my conscious awareness, from a physically fit athlete to a busy, weight-gaining, non-exercising non-athlete, and a non-self-respecting person caught up in "making a living."

Dramatically learning from a pathologist in medical school about the severe consequences of lifestyle disease, I described how I rediscovered the sense of well-being that came from changing my lifestyle back to one of disciplined physical fitness training. Like a master sculptor, the return to a disciplined life re-created feelings that once formed my sense of self, but I had not experienced that sense of self for ten years.

As a former athlete, I had a previously known the feeling of physical well-being that I needed to work towards achieving again. If you have not already been an athletic person, you will not know the sense of well-being towards which to strive. I do not doubt, however, that you will know the real joy of being physically fit when you discover it. It is a uniquely soothing sense that improves your perceptions, cognitions, and relationships. It is real. It is lasting only if you conscientiously maintain it with disciplined training or self-mastery.

"This is too real just to be in my mind," I said to myself upon rediscovering the sense of well-being associated with physical fitness. Clarification: I'm not talking about the "runner's high" or peak emotional experience. I'm not declaring that you must run a marathon to experience the sense of well-being I am describing, but I can't imagine a marathon runner who neglects physical fitness. I'm advocating a healthy lifestyle that includes reasonable attention to nutrition, physical activity, refreshing sleep, secure attachments to those you value and for whom you are essential, and spiritual restoration for the sense of inner peace. In a few words, seek and retain attention toward maintaining your physical, mental, and spiritual fitness.

References

Beck, A.T., Rush, A.J., Shaw, B.E., Emery, G. (1979). *Cognitive Therapy of Depression*. New York, NY: The Guilford Press.

Brown, R. S., Ramirez, D. E., and Taub, J. M. (1978). The prescription of exercise for depression. *Phys Sportsmed, 6*(12): 34-45.

Schuch, F., Vancampford, D., Firth, J., Rosenbaum, S., Ward, P.B., Silva, E.S., ...Stubbs, B. Physical activity and incident depression: a meta-analysis of cohort studies. *Am J Psychiatry, 175*(7): 631-648.

Jogging for the mind. (1978, July 24). *Time Magazine*. 112(4): 42.

CHAPTER 10

MY FIRST DEPRESSION RESEARCH

Fifty-Five People

I wondered if others, especially those people who felt depressed, could experience the sense of well-being I got from physical exercise. I ran an ad in the *Daily Progress*, the local Charlottesville, Virginia, newspaper, asking for volunteers to participate in a study of the effects of exercise on depression. It was a cold, rainy January night in 1971, nearly fifty years ago. Fifty-five people, ranging from 18 to 72 years of age, showed up and took a screening test for depression (the Center for the Epidemiologic Studies Depression Scale, CES-D).

They were advised to check first with their physicians to clear them for regular physical activity such as brisk walking, jogging, swimming, bike-riding, stepping on an elliptical, or moving on a treadmill. I gave them an exercise-recording booklet in which to record their exercise type, duration, degree of exertion, pre- and post-exercise pulse rates, and mood estimate using a 1 to 10 point scale, with 10 indicating the worst mood. I answered their questions, gave them my contact information, and asked them to return in six weeks. I promised to provide their depression scores at the end of the study when the CES-D results were available.

To my knowledge, no one sustained an injury or experienced other mishaps during the study. Of the 55 who started, 50 people returned six weeks later, took the CES-D, turned in their exercise recording booklets, and discussed the study results. As a group, the depression scores were elevated in the beginning and significantly reduced to normal at the end of six weeks of exercise. The sense of well-being from physical training was real, too real to be just in my mind, and thus I believed I was approaching an ideal treatment for depression. We know the old saying, "One swallow does not make a summer." One study was not proving my thesis. I consulted an expert for advice and guidance.

Dr. Fred Goodwin

In my opinion, Dr. Fred Goodwin, an American Psychiatrist and upcoming Scientific Director and Chief of Intramural Research, was a leading authority on depression in the 1970s and beyond. He remains a scholar, a skilled clinician, and a person I have always admired and respected. Dr. Goodwin agreed to meet with me and share his views about the unfunded research.

The monoamine theory, which was premised upon the notion of altered neurotransmitters— the brain chemicals connecting brain cells—was the foundation of antidepressant psychopharmacology and the dominant theory at that time in our understanding of the treatment of most cases of depression. Dr. Goodwin reasoned that if physical exercise was beneficial to depressed patients, it must be influencing neurotransmitters. Epinephrine was one of the widely studied neurotransmitters at the time.

Dr. Goodwin offered to study the urine of my depressed subjects before and after regular physical exercise regimens. Many University students in my Mental Health course volunteered to participate in the study. I collected urine specimens from my subjects, froze and stored the samples in my freezers at home. As time and opportunity permitted, Dr. Goodwin studied the samples in his lab at NIMH.

Epinephrine was a problematic neurotransmitter to study directly. MHPG, chemically known as 3-methoxy-4-hydroxyphenylglycol, is a metabolite of brain epinephrine activity that Dr. Goodwin studied. I drove frozen urine samples to Bethesda, and Dr. Goodwin, a busy scientist with many competing tasks, told me he found a trend in our urine samples that indicated physical exercise stimulated the release of epinephrine in the brain. Unfortunately, the study was necessarily delayed and never completed. We agreed that a trend was not reportable.

Combining Clinical Practice with Research

In the style of Thomas Edison following the complete loss of his plant to fire, I kept up the search for an ideal treatment for depression. All new patients who came to me for treatment completed the Paffenbarger Physical Activity Questionnaire (1986), an exercise inventory, along with a battery of psychological tests. Patients also completed a questionnaire about habits related to smoking history, alcohol ingestion, prescription and street drug abuse, and nutrition. Interesting to me was the fact that not a single depressed person was exercising. These patients were not physically fit. Moreover, they saw no connection between their health habits and their clinical depression symptoms.

Physicians obtain informed consent as essential requirement of all treatment beause it gives the patient full knowledge of all possible risks and benefits. With my own patients, I interpreted the results from the patient's questionnaire. Then I explained that the standard treatment for major depression at that time was administration of antidepressant medication and psychotherapy when available. If the patient agreed, I offered alternative therapies: physical exercise and cognitive therapy. If a need became apparent, we reviewed and decided upon a specific antidepressant. A minority of my patients wanted nothing more nor less than the standard psychiatric treatment for depression.

The exercise option that I advocate was and is based entirely on common sense. One comtemplating the option should ensure that his or her physician clears exercise for 30 minutes at least three times weekly, again ascribing to the notion to "start low and go slow," to be gradually increased to 150 minutes weekly.

Excessive exerise defeats the purpose. In the beginning, I prefer brisk walking on a level surface as a nearly ideal exercise. I caution one against exercising in congested areas with heavy traffic because exhaust fumes are not likely better for us than fresh air. While fitness involves more than regular physical activity, undertaking a more active lifestyle is an excellent place to begin. Once undertaken, I encourage saving a few minutes at the end of each exercise session to lightly stretch and meditate or pray.

Dr. Aaron T. Beck's Theory of Depression and its Treatment

Dr. Aaron Beck's 1979 book *Cognitive Therapy of Depression* describes the basis of the cognitive therapy option. I first read this book on the beach of the Outer Banks of North Carolina while vacationing with my family. It inspired me. Dr. Beck began his psychiatric education in the psychoanalytic theory of the mind, but he was disappointed in the results he observed. I also trained in the psychoanalytic theory of the mind and several of my fellow psychiatry residents went into analysis, following the examples of our professors. Fueling my interest in cognitive theory was a scientific article written by Dr. Beck nearly ten years earlier.

Dr. Beck does not know the cause of depression, he acknowledges, but he has proven that depressogenic thoughts, influenced by deeply held negative beliefs, keeps depression alive and well. His refreshing, clarifying ideas about depression intrigued me. Shortly after that, I met

Dr. Beck, a humble, kind, and most compassionate person.

After attending one workshop at the University of Pennsylvania on cognitive therapy, I enrolled in a two-year extramural fellowship in cognitive therapy. Each week, Dr. Judy Beck, Dr. Aaron Beck's daughter, listened to a one-hour tape-recording of my sessions with a depressed person in which I followed the cognitive therapy approach. Learning cognitive therapy was one of the most important and valuable decisions of my professional career. With time, cognitive therapy changed into cognitive behavioral theapy (CBT). Its effectiveness in the treatment of depression and some other mental disorders is unsurpassed. We will address the details of CBT later.

My Mental Health Class at the University of Virginia

With the consent of the director of the residency program, I was permitted, as a second-year psychiatric resident, to teach Mental Health. As a unique accommodation, in the event I was on- call Wednesday nights between 7:00 and 9:40, I first taught Mental Health in the Tumor Clinic

Amphitheater, a classroom near the Emergency Room, where on-call residents in psychiatry at the University of Virginia saw patients.

Fourteen students enrolled in my first Mental Health class, an elective course, listed as both an undergraduate and graduate course. The graduate students were required to write a special paper on an approved mental health topic in addition to passing the midterm and final exams with a grade of B or higher. The class was taught in a manner that fitness concepts were valued in its broadest meaning. Enrollment increased to 500 students each semester.

I believe two teaching methods I employed attracted and maintained the large enrollment it enjoyed for nearly 40 years. First, I took one of my fully informed patients to class with me. I selected patients whose stories needed to be heard. After the patient's story was told, a spirited round of applause always followed along with a round of student-directed questions to the patient. Without exception, the patients credited the class appearance as valuable and memorable. Second, because I am convinced that maintaining a sense of well-being requires personal commitment to fitness, I gave academic credit for exercise. I also shared my sobering experience of examining the consequences of lifestyle diseases on the cardiovascular systems of young adult men killed in traffic accidents.

Since its founding in 1819, the University of Virginia has amassed some well-earned traditions from which have sprung several enduring reputations. The one I stress here is the Honor System. As President of the School of Medicine Class of 1967, it was my privilege to serve on the Honor Committee (1966-67), the final arbiter in disputed matters of honor. Nothing was taken more seriously than the Honor System. Pledged work for any class fell under the Honor System. Its violation led to immediate expulsion from the University. The exercise option, a choice voluntarily made by any willing student in my Mental Health class, was pledged work. Other options included a self-reflection journal, dream journal, or library project.

Nearly all students selected the exercise option. In addition to exercising at least 30 minutes daily at least three days weekly, the exercise option required much more:

1. Depression tests were administered at the beginning and the end of the semester.
2. A two-mile run, weight, and vital signs were measured pre- and post-semester to assess physical fitness. These important occassions were observed and collected on the first day and last day at the track.
3. Each student maintained a pledged exercise journal, reviewed weekly by their teaching assistant. The exercise journal contained the essential details of the student's thrice weekly exercise experience, including the type of exercise, duration, intensity, and effect on mood.

Twenty-six teaching assistants, all having previously taken and excelled in my Mental Health class, were led by a graduate student who also had excelled in Mental Health. Twenty-five groups of 20 students, each with its teaching assistant, were formed out of the 500 total student enrollment. My graduate assistant and I met with the teaching asisstants one hour weekly before the class met. This commitment of time and effort proved safe and rewarding for all participants.

The data collected from the exercise option group firmly established an essential role of regular physical exercise in effectively reducing depression, a condition far too common among college students in this country today.

"What lessons can be learned from the Mental Health Class?" I'd sum it up to this: Any type of exercise is better than none and walking is an ideal form of exercise. Admittedly, many people are limited to little or no physical exercise owing to health factors beyond their control. To these people, I would extend the notion that innovation and creativity can prevail.

Those with challenges often derive ingenious ways to exercise, even when limited to moving parts of the body in isolation. If this descriptive applies to you, then I'd encourage you to do the best you can, taking pride in the fact that we can strive toward fitness goals using a variety of different methods. Exemplifying this was Christopher Reeve, a man who became a quadriplegic after being thrown from his horse during an equestrian event in Culpeper, Virginia. Despite the significant injuries, Reeve later rose in fitness status by finding the ways and means to work out daily despite his significant impairments. In my mind, he was the most physically fit person in the world at that time, even after becoming a quadriplegic.

The Idea Becomes Operational

I had been an athlete, but I was also reared under circumstances that required regular physical activity. I never owned a car before I was married. Walking or riding a bicycle was my ordinary means of transportation unless inclement weather forced public transit upon me. In looking back, poverty was a positive influence. I lived in a neighborhood in which all the critical activities of my life were within walking distance of my home. My friends lived nearby. I could see my church from my backyard, and my school was not more than a 15 minute bike ride from home. The athletic fields,

"fields of friendly strife," were no more than a 5 or 10 minute walk away.

I practiced psychiatry from 1971 to 2016. The last 11 years of my practice were spent working with the brave men and women of our military forces. In 45 years of psychiatric practice, I have never treated a physically fit depressed person. I wrote "The prescription of exercise for depression," "Jogging: Its uses and abuses," "Exercise and mental health in the pediatric population." I'm a believer.

Notwithstanding, I think that we should approach fitness reasonably and rationally. To do so, determine with your physician to what extent you may safely exercise. Also keep in mind that extreme physical activity is hazardous to your health. Excesses of all types are unhealthy and unreasonable. It is not a part of the physical fitness training that I'm advocating for the treatment and prevention of depression.

If Dr. Phillips and I have successfully achieved our goals in writing this book, you will understand depression more than ever before.

1. You will know the evidence for the usual kinds of treatments for depression.
2. You will be informed about the scientific evidence supporting how physical exercise influences the function of the brain.
3. You will become so sick and tired of depression that you will want to physically, mentally, and spiritually understand the condition so that you can find your way out of its grip, no matter how tightly or for how long it has held you in its ugly grasps.

Do you want to be released from depression? Not wanting to get better is not shameful; it is common to all who have encountered depression, a terrible state of mind, body, and spirit in which the will to fight often yields to the disease. We will return to this common characteristic of depression.

References

Brown, R. S. (1982). Exercise and mental health in the pediatric population, *Clin Sports Med, (1)*3: 515-527.

Brown, R.S. Jogging: Its uses and abuses. (1979). *Va Med, 106*(7): 522-529.

Brown, R. S., Ramirez, D. E., and Taub, J. M. (1978). The prescription of exercise for depression. *Phys Sportsmed, 6*(12): 34-45.

Paffenbarger, R. S., Hyde R.T., Wing, A.L., Hsieh, C.C. (1986). Physical activity, all-cause mortality, and longevity of college alumni. *N Engl J Med, 314*(10): 605-613.

Schuch, F.B., Vancampfort, D., Firth, Jl,Rosenbaum, S., Ward, P.B., Silva, E.S., Stubbs, B. (2018). Physical activity and incident depression: A meta-analysis of prospective cohort studies. *Am J Psychiatry, 175*(7): 631-648.

MY DEPRESSED PATIENTS

To Retire or Not to Retire

Like others in my situation, I felt too young to retire. No humor is intended, but I was only 85 years old when I stopped full-time practice. On the other hand, was I beyond my usefulness? As Shakespeare would say, "Aye, there's the rub." How does anyone know their capacity to be useful at anything? I wrestled with this question for weeks. Some attractive temporary medical practices were made available. "I don't think I want to see a psychiatrist who is as old as me," I told the recruiters. Thinking I was joking, they laughed, but finally stopped calling.

If I were writing a play, the actors would be instructed to be "serious" here. The thought of giving up being a physician saddened me. It is what I always wanted to do and what I loved doing. It is what I was called to do. The feeling of sadness would linger, I feared, unless I could find a way of working. How could I continue to contribute? Could I write encouraging words to help improve the health and well-being of others? I closed my practice and all other doors leading to employment. I decided to see if I could write about depression's response to fitness, self-regard, and rational thinking.

Secretary John O. Marsh's Influence Upon the U.S. Army

My wife and I had the distinct privilege of meeting the Honorable John O. Marsh, the former secretary of the army, who served under three U.S. presidents. He was an army paratrooper in World War II, where he had a distinguished career as an enlisted man. We were with him at a birthday party in Warrenton, Virginia, when he got the news that his son, a soldier, had been severely wounded in combat in Somali.

Thankfully, his son heroically overcame his multiple injuries and is now a country doctor.

One day, many years ago, Secretary Marsh asked me to meet him at a hotel in Charlottesville. I was pleased to hear from him but puzzled by the invitation. We went to the exercise and indoor swimming pool area of the hotel. He asked me to look around and make a rough count of the exercise machines in the area. Then he said, "All we need for the Army Fitness Test is a stopwatch and a pair of scales. The test can be conducted anywhere in the world."

Secretary Marsh was a man of few words, but what he accomplished for the Army is unsurpassed, mostly unknown and thus unappreciated. Quietly, he racially integrated the army, created family services for military wives and children, set up fruit and salad bars, and mixed eggs with Egg Beaters in all army dining facilities, required photographs of every candidate for promotion, mandated the Army Weight Control Program (AWCP), the Army Physical Fitness Test, and much more. In spite of these unrivaled achievements, he shunned all forms of publicity about himself or his work.

Encouragement

The real meaning and value of encouragement, the principal objective of this undertaking, came to me when I was taking the U.S. Army's Physical Fitness Test during Operation Desert Storm. At the time, the shooting was over because the ground campaign lasted less than 100 hours, and the army sent me to Walter Reed Army Medical Center, Washington, D.C., and then to Fort Lee, Virginia. Everyone who served in the U.S. Army knows the Physical Fitness Test is taken twice annually. Every Soldier must pass the test. After my weigh-in, a cause of much anxiety, I was tasked with sit-ups, push-ups, and a two-mile run, a part of the Physical Fitness Test that I knew would be difficult for me.

April in 1991 was a beautiful month, but it was humid and hot in the sun for those of us taking the Army Physical Fitness Test at Fort Lee, Virginia. Part of the two-mile run traversed the dark dirt roads through the Civil War battlefield where thousands had given their lives in the

Battle of Petersburg. Some say they can actually feel the spirits of the dead soldiers today in the park-like quiet areas of the battlefield. Imbued by those fighting spirits, I remember running out of the shade at a good pace, turning left onto Mahone Avenue, and then feeling the blast of the bright sun, a formidable force that was hotter than expected. I doubted, for the first time, whether I could finish the race at my pace. I could not yet see the finish line where several soldiers with stopwatches stood shouting out the time as each runner crossed the finish line on A Avenue. The finish line was another left turn away, although I could faintly hear them.

Unexpectedly, nearby, someone shouted, "If I can do it, so can you, Doc. Keep going, man. You look great."

Until I heard those words of encouragement, I didn't feel great; I was giving up, but the words were compelling. It was like a miracle out of the blue. It was as if someone understood. I was immediately comforted. A sudden motivation accelerated my legs and my will to win. It was like an unknown person was speaking; no, not talking, but shouting to my soul, "You may be 60 years old, but you are not giving up. You probably could have gotten out of the test, but you did not stay on the sidelines. You asked for no slack. You got up early this morning to do your best. You could have stayed home in the first place. You could have hidden behind your medical practice as an excuse, but you volunteered to serve your country during a time of war, willing to go anywhere and do anything your country needed to be done by you."

The stranger's words pulled and pushed me to a successful end of the run. In looking back, it reminds me of the observation made by Jesus about the value of small acts of kindness. "Truly I tell you, anyone who gives you a cup of water in my name because you belong to the Messiah will certainly not lose their reward." (Mark 9:41 NIV).

It is not the joy of passing the Army Physical Fitness Test 28 years ago that soothes my soul today. It is the memory of the encouraging words from an unidentified person that surprised me then, and moves me now to tears. As I read the above lines to two dear friends, Drs. Eleanor and

Terry Gagon, both retired physicians whose careers were spent mainly serving in the army, their thoughtful comments brought even greater fulfillment to the experience.

More Encouragement for Depressed Patients

"You sound heroic, Dr. Brown, but depression makes me think I'm the opposite of a brave soldier. I feel more like a failing coward. All I want to do is sleep, and I can't even do that well. I can't imagine running in a race. I could never be a Soldier. You were willing to go anywhere, but I'm not ready to leave my house. I can't stand the thought of being encouraged to do something I'd never dream of doing.

"Are you trying to make me feel worse, doctor? I don't believe a deeply depressed person can relate to what you are writing. You don't know what my depression does to me. Somehow, I know you want to help me, and you treated many depressed patients for many years, but are we sailing on two very different ships in entirely different directions? Are you trying to impress me with who you are and what you have done? I don't need to be impressed; I need to be understood."

It is true that being understood is immediately comforting, a valuable observation made by former Professor of Harvard Psychiatry, Dr. Elvin Semrad.   Yet by corollary, self-understanding is enhanced when we take the time to understand others."

Readers who respond to my writing as self-centered include my daughter, Nancy, an experienced reading and teaching specialist. I know there is some truth in what I'm being told here by my depressed reader as well, and I'm working on it. On the other hand, don't throw me out with the bathwater. Please continue reading to see if you agree there is value for those who are depressed in the approach I am taking. I shared my story about passing the Army Physical Fitness Test because I want you to experience the strong influence of encouragement. Try perceiving encouragement as one way you are understood. Few things are more comforting than being understood.

In the running story, I had to be in the race to be encouraged. Many depressed, as well as nondepressed, people know exercise is right for them, but they don't exercise. People who are suffering from depression need reminding that even a minimal amount of activity can have a substantial positive effect in reducing their symptoms of depression. Thus, consider this encouragement to leave the sidelines of life so that you can win the race for health.

Dr. Beck encourages his depressed patients to conduct a simple experiment. After listening to the patient, Dr. Beck would concur that the patient was depressed and then would very kindly ask, "Would you be willing to write down your mood in your daily log, on a rating scale from 1 to 10? An entry of 1 would signify no depression and 10 would signify feeling about as depressed as you imagine you could ever be. You could make the recording several times daily, always briefly noting what you are doing, such as sitting in a chair, lying in bed, watching TV—whatever activity occupies you. At least once daily, leave your house or apartment and go shopping or for a short walk. Note your mood from 1 to 10 again while you are out. Always bring your daily log to our treatment session."

Guess what happened? Every depressed patient's mood improved when they got in the race, using my metaphor, and became active. Further, the depressed patients were surprised by the fact that merely ambulating for short distances in their habitat, even for brief periods, improved their mood. Aristotle said, "Man is by nature a social animal." His statement underscores the fact that the minds and souls of men and women require companionship with and compassion from each other to remain compassionate and caring. In fact, humans must be loved by and attached to others to survive and flourish. When depression keeps us away from each other, it inflicts a most profound and severe damage. Bolstering the latter notion is evidence showing that deficits in a person's social networks decrease stress resilience and hippocampal BDNF.

A Season for Everything

There is a time and a season for everything. I'm approaching this new season in my life with the same dedication and compassion that guided me each day I went to my office, a hospital, or a military clinic to treat patients. I believe that what I learned about depression and its treatment may help others. I am writing for patients who may be depressed. I also want to help those who have a family member or a friend whose depression may respond positively to an in-depth, but practical, review of one of the most discouraging and prevalent illnesses of all time.

Two critical elements of my new endeavor are missing: the structure, tangible and abstract, of a medical practice, with its daily schedule, deadlines, and endless forms; and, most important of all, my patients. I present clinical case histories, a proven way of learning, that are instructive, but this is a matter that is not entered into lightly.

Confidentiality

Confidentiality is a patient's right that whatever he or she discloses to a physician remains confidential forever unless one of the few legal exceptions to confidentiality waives it. The patient takes the constitutioanl and common law right to privacy and confidentiality to his or her grave, respectively. These issues guided me as I wrote this book. I raised my right hand shortly after medical school graduation, while repeating the Hippocratic Oath, and promised not to harm my patients.

I present clinical case histories from my lexicon of patient encounters, anonymously, by omitting the elements of identification, while maintaining the integrity of the patients' symptoms of depression. I have put forth a conscientious, good-faith effort to exclude facts that may disclose the personal identity of my former patients. No potentially damaging identifiable information slipped in, as far as I could determine. In my professional opinion, within the limits of reasonable medical certainty, the benefit to suffering depressed patients outweighs the minimal risks to previously treated patients portrayed in the clinical case histories in these chapters.

How I Learned

University of Virginia professors were intellectually stimulating, even inspiring, but I learned more from my patients, especially my depressed patients. Their condition affected every part of their lives, from their appearance to their will to live.

All my patients are unforgettable, and the stories of patients in these chapters, selected from memory, not from medical records long-ago destroyed, reveal how depression afflicts the young and the old, the rich and the poor. A review of these patients' case histories, I believe, will be informative and encouraging.

My Objective

The purpose and objective of this composition is the encouragement of depressed patients who want to learn to heal from depression and prevent the recurrence of future episodes. You can do it. I've seen it happen over and over again. It is not magic, mystical, or challenging to understand. Yet it is demanding because it requires self-discipline; fitness of body, mind, and spirit; and thoughts that are as free of cognitive errors as possible. If it were possible, I would have you listen to a musical recording of Shakespeare's truthful statement, "... there is nothing either good or bad, but thinking makes it so ..." (Hamlet, Act 2, Scene 2) as we ponder the thoughts I'm sharing with you.

Healing Depression by Degree of Fitness, I repeat, is not a substitute for psychiatric treatment or medication when indicated. Please understand its uniqueness as the reminiscences of a student matured by age, informed by experience and study, and motivated by an earnest desire to comfort and encourage the depressed.

I sincerely hope you will benefit from my nearly five decades in the practice of medicine while specializing in psychiatry. I hope you will deepen your insight and understanding of the human soul from the decade I devoted entirely to the diagnoses and treatment of the complex psychological problems of Soldiers traumatized by combat in the war on terror.

My Perspective

I respect the views of all people who abide by the generally accepted interpretations of codified laws, particularly as presented in the Ten Commandments and United States Constitution.

I fight against prejudice in myself and the prejudicial behavior of others. Like Thomas B. Macaulay (1800-1859), I believe people everywhere are most likely to settle a question— including those pertaining to political, racial, and religious issues—when they discuss them freely. Accordingly, I welcome the opinions of others.

When the views of others are opposed to mine, I do not try to silence them by calling them purveyors of "hate speech." I seek the truth, proselytize for no religious group, and have almost no tolerance for ignorance, only sympathy, and I believe in God as depicted in the sacred scriptures of the Bible.

Depression does not favor one political party above another, but it is about beliefs, a central theme of this treatise. Gird up yourself to have the courage to critically face your ideas, including those in the past, present, and future. Get ready to examine your degree and capacity for self-mastery.

Self-mastery and rational thought are the hinge pins on which much of our health turns. These subjects are addressed in detail in discussions to follow. I hope you will come to see that good health is in your hands to a far higher degree than your physicians. Of course, you cannot be your own surgeon, but your need for surgery may be less likely when you are a self-disciplined, rational person.

Cancer and other catastrophic disorders remain unresolved, but specialists who devote their lives to the treatment of these conditions rely on a sentiment first put forth by Hippocrates, "It is more important to know what sort of person has a disease than to know what sort of disease a person has." Fascinatingly, it seems this notion was a presage to our current understanding of the brain and immune system which are intimately connected, readily influencing each other (Kipnis, 2016). Undoubtedly, modern neuroscience now shows that our thoughts and behavior influence our health to the degree opined by Hippocrates.

References

Kipnis, J. (2016). Multifaceted interactions between adaptive immunity and the central nervous system. *Science, 353*(6301): 766-771.

Louveau, L., Smirnov, I., Keyes, T. J., Eccles, J.D., Rouhani, S. J., Peske, J. D., Derecki, N. C., Castle, D., Mandell, J. W., Lee, K.S., Harris, T. H., Kipnis, J. (2015). Structural and functional features of central nervous system lymphatic vessels. *Nature*, 523(7560): 337-341.

CHAPTER 12

JIM, A DEPRESSED COLLEGE STUDENT

The Interview

The man on the phone, sounding anxious, said, "Dr. Brown, will you see my son? He's home from college for the fall break. I'm worried about him." The caller sounded distressed.

I saw the troubled man's son two hours after I got the urgent call. Something in the sound of the father's voice indicated that his son's situation, whatever it was, needed immediate attention.

The young man, Jim, was accompanied by his parents when they came to my office.

Jim sat directly in front of me, his mother sat to his right, and his father was seated to his left. All three people were distraught.

Jim's dad spoke first.

"Dr. Brown, we love our son, and we are very concerned about him. We want to do everything we can to help him, but we have reached our limit. Something is wrong, and we don't know what it is. Jim has changed; he is not the same person he was a couple of months ago. At the end of the summer, when he returned to MIT (Massachusetts Institute of Technology), he was an extraordinary college student, relaxed, poised, and self-confident."

Jim's dad's reddened face, quick jerking movements, and frequent sighing indicated that he was distressed; he was also cross and impatient. His eyes were opened wide, and his bulging neck vessels protruded over the tight-fitting collar of his starched white shirt.

Jim remained silent. He barely moved in his chair. His face, pale like a prisoner's unexposed to the light of day, and his slow, slumped-over gait when entering my office showed his feeling of profound despair. Devoid of curiosity, he gazed at the floor.

Jim's mother turned to her husband and said, "Honey, let me see if I can help explain it to Dr. Brown." A petite woman with early graying dark hair, Jim's mother was calm and composed.

Politely, I interrupted her. Speaking for the first time, I said, "Jim, by now, of course, you know my name and my profession. Do you object to your parents talking to me about you? If you prefer, I will see you privately."

Looking down at the floor, lacking energy, with indifference, Jim, speaking slowly and quietly, said, "It's okay." It appeared to me from Jim's partially opened mouth at the end of his brief statement that he wanted to say more, but he could or would not.

In poorly hidden irritation, shaking his head from side to side, Jim's father stared at him. He was thinking that Jim was not trying hard enough. He wondered if Jim was just "lazy," and needed to stop procrastinating. In a word, Jim's dad misunderstood depression and, after he failed to figure out what was happening to Jim, was left anxious and afraid. His impatience with his son was rapidly increasing.

After a long silence, Jim added, "I don't care."

Before Jim's mother could speak again, Jim's dad hastily said, "He had a complete physical exam yesterday with lab tests, and everything was fine physically. He's lost a little weight, but it's no big deal."

"How much weight did you lose, Jim?" I asked.

"Twenty pounds," Jim whispered.

"Over what period did you lose the weight, Jim?" I asked.

"Two months," Jim replied. His face was mask-like, empty, and expressionless, and he appeared frail and weak. He wore a white, wrinkled, unbuttoned dress shirt, a dirty, once-white T-shirt, un-pressed khaki pants, and an old, soiled pair of untied Nikes running shoes, without socks. He looked at me so infrequently it was difficult to see the color of his eyes, but I think they were blue. His uncombed sandy-colored hair fell over the left side of his forehead, and he stood nearly six feet tall. His unshaven face was youthful for his age. Most people would describe him as attractive, but thin and decidedly unkempt.

Finally, Jim's mother, touching Jim lightly on his right shoulder, speaking insightfully, said, "Jim took on too much this semester. He's president of his fraternity, and they put on a large social function that took a lot of his time. Grade competition is stressful at MIT. They do not inflate grades, but he always made the Dean's List.

"We knew he was busy because he called home much less often. We just learned that he stopped attending class and spent more and more time in bed. Occasionally, he drank beer but not to excess. I worry he may be having a nervous breakdown."

With his voice raised, Jim's father interrupted. Speaking sarcastically and resentfully, he said, "Jim has not had a nervous breakdown. I don't even know what that term means. It's old-fashioned. Nobody has nervous breakdowns anymore.

"Listen to me! He had a great summer job and next summer he is interning as an engineer with advanced electronic training including artificial intelligence, and he has already been offered a six-figure starting salary when he graduates. He can't be having a nervous breakdown! Please, stop using that term."

Jim kept his eyes closed as his father quarreled.

Finally, I got the floor again. "It's clear that Jim has loving and supportive parents. It's also clear that Jim has been a highly successful student in one of our nation's most prestigious universities. Jim's potential for the future is bright, but something has temporarily hindered him. Jim and I will work together to get him unhindered. At least, that's what I want."

Then I spoke directly to the patient and said, "Jim, what do you want from me? I prefer that you carefully consider your options before you answer."

Quietly and very slowly, but convincingly, Jim said, "I know what I want."

After a long, almost endless silence, speaking in a slow monotone, Jim added, "I want to stop suffering."

He covered his face with both hands and wept. His frail frame shook.

Respectfully, no one spoke or moved. It was Jim's moment.

No other word describes depression better than Jim's word, "suffering."

He later referred to that response as a "breakdown," but I saw it as a *breakthrough*, stressing the importance of correct labeling. It did not take a psychiatrist to diagnose Jim's depression. For many depressed patients, crying is not possible. For some depressed patients, crying is a highly valued relief. For Jim, it was the beginning of his commitment to treatment.

Jim's father was dumbfounded. His mother's tears did not stop, but she behaved as if she had done the forbidden, barely audibly saying, "I'm sorry. I'm sorry."

Jim quietly but competently assured me that he wished to live, he had never seriously considered suicide, and he had never made a suicide attempt. There was no family history of suicide attempts. I assessed his risk of self-harm as low at that time. However, all through Jim's therapeutic relationship with me, a period not longer than several months, I looked for evidence of suicidal thoughts or behavior, but found none.

Jim's plan to return to school after the fall break ended, just one week away, was unrealistic. Using the image of a broken limb, I helped him understand that all healing takes place by degree. He would not heal from his depression, his first episode, in a few days. If we were fortunate, he might be able to return to school by the beginning of the following semester. He reluctantly agreed.

Communicating with Jim's School

With Jim's consent, I contacted MIT and requested a retroactive medical leave of absence. I asked that the record of Jim's atypical academic performance for the semester be made void ab initio (void from the beginning of the current semester) because he was severely depressed and had been depressed most of the semester. MIT administrative officials approved the request. As a result, his academic record was unblemished by his depression, a second prominent landmark on Jim's road to healing. Now he could stop grieving over the lost semester, stop hating himself for failing to achieve his recent academic and social goals, and roll up his sleeves to get down to the hard work of restoring his health.

Jim's Treatment

For the first few weeks, I saw Jim daily. This case goes back many years from the time of this writing, but one distinct feature of the treatment sticks out in my memory. It was the contribution of Jim's self-discipline to healing his depression. He did what was asked of him, and he did it to the very best of his ability. As a 21-year-old man, he could physically exert himself more than an older depressed person, but the same degree of self-discipline is potentially present in everyone. Youth has its benefits, but the benefits for young and old are not significantly different when both are self-disciplined.

Successful treatment of depression requires self-discipline and rational thinking. All who experience depression complain of lethargy, low energy, failed interests, inertia, and anxiety. Depressed people know that exercise is right for them, but they don't feel like taking a walk. The less physical activity, the more the depression will increase. The more depression increases, the less the motivation to exercise. And thus, the cycle goes on. Fortunately, we can alter the sequence. Recommendations for this are spelled out in a section called, "How to Start Moving."

Self-Discipline

For years, the relationship between exercise, the mind, and mood fascinated me. This fascination partly stemmed from the recognition that I always felt better after exercise, yet I initially had failed to appreciate the importance of self-discipline as a vital precursor of exercise. The lack of discipline or inconsistent, partial discipline underlies many of the conditions that are decidedly unhealthy.

No one learns discipline without a good mother or father, coach, mentor, or respected leader. In a few words, we all need someone who cares and engages us; someone we want to please. The question is, how do we become self-disciplined? I don't think many of us understand just how to learn to become consistently self-disciplined. We fail to ask the question, "Who is in charge here?" The answer, of course, is "You, you, and only you." As Jim's story is told we will see how he answered the question of who is in charge.

Regrettably, anything can be perverted, including discipline, but I'm not going there because it is unfitting for this discourse, the healing of a depressed college student.

Jim had no family history of alcoholism or depression. It's important to look for a family history of both addiction and depression because either one can have a substantial genetic influence. Depressed people sometimes turn to the excessive use of alcohol to soothe severe anxiety, depression's constant companion, whether or not they have the genes related to alcoholism. Alcohol is a central nervous system depressant and worsens symptoms of depression. Jim's limited use of alcohol did not contribute to his depression, and he used no other drugs, two factors in this case favoring a good prognosis.

Genetic Predisposition to Depression

The role of genetic influence in depression is complicated. This fact can be the good news and bad news story. First, let's look at the good news. If a first-degree relative was depressed and responded favorably to a particular antidepressant medication, there is a better than even likelihood that the depressed offspring of that family member will have a similar favorable response to the same drug. Sounds simple but its importance is singular. Why? Unfortunately, often after numerous failed attempts, the reaction to antidepressant medication is less than satisfactory.

The bad news about the role of genetics in depression is that the relationship is not straightforward, meaning that the biologic factors and life experience also contribute. If you have a first-degree relative (mother, father, sister or brother) with a history of depression, it does not mean that inevitably you will also be depressed someday. Many, if not most, depressed people have no family history of depression. A vast majority of individuals with a family history of depression are not depressed. So, what's the worry? Factually, the chances of having depression are increased if a first-degree relative has depression. It increases your likelihood of becoming depressed by 1.5 to 3 times those who have no close relative with depression. However, the overall likelihood of inheritance of depression strongly suggests that factors other than genetics are involved.

Dr. Kenneth S. Kendler is the father of genetics in mental disorders. Until recently, his work has been limited by sparse data pools, a situation no longer the case. The question of "nature versus nurture" is being answered. "Recent advances in genomic research, coupled with large-scale collaborative efforts like the Psychiatric Genomics Consortium, have identified hundreds of common and rare genetic variations that contribute to a range of neuropsychiatric disorders" (Smoller, Andreassen, Edenberg, Faraone, Glatt, Kendler, 2018).

The work of Dr. Kendler, his colleagues, and others is calling into question the diagnostic boundaries espoused for the past 70 years and represented in the *DSM-5*. Thus far, the works of these pioneering scientists are determining that no single gene accounts for a mental disorder, and the mental disorders classification may be misleading. The near future in this exciting area of science increases the likelihood of discoveries that may substantially reduce suffering.

Abraham Lincoln's Depression

According to Joshua W. Shenk, author of *Lincoln's Melancholy: How Depression Challenged a President and Fueled His Greatness* (2005), Abraham Lincoln suffered from lifelong depression. He had a biological predisposition and environmental influences in common with many who are depressed. Both of Lincoln's parents, Nancy and Tom, were prone to depression. When Abraham was nine years old, his mother died. His childhood was harsh, and those who knew Lincoln best described him as "sad."

It is of our interest, although not reported elsewhere, that Lincoln's remarkable physical activity and physical strength, much celebrated by his biographers, was likely the single phenomenon that mitigated his depression. Lincoln did what most men were required to do in order to physically survive in the early 19th century, but he did more and famously won contests of physical strength, stamina, and endurance.

Had the neuroimaging tests of today miraculously been available in his lifetime, I am confident they would have showed that Lincoln's exercise-induced gains in BDNF fueled the conversion of his brain stem cells into neurons, and his self-education in the law then facilitated their integration into his hippocampus. Lincoln was proud of his self-taught law and was the only person of his time who passed the bar but had not studied the law in school or read the law with a practicing attorney. Perhaps unbeknownst to him was the fact that his practice of coupling exercise and study made him more resilient to depressive illness and enhanced his sense of self.

Jim's Genetics

There was no history of bipolar disorder in Jim's family. Bipolar disorder, earlier called manic-depression, is a challenging diagnosis to make, and it may present with vague psychological symptoms, remaining undiagnosed for 10 years or longer. Jim "took on more than he should," according to his mother. Excesses of any kind may be a symptom suggesting bipolar disorder, but one symptom does not make a diagnosis. Jim had no history of other relevant bipolar disorder symptoms. It is essential to distinguish between bipolar disorder, depressive state, and Jim's depression, which was major depression, because the treatment may be significantly different for each.

I diagnosed major depression. He had lost 20 pounds due to loss of appetite. However, not all depressed people lose weight. Many depressed people turn to food in an attempt to lessen depression, a strategy that fails. As a result, they gain weight.

Jim lost interest in nearly everything and, not having the word for it or the term *depression* to describe his condition, Jim's suffering was difficult to understand, as well as intolerable. One of the features of depression is its lack of apparent cause. As stated earlier, I've always found it helpful to search for a reason, though have seldom seen one, but when found the reason somehow seems to lessen the depression.

Jim's sleep---wake cycle was disturbed. For weeks, his mood was decidedly despairing. Nearly devoid of energy, he spent much of the day in bed and stopped attending classes. His physician found no evidence of significant physical health problems.

The Prescription of Exercise for Depression

I prescribed physical exercise for Jim's depression. I prescribed exercise for depression as early as 1971 and wrote about it in 1978, but it was approximately 20 years before Dr. Fred Gage at the Salk Institute provided the first convincing explanation of how exercise helps improve depression. Dr. Gage identified the role of BDNF. It is a human protein that causes stem cells in the brain to transform into brain cells or neurons. Remarkably, physical exercise induces the release of BDNF in the brain, and it does so robustly. This explanation is an oversimplification, but depression damages and destroys brain cells and impairs their essential function between brain regions, negatively impacting brain function and behavior. In contrast, physical exercise elicits BDNF and a host of other central nervous system factors to facilitate the regeneration of brain cells and optimize communication between brain regions, positively altering function and behavior.

As a former athlete, I knew the sense of well-being I got from regular exercise. Of course, I could not explain how physical activity produced its effects on my mind and mood. Now the mechanisms of action accounting for the antidepressant and cognitive effects of exercise are being clarified.

Depression and Sleep Disturbance

No one suffers from depression without also experiencing problems sleeping. Interestingly, depressed young people sleep or stay in bed much longer than usual. Older depressed patients sleep much less. Neither sleeping too much time nor too little is compatible with health. We learned from Jim's history that he spent so much time in bed that he stopped attending class.

I think depressed people stay in bed because it is warm there and safe. We know severely depressed patients have impaired temperature-regulating function in the brain. Some theorists postulate that the hibernating bear is a relevant animal model for the study of depression, one that mimics the neurobiological and metabolic changes found in depression: withdrawal from the environment, oversleeping, downregulation of energy production, loss of weight, decreased mobility, increased cortisol, and decreased neurotransmitter levels.

Undoubtedly, all theories aside, depression is a form of withdrawing from life. The withdrawal is assured by the severe anxiety so often accompanying depression. Activities that interfere with the withdrawal —such as antidepressants, mood stabilizers, and physical activity— produce their therapeutic effect by normalizing the various signaling systems, changes that restore proper behavioral functioning.

Depression and Anxiety

Recently, I invited the widow of one of my medical school classmates to attend our 50th reunion. Friends close to her had already informed me she was depressed; her normal grief having changed into a depression that was persisting. She declined my invitation: "Bob, it's this anxiety … It's so severe that I feel uncomfortable everywhere but at home." I understood.

Depression Is Often Worse in the Morning

In general, another pearl, depressed people feel worse in the morning, whether young or old. Jim's regimen would not unduly stress a physically healthy young person, so I prescribed early morning exercise for Jim. Daily, he went from his bed to his stationary bike and peddled at a comfortable pace for 30 minutes. He was back on the bike in the afternoon for another 30 minutes. Peddling for 30 minutes twice daily was his exercise schedule for the first two weeks. When he complained of a little muscular soreness, I referred him to a physical therapist who was also a trained masseuse.

Jim's Recovery

Slowly, Jim's appetite returned. We talked about eating rationally. The brain cells communicate with each other, their essential function, with chemicals called *neurotransmitters*. The so-called "chemical imbalance" theory of mental disorders is referring to the balance of neurotransmitters. You may well ask, "Where do these magical chemicals, these neurotransmitters in our brains, come from?" They are made entirely of chemicals derived from the food we ingest. Diet alone, unfortunately, will not cure depression, but a poor diet may contribute to worsening or prolonging of depression.

With improved nutrition, Jim no longer appeared frail. With improvement, we talked about the pleasure of sharing a meal with his family and friends. Jim had been away from home for the past three years except for a few weeks here and there. Coming home and being home were challenging for all who were involved, but the family made adjustments, and things were gradually worked out.

On his initiative, Jim added strength training. Slowly, his muscle mass increased and his body firmed up. We increased the bike exercise to three times daily for a total of 90 minutes per day. I cautioned him about avoiding activity for at least one to two hours before bedtime.

We maintained the same daily exercise routine for the remaining 12 weeks he was home except for Sundays. I recommended he make Sunday a day of rest. I also encouraged him to resume church attendance, something that he had stopped when he left home for college. He had been reared as Christian by Christian parents. Why not revisit his values and examine his deeply held beliefs? He accepted my encouragement, and I answered in the affirmative when he asked if I attended church.

Rational Thought (Cognitive Behavioral Therapy)

By using CBT, Jim learned how to find the connection between what he thought, how he felt, and what he did. One of the most significant psychological achievements or contributions of the 20th and early 21st century is Dr. Aaron Beck's

CBT. In simple terms, CBT is a way to discover the truth of one's situation.

First, the person learns how to identify his or her thoughts, the most basic of which are *automatic thoughts*, explained below. Then he or she learns how to take these automatic thoughts to the courtroom of his or her mind. Here, the evidence for or against the automatic thoughts is presented to the judge. The case of whether the thought is correct rests on the evidence. The person bringing the idea to court decides to what extent he or she believes or accepts the decision.

I am guilty of oversimplification of CBT, but my description is consistent with Dr. Beck's model. After mastering the fundamentals, it is intriguing to search our beliefs that give rise to what we tend to think. When it comes to identifying and, if necessary, changing our core beliefs, the job becomes more challenging.

Identifying Automatic Thoughts

Jim found it difficult to grab one of his automatic thoughts until I suggested he wait until he experiences an identifiable emotion. At that moment, he was to stop and ask himself, "What went through my mind just before I felt that emotion?"

Summary of Jim's Depression and Its Treatment

1. Jim's diagnosis, major depression, first episode, was confirmed.
2. Comprehensive risk assessments indicated a low risk of self-harm.
3. Medication was not needed nor desired by the patient.
4. A recent complete physical exam was normal.
5. No physical condition impaired his ability to exercise.
6. Stationary bike riding was the exercise used for treatment.
7. Indoor exercise was influenced by the weather
8. He went from his bed to his bike for 30 minutes six mornings weekly.
9. We gradually increased the frequency of his activity.
10. His mood, sleep, and appetite improved significantly.

11. Learning that he had a treatable condition helped his recovery.
12. He also learned the basics of CBT.

References

Shenk, J.W. (2005). *Lincoln's Melancholy: How Depression Challenged a President and Fueled His Greatness*. New York, NY: Houghton Mifflin.

Smoller, J.W., Andreassen, O.A., Edenberg, H.J., Faraone, S.V., Glatt, S.J., Kendler, K.S. (2018). Psychiatric genetics and the structure of psychopathology. *Mol Psychiatry, 24*(3): 409-420.

CHAPTER 13

J. B., A DEPRESSED WEALTHY BUSINESSMAN

Is Psychiatric Hospitalization Indicated?

Because he was a warm, self-confident, and competent physician, Dr. James B. Respess, Professor of Internal Medicine, University of Virginia School of Medicine, attracted VIP patients. Dr. Respess was also remarkably capable, kind, and friendly. This particular VIP patient was suffering from severe depression. Dr. Respess sent the following written request to the psychiatric consultation service: "J. B. is a very depressed 54-year-old married man. He has made two suicide attempts. Does he need to be transferred to the Davis Ward for psychiatric hospitalization? Please see him today and get back to me. The patient is in the hospital under my care on Barringer Two."

It was a beautiful May afternoon. Dogwoods blossomed, basked in the warmth of the bright Charlottesville sun, and swayed in the gentle breeze. Birds chirped happily. It was the sort of day I loved to be outside jogging. I looked at my watch, wondering how long the next patient would take.

I was a psychiatric resident at that time. Accompanied by a medical student, I knocked on J.B.'s Barringer Wing door.

A gruff-sounding voice replied, "Come in, but I don't need a psychiatrist," he said. He was annoyed. "Dr. Respess told me you were coming and I told him not to waste my time."

The anger in his voice was more significant than the passion in his demeanor. Surprisingly, contrary to how we were greeted, this patient wanted to talk.

"Sure, I tried to commit suicide, and I wanted to die. Yes, I tried it a second time. Any man in his right mind would do the same thing. I'm a complete failure; I always have been a failure, and I always will be a failure. Intelligent failures do not want to live. What good is the good in talking about it? I know my situation better than a stranger. Dr. Respess wants me to see you. I'm doing it solely out of respect for him and for no other reason. Do you understand?"

The Barringer Wing was a quiet, subdued, somewhat aristocratic area of the University hospital in those days. All its rooms were private. Today, it no longer houses patients, but its memory brings to mind one of the University's good old songs, "From Rugby Road to Vinegar Hill, we're going to get drunk tonight." It comes to mind now, not because I drank, but because it epitomizes two extremes of a dichotomy: the mildest versus the most extreme forms of mental illness. If the Barringer Wing was the Rugby Road of the song, the Davis Ward was the Vinegar Hill because it was where the severely mentally ill resided.

When a psychiatrist believes a patient is at risk of self-harm, such as suicide, or harm to others, or is unable to provide self-care, he or she must put into motion a series of steps leading, if necessary, to involuntary hospitalization. Would I be requesting a move from Rugby Road to Vinegar Hill for J.B.? This decision was on my mind from the minute I read the consultation request from Dr. Respess.

J.B. sat in a chair in his Barringer Wing room. He was a stocky man, not obese, certainly not shy, and not unduly upset. He could have been in a boardroom but for his hospital gown and bathrobe. He looked like the former U.S. Marine that he had once been, muscular, strapping, and sitting erect. His thinning dark hair was receding, his dark eyes conveyed sadness, and his deep voice resonated with authority, a cover, I later learned, for feeling insecure.

The patient opened the interview and kept control of it. The medical student stared at me as if to ask, "Do you see what this patient is doing and why are you letting him get by with it?" I nodded understandingly, but I had no difficulty with this patient exercising his control. It was easing his anxiety.

"Where are you from, Dr. Brown?"

"Norfolk, Virginia."

"Tidewater, Virginia?"

"Yes."

"I am a Failure"

J.B. was more engaging than most depressed patients; I did not know why, and it puzzled me. I wondered if he was lonely as well as depressed.

He said, "My wife has her own business in Chicago. She has her own life to live, I don't see much of her, and to be honest, I've failed as a husband, too. We have no children because we never wanted them. If she were here, do you know what she would say? She would tell you I drink too much, I isolate myself, and I'm too moody and irritable. The hell with her! That's what I say."

"Feeling like a failure must make you unhappy. Tell me what makes you feel like a failure."

"Get this straight. I don't feel like a failure. I know I am a failure!"

"You are making a distinction between feeling and thinking. Feeling and thinking are related, but of course, they are decidedly different, and that distinction is important, just as you correctly point out."

I said, "May I call you J.B.?"

"Hell, call me whatever you like. I don't care. I don't care about much of anything anymore."

"J.B., what is the evidence that you are a failure?"

Dear reader, this is not creative fiction; it is the truth. It is as precise as I remember it.

"I'm worth only 40 million dollars. My friends are worth at least a hundred million dollars. Would that fact make you know that you have failed? I have no office to go to. I go to the golf course, not to an office. I don't think I have ever actually succeeded at anything. At this point in my life, I don't believe I ever will. What is there to live for?"

J.B. was serious.

"What is the evidence that you are not a failure?"

"Sir," I asked, "What is the evidence that you are not a failure?"

He was taken aback, caught off guard, having never looked at his thinking in this way before. I could tell from his facial expression that he wanted to reply honestly.

"Are you asking me if there is anything in my life that I'm proud of?"

"Yes, that's it."

"I give money to an educational fund for a U.S. Marine Corps Academy in Texas. That helps me feel good for a while, but the feeling does not last long."

"It sounds like you are a generous person. That's a splendid reason to feel proud. I'm making a list of the evidence that you are not a failure. I'm putting that on the list. What else can we add to the list?"

"President Richard Nixon asked me to join a group of businessmen on a flight to China. I think it was the first time American businessmen were sent to China since it became a communist country."

"I remember reading about that China trip. It was a historical landmark. Should I add the China business trip as evidence that you are not a complete failure? Or was it a trip solely for businessmen who were widely recognized, to use your term, as "intellectual failures?"

To see a depressed person smile is a tremendous relief and an enormous treat. J. B. began to smile. And as odd it sounds, he looked 10 years younger when he smiled.

"I see what you are doing. You are trying to distract me so that I won't stay bogged down in my depressive thoughts, are you not?"

"I want you to look at the evidence for your ideas."

"Distract you? No, I do not want to distract you. Just the opposite: I want you to look at the evidence for your ideas. Suppose that I also believed that my life was an utterly hopeless failure, I might do what you did. I would be acting on beliefs that are not true. It would be like finding a suspect guilty of a crime and executing him without a trial, without looking at the evidence.

"All our behavior and most of what we feel are influenced by what we think. I want you to challenge your thoughts, asking yourself, 'What is the evidence that what I am thinking is correct? What effect will it have on me if I believe my thoughts are real when they are false or untrue?'"

"Search for the evidence that your view may be wrong."

"J.B., you are one of the least likely people I ever met who is or ever will be a failure."

A glint in his eye suggested that our discussion piqued his curiosity. Addressing his thoughts, not me, he said, "Have I been lying to myself about who I am?"

After several days in the hospital, J.B.'s depression began to lift, transfer from Rugby Road to Vinegar Hill proved unnecessary, and we soon developed mutual respect. An amiable person, J.B. chose to see me frequently after his discharge from the hospital. I was young in my training and less informed about boundaries, and J.B. would have his chauffeur drive us from my office to the university cafeteria, one block away. He even followed my family and me to Virginia Beach, our vacation spot that summer. He stayed in a nearby hotel, and I saw him daily for discussions about his identity and how he could become more authentically himself. When I last heard from J. B., he was all right.

In retrospect, my approach to this lonely depressed patient was a previously new form of CBT and relationship therapy for me. He responded to the truth of his situation: He was never a failure, but a generous, heroic figure who needed someone he could respect to respect him. Boundary crossing or fraternizing with a patient was frowned on by my supervisor. I did not recognize all the risks, but I believe we enriched his memory with the truth of the remarkable life he had led. Depression closes the door to positive memories and floods the awareness of the mind with a deluge of negative memories. The negative memories are magnified, assigned a significance they never deserve. The negative, irrational memories create an ever-increasing excessive emotional weight only lifted and removed by restoring the truth.

I did not push him during his therapy sessions. It took time getting to know each other. We set an agenda for each meeting, and each of us would discuss the items placed on the list. We reviewed the agenda at the end of the session. Rapport developed slowly. This episode was not his first episode of depression, but it was his first encounter with psychological or talking therapy. We had agreed on the agenda before each session started. In several ways, I imagine, it was like a tutorial that has been the traditional form of learning for hundreds of years at Oxford University.

Physical Exercise and Well-Being

I regret that I treated J.B. early in my career as a psychiatric resident, long before I fully valued the critical importance of exercise to clinical depression. He frequently played golf but used a golf cart. He rarely walked anywhere. But as a former U.S. Marine, J.B. knew the sense of well-being inevitably associated with exercise. Would he remember what to expect from physical fitness now that he was depressed? The answer was "no," he had not remembered.

I would have tried to get J.B. to remember the way he felt years ago while serving as a U.S. Marine, the days he was physically fit. He could have gradually increased his exercise by first giving up his golf cart, knowing what his objective would be, a transforming experience. Had he had not previously identified the sense of well-being from physical fitness as a U.S. Marine, the endpoint would be unknown, unfamiliar, making it more difficult, but not impossible to reach.

The sense of well-being associated with fitness is not a runner's high. It is not transient or short-lived. It is much more enduring, much more complicated, and its causes are multiple. It is a feeling of satisfaction, a sense of doing right, and some report an awareness of spiritual gratification. It is indeed more than an endorphin (neurotransmitter or brain chemical) boost.

Regrettably, there is widespread misunderstanding about endorphins. It arises from a small study of seven young women exercising on stationary bikes. At the conclusion of the study, there was a seven-fold increase in their endorphins (Carr et al., 1981). The widely publicized article is misleading. A less publicized investigation (Chung & Dickenson, 1980) revealed that an endorphin-blocking agent injected after a race did not affect the runners' report of a sense of well-being. Be sure to correct their mistake when your friends talk about endorphins as if they were solely responsible for the sense of wellbeing of physical exercise. It will help them realize how little they know about the effect of exercise on the three-pound organ called the brain. Perhaps you can encourage them to learn more by reading this book.

Dr. Phillips resolves this riddle in her pool game analogy. "My gestalt brain sees endorphins, neurotransmitters, peptides, neurotrophins, neurogenesis, etc. like a game of pool. Stress (which can include exercise) is the cue ball that starts the cascade. Whether the depressive eight ball falls early or late depends upon the position of the other balls and the skill (resiliency) of the player. Therefore, I think that mood-elevating effects might come from optimized levels of stress hormones, peptides, BDNF, and neurotransmitters

... and if dopamine and serotonin are involved ... then a partial 'high' from moderate intensity exercise occurs. But if I'm running for more extended times, then endorphins kick in."

References

Carr, D.B., Bullen, B.A., Skrinar, G.S., Arnold, M.A., Rosenblatt, M., Beitins I.Z., McArthur, J.W. (1981). Physical conditioning facilitates the exercise-induced secretion of beta-endorphin and beta-lipotropin in women. *N Engl J Med, 305*(10): 560-563.

Chung, S.H., Dickensen, A. (1980). Pain, encephalin, and acupuncture. *Nature, 283*(5744): 243-244.

CHAPTER 14

CATHERINE, AN ELDERLY DEPRESSED WOMAN

Dr. Harvey Smallwood, a remarkably fine Internist, practiced for many years in Charlottesville. He referred Catherine Stockton. "You will like this patient. She is a very bright 80-year-old, educated, articulate woman who is as stubborn as a mule. I can't do a thing more for her. She is depressed and has been as long as I have known her. Good luck." This busy, friendly physician had no time for small talk. He hung up the phone as fast as a relay runner who handed off the baton to the next dashing runner. I was not offended by his rapid-fire brief phone call; he honored me, entrusting one of his patients to me. He also knew I was busy. Neither of us had time for chitchat.

Mrs. Catherine Stockton

Mrs. Stockton came to her first session accompanied by her 83-year-old husband, a prominent man, respected by the community. She also arrived with a large paper bag nearly filled with her medications, some dating back 10 years or longer. I could not say she looked like a depressed person, only that her facial expression was unchanging, nearly expressionless. Her frugality of speech and attention to detail were consistent with her Scottish heritage.

Dr. Smallwood was correct; there was something I liked about this patient from the first day I met her. Even now, years later, it is difficult to say precisely what it was that was so likable. As I reflect on the question, I believe I respected her and found her heroic and courageous. She had carried the heavy burden of lifelong depression, but I never heard her complain about it during all the years I treated her.

Mrs. Stockton's Medications

We reviewed each of her medications. Realistically, she was currently taking a small number of the medicines carried in her brown bag. It is not uncommon, but unwise, for patients to keep their prescriptions, old and new, after their course of treatment has expired. For some people, having their doctor's name on their bottles of medications is reassuring, another way of linking themselves to their doctors. I did not want to come across as critical of my new patient, but I needed to alert her to the dangers of amassing a large collection of expired medicines.

"Mrs. Stockton," I commented, "Benjamin Franklin said, "The best doctor gives the least medicines." My grandfather, Benjamin Franklin Browne, justifies my addendum to old Ben's advice: 'Don't keep old medication around, either.'"

Mrs. Stockton nearly smiled. If I exaggerate, it may be said that a small smile momentarily and spontaneously visited her face.

"Hogwash," she said. "May I quote myself? I brought my old medications so that you can see all the antidepressants that failed to help me!"

"Very good."

"Dr. Smallwood gave up on me."

"But I'm angry with Dr. Harvey Smallwood for giving up on me and sending me to you!"

"What is the evidence that Dr. Smallwood gave up on you?"

"He sent me here!"

"Is there any other evidence that your internist gave up on you?"

"He could keep trying!"

"That's true. What is the worst reason Dr. Smallwood would send you here?"

"He never wants to see me again."

"Will he still be your internist or family doctor?"

"I hope so."

"How could you find out his reasons for sending you to me or refusing to be your internist?"

"I could ask him."

"Do you want to ask Dr. Smallwood why he sent you here?"

"Yes, I do."

"Do you want to ask him now?"

"Do you mean right this very minute?"

"Yes. I have Dr. Smallwood's unpublished phone number."

"Okay," she replied cautiously after looking at her husband, who nodded his approval.

I dialed the number and passed the phone to the patient.

"Dr. Smallwood, this is Catherine Stockton. How are you today? I bet you are; I won't keep you on the phone but one minute."

"Why did you refer me to Dr. Brown? I want an honest answer. As you know, I'm a strong-willed person. I can take it, whatever the answer is. You know me after 35 years."

"Is it 36?"

"Is that the truth? Will you still be my internist?"

"Thank you. Your answer helps me."

She passed the phone back to me.

"What did Dr. Smallwood say? Why did he refer you here?"

She sat silently. Both her husband and I sensed her relief from the way she was no longer frowning or verbally combative.

Finally, she spoke: "I think it best to keep my conversation with Dr. Smallwood to myself. Move on to another topic, please."

"Sweating is never ladylike"

She continued, "I am Episcopalian, but I do not drink alcohol. Of course, I never used drugs, and I never smoked. I never exercised. In my generation, Virginia ladies did not exercise. Sweating is never ladylike. Besides all that, I have an advanced stage of arthritis, the kind that severely limits physical activity. I get by with a cane; the probability of falling causes me extreme fear."

"Have you considered seeking the care of a physical therapist? Has Dr. Smallwood ever suggested that for you?"

"He always brings it up, but I see no sense in it. Why go?"

"I know an excellent physical therapist. I believe Rick Moore can make a positive difference in your ability to move about with less discomfort. My secretary will give you his name and phone number. I will also make a referral for 15 treatment sessions. His secretary will call you before each session. It will be our first step in treating your depression."

"I'm going to go to prove you wrong."

Choosing to ignore her defiant statement, I said, "As I understand it, you have distinct and separate episodes of depression, no symptoms suggesting bipolar disorder, and between your episodes, you feel pretty much like your normal self."

"Yes."

Homework

"I'm going to give you a homework assignment. Will you and your husband write down in a journal the date the next episode begins and when it ends? I can give you a booklet to make the recording easier.

Mrs. Stockton, mother of three adult children, enjoyed telling me about their accomplishments. Her son lived out of state. One daughter lived in town and her other daughter, an accomplished literary critic and research assistant at the University, resided with the patient and her husband.

Mrs. Stockton was reared by educated and refined parents, lived a quiet life enriched by reading widely, and enjoyed her family. Owing to a combination of her personality and her husband's public office, she sought anonymity.

"I must say this has been a most interesting and challenging session. I'm giving you my cell phone number. I want you to know you can call me at any time."

"Please tell my secretary I want to see you every two weeks."

"Change none of your medicines now. They are safe. We will put medication at the top of our agenda for our next session."

I continued, "I'm looking forward to being your psychiatrist."

I removed the several current medications and passed the large brown paper bag, weighing several pounds, to Mr. Stockton, saying, "Sir, can you be our magician and make these useless, possibly dangerous medications, disappear?"

"With pleasure," Mr. Stockton replied.

Mrs. Stockton's "Progress"

At first, I saw Mrs. Stockton every two weeks; then she reduced her visits to "as needed." She never went to a physical therapist and never increased her physical activity. Mrs. Stockton's exercise was minimal initially. Slowly, like her appointments, her exercise gradually became as needed, meaning attending to bathroom needs and walking to the kitchen table to eat.

Always friendly, but aristocratic to the degree required by her cultural heritage, she never argued or directly refused to exercise. Politely, she declined to talk about it. Almost parenthetically, she reminded me that Southern ladies do not perspire in public or privately. In a word, without saying it, I was given to understand that she and her generation would never stoop to the level of exercise that would cause core body temperature elevation consistent with sweating.

The Last Time I saw Mrs. Stockton

The last time I saw Mrs. Stockton, always with her husband, she was using a walker. After years of on-again off-again treatment of Mrs. Stockton, I departed for another city to treat combat Soldiers. She understood, but it was a sad parting. I think we had grown fond of each other, and our mutual respect had solidified. Regrettably, Dr. Smallwood passed away. She had made a satisfactory adjustment to one of Dr. Smallwood's partners. I found another psychiatrist for Mrs. Stockton to replace me, but she declined the referral.

Several years later, Mrs. Stockton passed away, soon after the death of her husband. Both died of natural causes. Truthfully, I still miss the strong-willed, articulate Scottish lady who lived heroically despite the heavy burden of chronic recurrent major depression. Strong Southern ladies neither "perspire," nor let others know they get depressed.

Dr. Phillips observes, "Intermittent caloric restriction could be used to increase hippocampal BDNF in a patient like this; alternatively, water aerobics could be beneficial from an exercise and arthritis perspective. In the near future, drugs currently under development may mimic the effects of exercise. For example, Metformin partially works by lowering inflammation and optimizing BDNF levels." Sadly, this scientific data was unavailable years ago during the course of Catherine Stockton's treatment.

References

Eyileten, C., Kaplon-Cieslicka, A., Mirowska-Guzel, D., Malek, L., Postula, M. (2017). Antidiabetic effect of brain-derived neurotrophic factor and its association with inflammation in type-2 diabetes mellitus. *J Diabetes Res*, 2017:2823671.

CHAPTER 15

SELF-MURDER

Diane

Christmas is four days away. Our days are shorter.
Our nights of darkness are longer, and for most
Americans, Christmas is a special time of the year.
We had a 10-inch snow last week, but the
weather has warmed up and heavy rain is falling
in Crozet (cro-ZAY), a rural community 12 miles
west of Charlottesville. Crozet is named for a
French military engineer, Claudius Crozet, who
migrated to the U.S. after Napoleon's defeat and
taught at West Point. Colonel Crozet, for his time,
1789-1864, rather miraculously dug a railroad
tunnel through the base of the Blue Ridge

Mountains that opened in 1858. It was the longest tunnel in America in 1858 but later fell into disuse and finally into decay. Recently, there is news of its reopening, not as a railroad tunnel but as part of a park and recreational facility.

Gray-haired citizens faithfully gathered today for their Friday morning exercise class at the Crozet Baptist Church. Gloomy weather probably accounted for the sparse attendance of nine, instead of the usual 14 or more. The group trickled in slowly, as if indecisive about coming out in the rain. I was the second to arrive.

Diane's hair is white. She was the last member of the exercise class to arrive. Tri-focal wire-rimmed glasses were prescribed after her cataract surgery. Today, she walked with a peculiar gait, as if one leg was stiff. A multicolored Christmas wreath knitted onto the front of her dark green sweater drew favorable comments from other women in the exercise class. Diane's expressionless face remained fixed despite the compliments.

I had an opportunity to briefly chat with Diane during the 10-minute walking period. Diane had been walking in the unlit church sanctuary, while I remained in the exercise room. "I noticed you were walking differently today," I said.

"Thank you for noticing that," Diane replied. "I woke up today with a stiff hip … but I felt disoriented in the sanctuary. I believe it's more in my head than my hip. I'm so tired of feeling this way. I've been wondering if it's worth hanging around. I'm getting tired of life."

Trying to be reassuring, I asked if she had tried hip exercises in bed. Our exercise leader, Rick Moore, is a competent physical therapist. Most of us in the exercise class are Rick's patients and were referred to the class by him. We've been instructed how to exercise in bed before getting up each morning.

"I've heard about the exercises, but I haven't been doing them … just haven't felt like doing much of anything. I almost missed this class today, but at the last minute I decided to come."

To my surprise, Diane said, "You are an inspiration to me."

I am not good with compliments, giving or receiving. Her comment made me feel awkward.

Scrambling for words I said, "I guess it's because of being 87, the oldest person attending the exercise class at this time." Quickly, I moved the topic back to her feeling disoriented walking in the darkened church sanctuary and said, "Bifocal eyeglasses can make walking more difficult."

Over the next few minutes, Diane spoke and I learned that she wore trifocal eyeglasses, has poor near-sight vision following cataract surgery, could not recall her surgeon's name (making her feel ashamed) and that these impairments and more were contributing to her tiresome feelings about living.

Diane perceived that her statements about being tired of living concerned and puzzled me. She tried to reassure me. "I'm not planning on leaving now. I'm just tired of the way everything in life is going."

What is my duty, if any, to a limping, nearly equally elderly, white-haired fellow member of my exercise class, one we both have been attending for several years, whose name I had not found important enough to ask until today?

When Someone Tells You, "I'm Tired of Living"

I believe we have a moral duty to care about others. As a seasoned psychiatrist, unlike a person unfamiliar with behavioral health, I know that no one murders one's self without first mentioning it to someone before they act. References to suicide, a relatively new term historically for self-murder, are made in many different ways. Trained to "listen with the third ear," I am more attuned to indirect references to suicide. You are not. But you are armed with intuitive feelings, a sense of something different or not right, upon observing that someone you know well does not seem like his or her usual or normal self.

You need not become the Sherlock Holmes of suicide detection, but you can readily learn a few things about people who have suicide on their mind. First, foremost, and basically all that is important is the abiding first principle of suicide detection: Take every reference to suicide seriously. The second abiding principle of suicide detection: No one can predict suicide.

Nevertheless, one need not feel entirely helpless in this sensitive and challenging matter.

Risk Factors

No one can predict a heart attack, but the death rate from heart attacks has dramatically decreased since the risk factors of heart disease have been studied and identified, and the knowledge about heart disease has been publicly disseminated. Our 65-year-old neighbor Becky knows her LDL (low density cholesterol) score, her HDL (high density cholesterol, the "good one") score, and her triglyceride level. Her physician told her how to optimize these important components of her circulating blood. The likelihood that these fat globules will not clog her blood vessels, causing a heart attack, is now more favorable than it was before she followed her physician's suggestions.

The risk factors of suicide are being identified and are employed in the service of reducing suicide, always among the top 10 leading causes of death. High on the list of risk factors of suicide are major depression; prior suicide attempt; alcohol or substance abuse; isolating behavior; being single, widowed, or divorced; marked or severe anxiety; psychosis; dementia; recent humiliation; and others, such as physical pain. My list is not intended to be exhaustive.

"If She Dies, I Will Kill Myself"

A young engaged couple traveling well over the speed limit crashed their motor cycle into a tree. The driver's fiancée was seriously injured and flown to a university trauma center. The driver, fraught with overwhelming guilt, raced to the university emergency room. His clothes were torn and despite having no serious injuries, he was covered with blood. He entered the trauma room where bright lights revealed the limp form of his fiancée. As he was ushered out of the trauma room by two large muscular attendants, he shouted, "If she dies, I will kill myself." An emergency room nurse addressed him harshly and said, "If you kill yourself do it outside, not in here." Moments later, the desperate young man shot himself to death in front of the hospital.

What About Diane's "Tired of Living" Statement in the Exercise Class?

Diane's statement was subtle, but troubling. She did not utter the word "suicide" during her five-minute conversation with me earlier today, but her statement, "I'm tired of living," preyed on my mind. If I have any duty to Diane, it is a moral, not a legal one. My knowledge of Diane was limited. Did she live alone? Did she have a supportive family? What could I do, if anything, under the circumstances? My concern was experienced as a slowly evolving anxiety.

I called Amy, a neighbor who has been attending the exercise class years before I joined, but I had to leave a voice message to return my call. I then called Barbara, another neighbor and fellow exerciser who coordinates the class. I learned that Diane lived near her family with whom she had her evening meals. Barbara said Diane would likely welcome a phone call from me and she would not view it as inappropriate or intrusive, according to the way I framed my question.

About 8:15 PM I reached Diane by phone. I said I called out of concern for her statements to me earlier in the day during the exercise class. She welcomed my call and said, "Thank you for your concern. I'm tired of watching the news. I don't know … I can't explain it exactly. I guess you could say I'm in a rut. There are just so many changes … so many things going on in my life. I'm so tired of pain. Either my hip or my knee is always painful. I'm just so tired of all that."

"Diane, are you having thoughts of harming yourself?" I asked.

Diane said, "No, I would never do that. But I know one thing for certain. I will not go out of my way to live to be 100."

Suddenly, Diane sounded less burdened, less bogged down. I can't say she was immediately transformed into a lilting, happy-sounding person, but I sensed a lifting of wearisomeness in her voice.

"Bob, I am concerned about your family. I understand your son has been very ill and your grandson fell on the ice and broke several bones in his leg."

I thanked her with reassurance that my son and grandson were mending.

I called to offer help to Diane, and she offered me help through an expression of concern for my family. We both felt better.

Suicide and Ambivalence

An argument for "rational suicide" or "assisted suicide" is not part of this text. As a physician, death by suicide is abhorrent to me. If there is a thread or theme woven throughout these pages it is simply this: Life is a precious gift and it may be enjoyed fully by most people of all ages and states of health.

I stated earlier that suicide notes provide evidence that most people who take their life are thinking irrationally at the time of death. Nearly half of completed suicides have elevated blood alcohol levels, and many also are using substances of abuse. Half those who were rescued after jumping from the San Francisco Golden Gate Bridge said they changed their minds about suicide half-way down to the bay.

There are several reasons why people mention suicide to others before they act. They are ambivalent—a gripping symptom of most depression—about most things, including the thought of ending their life. There is also a "coin-flipping" component of the ambivalence; almost a magical-thinking element that goes like this: "If God wants me to live, He will give me a sign." There is also the "who cares" component: "If I glibly mention suicide, will anyone care enough for me to do something to keep me alive?" The statistical fact that suicide attempts far outnumber completed suicides also suggests ambivalence.

Talking to a Person at Risk of Suicide

"Hi. Good morning, are you going to kill yourself? Have a nice day!" is not the best way to conduct a meaningful suicide-risk assessment. You may find it difficult to talk about suicide, but contrary to what you may think, people with suicidal thoughts welcome an opportunity to discuss the subject with a caring person.

It is useful to think about an informal suicide-risk assessment as having a beginning, middle, end, and context. Each phase is important, but the context, that you care, is critical. An example of the beginning phase of a suicide-risk assessment goes something like this:

1. I notice that you seem less like your usual self.
2. You seem to prefer to be alone.
3. I can't remember when I last saw you smile.
4. You look tired and worried.
5. If there is something on your mind worrying you, please know that I care and I want to hear it.

The middle phase of a suicide-risk assessment may go something like this:

1. Have you lost interest in things you once enjoyed?
2. Have you become tired of living?
3. Have you thought about giving away your prized possessions?
4. Have you seriously considered taking your life?
5. Do you have a suicide plan?

6. Have you rehearsed your plan?
7. Do you have the means of taking your life?
8. Have you ever made a suicide attempt?

The end phase of a suicide-risk assessment may go something like this:

1. Dear friend, I hope you know that I care about you.
2. Your honest answers to my questions concern me.
3. I believe you are depressed.
4. I know there are ways I can help.
5. There are also ways professionals can help.
6. I want to stay with you until help arrives.
7. Shall I call your minister, priest, religious leader, family doctor, or good friend?
8. I will call whomever you wish or take you to them, but I will not leave you alone.

Here is the take away point: If you suspect someone is at high risk of committing suicide, do not leave them alone for any reason, including their request to use the bathroom. Assure them of your concern as you call for help on your cell phone. If you do not have access to a cell phone, you must find assistance some other way. Such a situation may be challenging, but do not handle the crisis without assistance and do not leave the high-risk person alone.

Why Do We Hear So Much About Suicide These Days? Is There a Suicide Epidemic?

These important questions about suicide, unfortunately, have complicated answers. It seems that human life has been devalued since World War II; or, more precisely, since the degree of evil that made the use of nuclear weapons necessary to end World War II. The phenomenon of devaluing human life is global. The theme song of *MASH*, for example, one of the most popular television series in history, shows this trend: "Suicide is painless; it brings on many changes. And I can take or leave it if I please."

Recent suicide statistics for young people between 18 and 24 indicate a marked increase in self-murder. However, the risk of death by suicide for men increases with the life span: A 90-year-old man is more likely to take his life than a 20-year-old man. On the other hand, the risk of suicide among women steadily increases until the mid-50s and then trends downward.

Young Black males are also trending upward in suicide, a new finding. Black women, especially older African American Black women have the lowest suicide rate of all races and genders. I believe the low suicide rate of older Black women reflects their spiritual strength, making them a stable resource in Black American families today. When I shared my opinion about older Black women's spiritual strength and leadership with Black Soldiers, they found it humorous and declared that their low suicide rate is entirely explained by "their meanness ...older Black women are as mean as hell." I suspect they confused "meanness" with firmness.

Here is the bottom line: Life is precious but suicide is a pernicious, malicious, and the destructive consequence of biopsychosociological factors. The use of such a multisyllabic word is a feeble way of saying that suicide is the result of biological, psychological, and sociological influences that demand our attention immediately.

It's easy to get caught up in the statistics of suicide and, in so doing, distract our attention away from appreciating the pain and suffering the victim of self-murder wants and feels compelled to end.

A Surgeon with Useless Hands

Years ago, I was urgently called to the home of one of my patients. I arrived just as the local rescue squad reached the home. My patient, the rescue squad, and I immediately went upstairs. Lying dead on the bed was my patient's husband, a renowned surgeon whose extremely rare hand disease had been diagnosed by one of my classmates. It was a devastating blow to a skillful surgeon to have useless hands. He had undergone other recent significant life changes, but this change, this loss of two once useful hands that were no longer capable of performing surgery as they had for so many satisfying years, was devastating.

He had called in a prescription for himself to a pharmacy in another town. His body was still warm, but he was dead from an overdose. It was a very sad time for all who knew and cared for him, but those closest to him were aware of his suffering and were not angered by his deed.

To her credit, his wife was strong enough to go on with her life. She and his family grieved for him, and everyone wished he could have found a successful way to live without continuing his life as an operating surgeon. Robotic surgery, a surgical technique relying less on finger dexterity and more on the kind of dexterity required by computer games, was introduced well after this man's life ended so sadly. But he felt the need, not to leave his loved ones, but to end a degree of suffering only he understood and could no longer bear.

When Necessary, Involuntary Evaluation Is Available

If you have a relationship with a depressed person, follow the suggestions given above to make suicide-risk assessments as needed, based upon that person's symptoms. When that approach fails, you must contact a professional who, if necessary, can request a court-ordered evaluation. Laws are in place protecting those who undergo court-ordered evaluations from harm to self, harm to others, or inability to care for self. An attorney is appointed to serve as the evaluatee's legal defense attorney. Laws specify the timeliness of the evaluation and how long, if necessary, people can be detained beyond their will. In other words, authentic concern for those who may harm themselves can lead to appropriate legal action to prevent needless death.

If you sense the need of assistance before taking the legal approach, call the legal aid society in your community, or your family attorney, and seek advice. Most communities have a magistrate whose office initiates the involuntary evaluation order.

What to Do When You Are Thinking About Suicide

It is troubling when thoughts of suicide are more than merely transitory. It is time to review these thoughts with someone whose opinion you respect and trust. "I trust no one," an acquaintance once commented, "and I have good reasons for doubting others." Understandably, people who were abused naturally deal with ongoing trust issues. They also have higher rates of suicide than those never abused. The abused person will require a suicide-risk assessment conducted by a sensitive and skillful person. Nonetheless, the risk of death by suicide must be construed as a psychiatric emergency, and if necessary, an intervention may be urgently required.

Finally, if you are the one in need, the one having suicidal thoughts, though still functioning, trying to get by day to day with your depression, why not take the easy, simple, nonlegal approach by calling a friend, church or religious leader, family doctor, or local hospital and honestly state, "I'm having thoughts of harming myself. I do not want to burden my family. How can you help me?"

The Importance of Risk Factors to Health

Acute coronary occlusion or heart attack in the 1930s and 1940s was commonly mistaken for "acute indigestion." Cardiologists, armed with advanced diagnostic instruments, nowadays readily diagnose heart attacks from the history of the patient's complaints and a few tests. Public education about the risk factors associated with the prevention and treatment of heart disease has led to an impressive reduction of morbidity and mortality associated with this leading cause of death in this country in the early 21st century. It was the identification of risk factors of heart disease and the widespread dissemination of this information that is largely responsible for the remarkable progress in this field.

As stated earlier, risk factors associated with suicide are being identified, but compared to cardiology we are still in the early stages, the stage of the 1930s and 1940s. What's worse, there is strong negative bias against those who experience mental illness. Mental illness has a terrible press. Whenever something horrible is publicized, too often the public is misled to believe the actor was "crazy."

A severely depressed person's illness may progress into a stage where he or she is no longer competent to perceive the sense of needing or seeking professional help, but it is the general consensus that no one commits suicide without first telling someone about it. If there is a takeaway message here it is for all to listen "with the third ear" when anyone mentions suicide or its equivalent. For public information this is the seminal risk factor of suicide.

It may surprise you, but there are many people who want to and will help those having thoughts of suicide. You need not feel ashamed to admit that life no longer seems appealing to you. Just as Freud predicted a century ago, neuroscience is revealing that many psychological disorders have a physical or organic cause. Limitations of scientific knowledge are less restrictive today. With time, prejudice against mental illness will lessen. We will freely discuss depression in the way we discuss pneumonia today. Suicidal thoughts will be known to have their origins in treatable conditions. No depressed individual or person at high risk of self-harm will need to suffer in silence or sense the need to withdraw from others when the stigma disappears. Psychosis or extremely irrational thinking remains to be more fully understood.

A significant part of the psychic disturbance—the "pain of pain" of depression— that causes thoughts of self-murder result from stigma or the public's disdain for the mentally ill. Many depressed people believe that others see them as weak, unhappy, failures. Historically, even the Church unfairly condemned those who committed suicide and prohibited burial in church grave yards. How sad it is that for centuries, society created and assigned these erroneous, unspeakable notions to those suffering from treatable conditions like depression.

Suicide and War

During the Golden Age of Pericles, circa 500 BC, Athens made significant advances in politics and architecture. It was also a time of relative peace. Democracy was enjoyed by nearly all. I envision a relatively happy period in history, one not unlike we are apt to compare America today with Athens of Pericles Golden Age. Like America's early twenty-first century Athens also had its suicides.

In her thoroughly documented study of suicide in ancient Greece, Elise P. Garrison provides an in-depth summary of the social attitude toward suicide in that age: "The aim of this discussion has been to clarify our understanding of the view on suicide in classical Greece. In all cases, a corpse is powerful and dangerous, and in some forms of violent death the implements used acquire additional danger. But the evidence suggests that, though a variety of responses to suicide existed, the importance of shame and honor meant that a distinction between honorable and cowardly suicide was widely recognized, the first acceptable and even praiseworthy, the second to be condemned" (p.34, Garrison, 1991). Deferring to Durkheim's definition of suicide, Garrison defines suicide as any death which is the direct or indirect outcome of a positive or negative intentional act is suicide. Within that context, suicide arose when a person was restoring social equilibrium to society or, alternatively, felt inadequate. Whereas suicide that was a form of self-sacrifice during social obedience to military service was deemed heroic, suicide that occurred from cowardice or laziness was condemned (Wright, 2016).

Today's unusually high suicide rate among veterans is sobering. Recent work by the Department of Veterans Affairs reports that suicide rates of veterans from 18 to 34 years of age steadily increased from 2006 to 2016, a trend that resulted in the highest rate among any age group. About 20 veterans a day take their own lives, accounting for 14 percent of adult suicides in the U.S., a rate that is 1.5 times higher than those without military service, with the branch of the army being most affected. Notwithstanding, since the majority of veterans are older, the majority of suicides occur in older veterans: Nearly 60 percent of veteran suicides occurred in people ages 55 or older (Shane, 2018).

Having worked with this population during our War on Terror in the Middle East, and with the family members of our military, the suicide statistics are puzzling. The suicide rate is equally high among the combat-deployed and the non-deployed. I believe it is too soon for society to develop either a rational understanding or an understandable attitude toward our present military suicide rate. Particularly interesting is the shift in society wherein suicide rates have failed to drop during times of war and peace.

Suicide and the Weather

There is an association between suicide and the seasons. Seasonal affective disorders, thought to be depressive disorders related to availability of sunlight are not included in *DSM-5*, but is now identified as Major Depressive Disorder with Seasonal Pattern. In Shenk's *Lincoln's Melancholy* (2005), Lincoln said he frequently had suicidal thoughts and described a touching moment following the death of Ann Rutledge with whom he enjoyed a close relationship. She died on August 25, 1835. Shortly after her death, the weather turned bad. Lincoln told others he could not bear the thought of rain falling on Ann's grave. Lincoln's friend said that after this statement, he changed; and that "he seemed retired and loved solitude." Lincoln later wrote that "exposure to bad weather," based on his experience, proved "to be very severe on defective nerves."

Many people report they are depressed during the Christmas season, but suicide rates in America are highest in the spring of the year. Ongoing research suggests a causal relationship between suicide rates and seasonal factors, but I am aware of no completely rational explanation for the seasonality of suicide, as it is complicated by numerous variables including gender. However, consider late spring time and early summer some a suicide risk factor.

Suicide and the Economy

Included in a long list of contributing factors outside the depressed person who commits suicide is the economy. Suicides rose steadily during the Great Economic Depression. Many depressed patients have told me, "My family will be better off financially with my death." When I hear statements like this, I argue firmly with the patient, "Your family would never fully heal from the lasting devastation they would experience from your suicide. No amount of money can replace a father, mother, son or daughter. Your family's love for you is enough to strengthen you through this depression. Do not give up on your family. Do not give up on yourself."

Suicide and Faith

I remind a person of faith that he or she is never alone. Jesus, born when Quirinius was governor of Syria, promised, "I will never leave or forsake you." Jesus offered immediate and long-term care. Jesus, described as "a man of sorrows and acquainted with grief" (Isaiah 53:3 NIV) said, "Come to me all who are weary and burdened, and I will give you rest. Take my yoke [wisdom] upon you and learn from me for I am gentle and kind in heart, and you will find rest for your souls" (Matthew 11:28-29 NIV).

In Somerset Maugham's *Rain,* published in 1921, a minister commits suicide. Maugham was a British writer who was a nonbeliever and remained an agnostic regarding the existence of God. Sinclair Lewis, an American Nobel laureate in literature, published *Babbitt* in 1922. George Babbitt asked his minister to offer a special prayer for him during a major crisis he was experiencing. Babbitt was asked to get on his knees in the minister's office, whereupon his minister first made a business phone call before attending to him. There is never a shortage of critics of religious beliefs and practices. Nearly 100 years since *Rain* and *Babbitt* were published, consider the criticisms as well as the stressors ministers and other religious leaders endure as they follow their calling.

Postmodern Deconstruction and Faith

Twentieth century postmodern deconstruction, a systematic method of searching for injustice, questions all the assumptions of Western culture. Its degree of influence on education since the middle of the last century is profound. In the 1960s, some deconstruction theologians were known as the "Death of God" theologians.

At the risk of oversimplification, some postmodern deconstructionists encourage believers to denounce faith as superstition, fit only for the less intellectually curious and honest. The Pew Research Center (2018), a nonpartisan fact tank, reports a downward shift in church attendance and from faith in God to a self-identification as a "spiritual person." Nonetheless, at least 80 percent of Americans continue to believe in God. Only 10 percent of those surveyed said they do not believe in the God of the Bible or a higher power.

A Local Minister's Suicide

Several years ago, in our community, a Christian minister took his life. His family and his congregation were gravely concerned and plainly shocked. Everyone asked, "How could a man of God do this to himself and to the members of his church?" No one asked, "How could a man of God become ill, get pneumonia, break his leg, suffer with terminal cancer, or die in a car crash?"

Sadly, even intelligent, educated people do not believe depression is a disease. Too many people mistakenly believe depression is something you get over by trying harder and that suicide is an inexplicable, selfish act committed by weak characters. If you believe either one of these unsubstantiated and untrue statements about depression and suicide, you must examine the evidence that depression results from mental and physical diseases that affect the brain and that suicide is a complication of depression. For some, depression is a terminal illness.

The Most Encouraging News About Depression

The most encouraging news about depression, documented repeatedly, is that comprehensive psychological treatment coupled with physical activity can help heal the depressed brain cells damaged or destroyed by toxic depression.

As Barney Fife of the ever-popular *Andy Griffith Show* television series, still one of my favorites, would say, "Now put that in your smoke and pipe it!"

A well-written article, "The Challenges of Improving Treatments for Depression" (Cuijpers, 2018) brings to our attention the fact that "54% of patients responded to antidepressants, whereas 38% responded to placebo. Comparable numbers have been reported for psychotherapies with response rates of 54% compared with placebo response rates of 41% across control conditions." These response rates are based on his review of reported research.

Absent from the important Cuijpers article in the world's most frequently read scientific journal is the research of Fred H. Gage of the Salk Institute and the comprehensive research reviews of neuroscience by my co-author, Cristy Phillips, and others, that establish major depression as a disorder of the brain that can be healed and prevented by exercise-induced neurogenesis and synaptogenesis. It is sad that we have for too long espoused a dichotomous way of thinking that excluded from clinical and scientific practice the undeniable relationship between mind, body, and spirit in the treatment of illnesses like depression.

References

Cuijpers, P. (2018). The challenges of improving treatments for depression. *JAMA, 320*(24): 2529-2530.

Garrison, E.P. (1991). Attitudes toward suicide in ancient Greece. *Transactions of the American Philological Association*: 121: 1-34.

Shane, L. (2018, September). VA: Suicide rate for younger veterans increased by more than 10 percent. Retrieved from https://www.militarytimes.com/news/pentagon-congress/2018/09/26/suicide-rate-spikes-among-younger-veterans/.

Shenk, J.W. (2005). *Lincoln's melancholy: how depression challenged a president and fueled his greatness*. New York, NY: Houghton Mifflin.

Wright, R. (2016, September). Theatre of war: Sophocles' message for American veterans. Retrieved from desk/theatre-of-war-Sophocles-message-for-American-veterans.

CHAPTER 16

GETTING TO KNOW YOUSELF

Imagine you've come to my office seeking treatment for depression. It is something you knew you needed to do, but before now you lacked the energy to make the effort. You also delayed seeking professional help because you were afraid of the unknown, did not want the stigma too often attached to mental illness, and shared the widespread irrational perception that "only crazy people see a psychiatrist."

As you are seated in my consultation room to discuss your interest in the treatment of depression, many anxious thoughts may multiply in your mind. "What information do I want to disclose about myself? What do I wish him not to know at this time? What are the reasons I want to remain silent about the hidden information?"

Pedagogue and Student

In this manuscript, I'm serving as your pedagogue, or teacher, walking beside you, explaining how depression can be healed. Ours is a unique mission because I will also describe what is going through the mind of your psychiatrist. He is a person well known to me. I stare at his face in the mirror each morning. I've supervised his work as a mentor. I will know what he is thinking. I'm going to explain his thinking to you because we must understand our roles as teacher and student. My task, done successfully, will demystify the treatment of depression, and optimize the clarity of your objectives. In the beginning, it is no more comfortable for the psychiatrist than for the patient who is depressed.

Let's assume you have adequate health insurance, a topic of considerable importance in this second decade of the 21st century, but too unsettling and far too complicated for us to fully contemplate here. Suffice it to say that emergency psychiatric care is made available to those who have no health insurance: A medical institution, such as a university receiving a federal grant, must provide emergency health care to all who seek it regardless of their ability to pay. For non-emergency care, most universities will work with the uninsured and underinsured to obtain coverage from various federal or state programs or, alternatively, to develop a fair, practical, and personalized means of making payments. In private practice, I never declined to treat patients who were unable to pay.

Screening Psychological and Other Tests

Assume that a nurse or assistant has already obtained your necessary information and your vital signs (blood pressure, temperature, and pulse rate). You will also have completed several screening questionnaires so that your scores on the Beck Depression Inventory (BDI) (Beck, 1961), the Beck Anxiety Inventory (DAI) (Beck, 1990), the Beck Hopelessness Scale (BHS) (Beck, 1974), the Paffenbarger Physical Activity Questionnaire (Paffenbarger, 1986), and the Complete Life Inventory (Brown, Snyder, & Peterson, 2002) are made available. We will review these informative measures, and I will ask if they accurately reflect your feelings and thoughts now and for the past one or two weeks or longer.

If you conscientiously and honestly completed the questionnaires and screening psychological tests, I will know just how depressed, anxious, and hopeless you report that you have been feeling for the previous one to two weeks. I will also learn how often you exercise, and whether you identify yourself as a person of faith.

Seizing Up Each Other

You and I, your psychiatrist, will be sizing up each other. You are making up your mind as we proceed whether you can comfortably talk with me about your sense of despair. You wonder if I'm competent to treat you and whether I will listen and think carefully about what you tell me. Or do you find me easily distracted, appearing preoccupied? Do you judge me sensible as well as understanding? You contacted the American Psychiatric Association before your first appointment and verified my professional qualifications.

You question whether you have the energy and the level of trust sufficient to seriously consider working on your depression if that is what you have. Your task is not easy because depression makes decisions of any kind almost overwhelming. It's hard to think clearly with depression. If you are like most depressed people, you are nearly mentally paralyzed by ambivalence and have little or no confidence in yourself. Your anxiety level is very high, often confining you to the security of your home.

Your psychiatrist will be deciding if you are competent to give and withhold information about suicide, every psychiatrist's nightmare in treating depressed patients. Together, we discuss suicide, with the understanding that my first and ongoing concern is your safety. I will make a suicide-risk assessment, asking if a first-degree relative such as your father, mother, sister, or brother ever attempted suicide. If you answer in the affirmative, I will want to know the details. I will ask if you have ever felt so depressed or upset that you came close to making a suicide attempt, but stopped short of it. If this happened, I would need to know what prevented you from taking your life. In particular, what gives meaning to your life?

Psychiatry and Forensic Psychiatry

As a board-certified psychiatrist, I will make your diagnosis in the first three minutes of the interview and spend the remainder of the hour mentally confirming or refuting my diagnosis. As a board-certified forensic psychiatrist, I will look for secondary gain. Unknowingly, are you reaping a benefit from your symptoms? Has a third party injured you? For example, have you been in a motor vehicular accident for which litigation is looming in the background?

I hasten to say that it is highly unlikely that secondary gain or malingering is relevant in most cases of depression. I will also state here that it is disadvantageous for the patient to ask the treating psychiatrist to become his or her forensic psychiatrist. Dr. Thomas Gutheil, Harvard Medical School forensic psychiatrist, has written convincingly on this topic and referred to it as "wearing two hats." It doesn't look right, feel right, or turn out right when this breach occurs in the doctor-patient relationship. The court may determine that a qualified expert witness, the only witness permitted to render an opinion, is more likely to be objective than a treating therapist.

If your case has a forensic or legal element, retain an attorney and assure him or her of the necessity of a forensic psychiatrist. If your attorney assumes the treating psychiatrist brings your best interests to court, he or she is misinformed. A treating psychiatrist has a doctor – patient relationship with the patient. A forensic psychiatrist does not establish a doctor – patient relationship. As a consequence, a forensic psychiatrist attempts to rid himself or herself of bias and subjectivity, a requirement of an expert witness's testimony.

Why Depression

Do you know why you are depressed? One of the truly depressing things about depression is the real fact that its cause is seldom identifiable to the one who is affected because it results from a combination of genetic, psychological, and medical factors. Nonetheless, as I wrote earlier, it is time well spent to look for its origins. The cause of some depression is identifiable almost immediately by a skilled observer. For example, the previously mentioned hypothyroidism or low thyroid function is quickly diagnosed with a blood test and treated with synthetic thyroid replacement (thyroxin or Synthroid) treatment, and it is a common cause of clinical depression. Interestingly, some physicians resort to the use of a low dose of a synthetic thyroid hormone, even without primary hypothyroidism, to supplement antidepressant medication, an attempt based on knowledge that subtle thyroid dysfunction often accompanies depression. Although rare, some cancers present with depression as its first sign, sometimes the putative result, at least in part, of stress-related increases in inflammatory molecules called cytokines that stimulate behavioral symptoms via the vagus nerve.

Let's assume that a recent physical examination, including a battery of blood tests, was normal. Let's also imagine that you can find no plausible explanation for your depression. You feel a little relieved to learn that your case is like the majority of depressed people: You are physically healthy, and you cannot readily identify a physical cause(s) of your depression.

At this point in my evaluation of depressed patients, I ask "Are you physically fit?" The answer is nearly always, "No." Responses to the Paffenbarger Physical Activity Questionnaire inform me that depressed patients rarely, if ever, exercise on a regular basis. Some athletes frequently report they are "feeling down," but it is commonly the result of their poor performance or their team record that explains why they feel down. Some high-performance athletes are simply physically exhausted from over-training. These instances are not the same as depression.

How Well Is Your Mind Working?

If there are no identifiable physical causes of your depression, I will now take a look at your Mini-Mental Status Examination (MMSE) results. Strange as it may seem, as we talk, I will be observing how you make me feel. It is nearly universal to feel depressed in the presence of depressed people. This "contagious" element of depression is experienced by children and adults alike, often at a partial level of awareness, often without a word of explanation for it. It is the nature of the disorder, wholly unintended, but real.

Contagious is not the best term for it, but other psychological conditions are even more transmissible to others. I have acquired a full case of posttraumatic stress disorder (PTSD), for example, from intensively treating hundreds of combat Soldiers with a PTSD diagnosis. My PTSD symptoms make it difficult at times for my family members to understand my jitteriness, temperament, and horrendously exaggerated startle reflex.

The MMSE is a standardized list of questions that are commonly used to document the cognitive decline that is seen in dementia. Its administration takes 5 to 10 minutes. It is a questionnaire. If your results are within the normal range during your initial evaluation, it can meaningfully help eliminate concern about dementias such as Alzheimer's disease. Pseudo-dementia looks like Alzheimer's disease, but it is no more than severe depression. The "dementia" resolves with successful treatment of depression.

Your psychiatrist will conduct a Mental Status Examination (MSE), in addition to the MMSE, because he wants to determine your degree of orientation to time, place, person, and circumstances. He will decide if your memory and judgment are intact. He will also inquire about disturbances of your thinking due to delusions or hallucinations, and the degree of impairment of self-care. Severe depression may be accompanied by psychotic features such as auditory hallucinations, consisting of hearing voices without the presence of others. Auditory hallucinations in severe depression usually include hearing berating and severely critical voices that sound real. Major depression with psychotic features is rare, but it usually responds to either antipsychotic medications or electroconvulsive treatment.

As your psychiatrist, I want you to tell me about yourself, but I also know that you may not have the energy or interest to say much of anything. I do not want to add to your despair. I will not pressure you to speak. I will reassure you that I am ready to listen when you are prepared to talk. Deep depression may cause strong feelings of worthlessness or cause you to have inappropriate, irrational feelings of guilt, thus making it difficult to be open about yourself.

Irrational Guilt

Inappropriate, irrational guilt feelings over trivial matters commonly fill the minds of depressed patients. Years ago, for example, I treated a very depressed man who was an acknowledged expert librarian of ancient texts. When depressed, minor mistakes he thought he had made 20 years earlier as a young bank teller haunted him. Memories of the small errors became vivid and disturbing. He may have reported that all the accounts he managed one particular day were balanced, when upon his guilt-prone retrospection, he thought his report may have been in error. He was not certain of it, but he strongly felt like it was in error. Convincing evidence to the contrary felt unconvincing. In reality, no error was ever discovered in his case, even after 20 years. He was a brilliant man, successful in a new profession requiring detailed, flawless memory. The incident is cited here to show how powerfully depression can affect the innocent.

The depressed librarian's case demonstrates that supposed misdeeds of the past, trivial or significant, often occupy the mind of a depressed person. Irrational regret and irrational guilt worsen the symptoms of depression. Rational guilt reflects one's moral standards of conduct. Irrational guilt is a form of negating one's worth.

A Meaningful Connection

Your psychiatrist wants to "reach" you to establish a meaningful connection and working relationship. Depression impairs your ability to respond to people. In a word, you want to be left alone like a bear hibernating in a cave all winter, to remain in a safe place, undisturbed by changes or people. Your psychiatrist wants to gently wake the bear, encouraging you to leave your comfort zone and metamorphose into a more natural and mature form of yourself. Hiding from fear never works. Withdrawing from and avoiding others worsens depression.

On the other hand, there is a part of you that realizes one remains human by being with and around other human beings. The circle of relationships for depressed people is small. There may be only one person you perceive as safe or even necessary to be around. I cite another incident of a depressed patient in which depression was like an octopus, missing no opportunity to wrap its tentacles around any and every aspect of life. In this case, depression led to excessive dependence on others.

Caroline

Caroline, the middle-aged wife of a community religious leader, suffered from chronic depression. None of her treatment from past therapists in the various communities where her husband's work required them to live had been successful. Caroline's dependence upon her husband was taxing and ultimately, he concluded he could no longer tolerate it.

Caroline's husband turned to other women for affection, making his wife's dependency worse. She required psychiatric hospitalization when, after a long marriage, he divorced her. Had Caroline not been depressed or extremely dependent upon her husband, she could have divorced him for adultery, ruining his career, but dependence on him kept her with him. After a long, painful period of her life and successful management of her chronic depression and chronic dependence, Caroline discovered she could survive without her husband. A well-trained psychiatrist would be sensitive to Caroline's tendency to transfer her "needy" dependency onto him or her. Teaching Caroline to value healthy independence became the primary challenge of her therapist.

Betty

Many years ago, I treated Betty, a depressed young single mother. Her life was left in ruins when her husband ended their marriage. She believed her life was destroyed. Like a tornado, the trauma was sudden, unexpected, and desolating. Her husband left her and their young son for another woman. His announcement was incomprehensible: "I don't love you, and I do not believe I ever loved you! I found someone that I truly love. That is just the way it is."

Betty said to me, "I thought we were a happy family. I was pleased. I enjoyed my roles as wife, mother, and elementary school teacher. I thought he was just as happy and fulfilled. He was completing his MBA degree, and he had accepted an ideal-sounding position in another state. We had already selected a new house, but he never intended to live in it with me and our child. Our divorce was messy and prolonged. I could barely function.

"I would have committed suicide, but my son needed me," she said. It seemed as if her tears would never end. They came from a badly broken heart. She faced an entirely new and unknown life, one she never expected to live without her husband.

As an alternative to psychiatric hospitalization, I saw her twice weekly in my office for two years. She slowly recovered. She came to understand that she was betrayed by her husband, a person lacking virtue. She had been a good wife and a good mother. The responsibility for the end of her marriage rested entirely in her husband's hands. She and her son were better off without a person in their lives who behaved like her husband. These realizations came slowly, but she ultimately believed them 100 percent.

At the end of her therapy, Betty moved to a better job in another state. Her sense of intrinsic worth returned. She was ready now to step up and move on. Betty brought her son to meet me at her final session. I was about to make a discovery that changed my method of evaluating a new patient. I was stunned by the shocking disclosure.

I congratulated Betty for having such a handsome young son. As I recall, he was about five years old, with large blue eyes and neatly trimmed blond hair. I knelt down and spoke directly to him and called him by his name, having heard about him over a long period. "When you and your mother move to Kansas," I said, "I hope she will find a nice Sunday school class for you in a church where the Bible is taught." He seemed pleased, if not excited, by what I said.

Betty, a kind-hearted person, said sharply, "Dr. Brown, I am surprised! After treating me for two years, you do not know that I am an atheist?"

I learned from that encounter with Betty and her young son that I needed to add a spiritual inventory to my intake evaluation of all new patients. It is not my job to influence my patients' religious beliefs, but I must know what they are, how they shape their lives, and whether they are a source of comfort, confusion, irrational guilt, or all the above. My patients also have the right to know my religious beliefs, and when asked about them, I reply honestly.

Over the years, before I developed a spiritual inventory, I noticed but paid little attention to something I found difficult to understand: Patients readily told me the most intimate details of their sexual history but refused to disclose what they prayed about. "What I pray about is too private to share," was the reply I received. Upon reflection, were patients saying that sex has lost its meaningfulness, but prayer remains a sacred communication between them and God alone?

Reluctance to permit a psychiatrist into the sanctuary of the mind is an intriguing phenomenon. I suspect some might say that the matter of open discussion of sexuality between a patient and his or her psychiatrist is socially acceptable, whereas open discussion of personal prayer between a patient and his or her psychiatrist is not expected and is viewed by some as suspect. Historically, theology and psychology were nearly indistinguishable. The subject matter was the same; hence, *psyche* meaning *soul* had only twinges of differences until social and cultural changes swept across Western civilization.

Spiritual Inventory

A portion of the *Brown-Peterson Spiritual Inventory* was first introduced in *Textbook for Mental Health, A Narrative Approach* (Brown, Snyder, Peterson, 2002). Honest answers to questions comprising the spiritual inventory provided information about my patients that helped identify beliefs, practices, and values. For the most part, the spiritual inventory was willingly accepted by patients as part on my evaluation.

Directions: Use one of the following numbers to identify how each of these statements best apply to you:

Almost Always (5)
Often (4)
Sometimes (3)
Seldom (2)
Almost never (1)

1. I believe in God. _____

2. I believe God is working in my life. _____

3. I attend religious services. _____

4. Religion fills a need in my life. _____

5. I am hopeful about the future. _____

6. I can take my place in line without fretting or pushing. _____

7. I can cope with being last. _____

8. I am not perturbed when others are unavoidably late. _____

9. I make an effort to help neighbors and friends whenever I can. _____

10. I follow the "Golden Rule" to treat others like I want to be treated. _____

11. I try to do the best I can in any task I undertake. _____

12. I meditate or pray regularly. _____

13. I read the Bible and/or meditative materials. _____

14. I am prepared to face hardships and death. _____

15. My faith is vital and personal. _____

16. I practice what I believe consistently. _____

17. I feel empowered to do right. _____

18. I seek wisdom beyond myself and peers. _____

19.   I enjoy internal freedom.   _____

20.   I keep the 10 Commandments _____

Scoring

Total your score above. Note two things: 1) 84 or above indicates that your life is probably spiritually fit; a score between 63-83 indicates your spiritual life needs work. A score of 42 or below indicates that you may want to seek counsel from a respected mentor, clergyman, mental health professional, or relative. 2) Examine the "Almost Never" responses. These areas need to be addressed regardless of your level of spiritual fitness. Keep a record of your score in order that you might use it to measure your progress at a later time (Brown, Snyder, Peterson, 2002).

Permit me to offer a word of caution regarding the relationship between spiritual fitness and clinical depression. Depression causes people to question all things, even the reality or existence of

God. Doubt, fear, skepticism, and anxiety form dark clouds of ambivalence in which the depressed uncomfortably exist. In other words, it is very difficult to maintain a desirable level of spiritual fitness when you are clinically depressed. If you can manage to attend religious services by overcoming your fear of contact with others, you will find that it is often rewarding. If you are a person of faith, by all means, inform your minister or religious leader about your condition, and request a home visit and prayer.

Review of Your Session

By the end of your first session with your psychiatrist, you decide you can work with him. That decision brought a feeling of relief. It was not his credentials, but his ability to listen, understand, and care that convinced you that the right selection was made. He did not appear distracted. You did not find that he wanted to "get you out" as quickly as possible. He permitted no interruptions of the session, indicating its importance to him. Somehow, he made you feel valued, someone he wanted to understand and help onto the path of healing.

Your psychiatrist found you competent to give and withhold information about suicide. There was no family history of first-degree relatives attempting suicide, you had never attempted suicide, and you agreed to a plan to contact him if suicidal thoughts occurred. He gave you his phone number and instructed you to call 911 if you failed to reach him. He believed you were honest with him in all matters discussed.

He made his thoughts clear to you that his first objective was your safety. He explained that his concern about your safety would be ongoing. Your psychiatrist could pass the "toss and turn test" at night, able to sleep soundly, trusting you accepted a safety plan to which both of you were committed.

He summarized your history, appearing to have correctly understood your case as you shared it with him. He provided you with the results of your psychological tests and carefully explained their meaning, assuring that you understood. You and your psychiatrist agreed that your diagnosis is major depression.

He explained several treatment options: medication, psychotherapy, and physical activity, or a combination of all three. You raised questions about the benefits and side effects of each treatment. He discouraged you from making a rash choice between the treatment options but confessed his preference for fitness because recent research strongly supports its role in the prevention and treatment of depression. Dr. Brown's preference for cognitive behavioral therapy (CBT) was based on his experience with it, its measurable results, its relative short term of an average of 12 weeks, and the wide range of research supporting its effectiveness in depression. You understood the fact that there is limited available evidence supporting the combination of all three types of treatment. Your psychiatrist, not following the common practice, prescribes medication for depression as a last resort. The plan you accepted is the combination of reasonable physical activity and CBT.

He wants you to return next week. He urged you to walk each day and to record your mood from 1 (no depression) to 10 (the most severe depression possible) before and after walking. You want to cooperate, but confess that you have rarely left your home for the past month. "If you can't leave home, go for a walk inside your home. See if you can walk 15 minutes," he said. "Just make certain you can walk inside in a safe pathway." Your family physician found no health contraindications to exercise.

At the end of the first session, your psychiatrist is encouraged. He believes you are motivated to get better. He found that he could rely on your statements as honest. He judged your risk of harming yourself, his chief concern, to be low at this time. He detected no hidden agendas. He saw that you were not only depressed but isolated, lonely, and highly anxious. He thought you would benefit from group therapy, a form of psychotherapy he will introduce later. Most of his patients also attend his group therapy sessions. He found your superior intellect, excellent verbal skills, and motivation to be strong indicators that your response to group therapy will likely be favorable. He saw you as authentic, and he looks forward to your next session.

Practicing What You Learned

As you return home, you wonder why you did not see a psychiatrist earlier. Your mood is improved because you sense a basis for hope, the imperative that precedes change. A plan is set out, and you intend to follow it, knowing one session has not cured your depression. You open the blinds, take out the exercise and mood journal just given to you by your psychiatrist, and record a score of 7 for your pre-exercise mood. Your score indicates a moderate to severely depressed mood. You walk fifteen minutes inside your home, careful not to fall. At the end of your walk, your mood did not change. "At least it got no worse, and 15 minutes is probably not long enough," you correctly reason to yourself, and at least you started.

All in all, you decide it was a good day. You saw a doctor, you are not "crazy," and you have a plan. Most of all, you have made a full commitment to healing. The doctor also mentioned *spiritual fitness*, a fascinating concept. You're going to think about that idea. You decide to put spiritual fitness on your agenda for next week's session, and you like the idea of having an agenda, knowing what you want to discuss before each treatment session.

References

Beck, A.T., Depression Inventory, Philadelphia: Center for Cognitive Behavioral Therapy, 1961.

Beck, A.T., Hopelessness Scale, Philadelphia: Center for Cognitive Behavioral Therapy, 1974.

Beck, A. T., Anxiety Inventory, Philadelphia: Center for Cognitive Behavioral Therapy, 1990.

Brown, R. S., Snyder, D. M., Peterson, D. (2002). *The Brown-Peterson Spiritual Inventory in Textbook of Mental Health, a Narrative Approach.* Boston, MA: Pearson Custom Publishing.

Paffenbarger, R. S., Hyde R.T., Wing, A.L., Hsieh, C.C. (1986). Physical activity, all-cause mortality, and longevity of college alumni. *N Engl J Med, 314*(10): 605-613.
Strasburger, L.H., Gutheil, T.G., Brodsky, A. (1997). On wearing two hats: role conflict in serving as both psychotherapist and expert witness. *Am J Psychiatry, 154*(4): 448-456.

CHAPTER 17

HEALTH AND SPIRITUAL FITNESS

Language of the Human Spirit

This chapter introduces the language of the human spirit, as used in this manuscript, and its attachments and losses.

The Thought of Spiritual Fitness

The thought of spiritual fitness may not occur to you in the way I mean to convey its importance to healing depression, and as a general principle of good health. Not wishing to offend, I will necessarily address spiritual matters, recognizing that they encompass the most personal, private, and sacred part of our being. My biases, in-so-far as I can identify them, are delineated throughout this chapter. Perhaps you can identify your own biases as we proceed. Writing your biases may prove beneficial.

I am not attempting to proselytize, change your religion, or invite you to accept a specific religious doctrine, practice, or service. I simply want to persuade you to consider the value of applying the ideas and habits of fitness to your spirit, just as I have advocated physical and mental fitness.

I recognize the importance of the meaning of terms used in a discussion of a sensitive topic such as the human spirit. I use spiritual fitness as a means of achieving and maintaining spiritual health. At the core of the topic of spiritual fitness and spiritual health is the importance of an acceptable meaning and understanding of two words, *spirit* and *soul*.

The terms *spirit* and *soul* are frequently used in various circumstances as if their meanings were commonly understood. And to a certain degree these words are commonly understood. I take the precaution of limiting my use of the terms to decrease the likelihood of misunderstanding.

The original use of the word *spirit* was related to breath. In this sense, spirit is the "breath" of life or the force or principle believed to animate living beings. When I go outdoors on a cold morning, I can see my breath, but I am not seeing my spirit. One does not see one's spirit. It is an essential but invisible, immaterial, nonphysical presence. When death occurs, breathing stops and the spirit leaves the body. When she died, I was standing at the bedside of my mother-in-law, who resided with us the last five years of her life. "Kay Kay," as our children called Kathleen, smiled and exhaled her last breath. She was 92 years old and a wonderfully kind person. Clearly, she was no longer alive. The spirit of this devout Christian woman left Charlottesville for her new abode in Paradise. Specifically, the soul or life-giving part of Kathleen Hinkle left her lifeless body.

Those who prefer may substitute *inner self* or *essential being* for the word *spirit*. By making such a substitution, you may find that some of the poetry and beauty of the spirit is sacrificed.

I believe God is the Holy Spirit, and I believe every human being has a spirit. I don't believe in the spirit of St. Louis or the spirit of Los Angeles in the same way, as great as they are, as I believe in the Spirit of God and the spirit of mankind.

As mentioned earlier, the notion of *spiritual fitness* may be a term with which you are unfamiliar. The idea that one's spirit can become fit may not have occurred to you. Let me explain what I mean by fitness as used in *spiritual fitness*. Theologically, the righteous are those who are right with God. The close similarity between righteousness and fitness cannot be denied. King David reminds us that "Love and faithfulness meet together; righteousness and peace kiss" (Psalm 85:10 NIV).

By fitness, I mean trying to be the best and staying your best for your situation and unique set of circumstances. Physical fitness is defined as "the ability to carry out daily tasks with vigor and alertness, without undue fatigue, and with ample energy to enjoy leisure-time pursuits and respond to emergencies," according to the Centers for Disease Control and Prevention (CDC), You may already be doing your best to become and remain physically and mentally fit. But how spiritually fit do you consider yourself? Is there room for your spirit to improve? As you understand it, do you want to be spiritually fit? Most important, should you wish to become more spiritually fit, how would you go about it? Some answers to these important questions are found later in this chapter and also in Chapter 18, "Achieving Spiritual Fitness."

Human Spirit and Values

Try conceptualizing the human spirit as where your values are kept alive by rationale active practices that lead to healthy (or virtuous) habits of the mind and body. In secular terms, the manifestations of the human spirit (or character traits) are generally considered to affect personal awareness, insight, understanding, and judgement; in religious terms, the human spirit (or Christian character) is considered to represent an element of God in the nonmaterial make-up of humans. In both contexts, excellence of the spirit [or character] is marked by choices that eschew both excess and deficiency. According to Kant, the cardinal virtues of prudence, justice, fortitude and temperance are strengthened when we obey the dictates of duty.

Later, a list of seven virtues that opposed the seven deadly sins appeared in a poem entitled *Contest of the Soul* by Aurelius Prudentius (410 A.D.) Identified among the seven virtues were purity, temperance, charity, diligence, patience, kindness, and humility. Proponents of a virtuous life maintain that the persistent practice of virtues guards against temptation of the seven deadly sins, namely lust, gluttony, greed, laziness, wrath, envy, and pride. Speaking to these nuances, Aquinus underscored the importance of the unity of virtues, a notion that suggests that both the ends and methods to obtain the end are important. Cardinal and theological values differ in that the latter are believed to be accessible only with the assistance of God.

The Beck Institute reminds us that "Values can be an antidote to suicide" (Cotterell, 2016). The value that we give to life stems from unspoken values that reify as lived behavior. Unfortunately, stress and crisis often subvert espoused values over time. During the process, sources of spiritual security are increasingly abandoned as waves of unexpected threat fracture our attention and focus, ultimately enfeebling our attempt to lead a virtuous life and damaging our credibility along the way. Both the opportunity for death and recovery lies juxtaposed alongside the crisis. Re-alignment of belief and choice becomes paramount for the process of recovery, particularly amidst changing circumstance.

The idea of realigning belief and choice is patently evident in the Beck Institute's work on suicide wherein they illuminate a common wish for a life of comfort and joy as opposed to one of pain and suffering. By helping their patients to re-channel their frustrations, they promote fitness and spiritual health. As an exemplar, they point out that a person who cannot produce professionally can re-channel their energy to family and community. A person who wants to run away from a particular circumstance can find alternate outlets for engagement. By rechanneling aspirations in ways that are congruent with values, the Beck Institute underscores how we can find alternative paths that are congruent with personal values. In this way, the highlighting of values becomes an antidote for suicide.

Otto Warmbier

Held prisoner in North Korea, from January 2016 to June 2017, University of Virginia undergraduate Otto Warmbier was released on June 14, 2017. He had been on a college student tour sponsored by a Chinese travel agency. After spending five days on an organized tour of the authoritarian state with a group called Young Pioneer Tours, he was falsely accused of a trumped-up charge and sentenced to 15 years of hard labor. For the 17 months after his sentencing, his condition was unknown by his parents whose contact with him had been forbidden by North Korea. On June 13, 2017, it was announced that the State Department had secured Warmbier's release at the direction of President Trump's behest. Later that evening, Warmbier arrived in the U.S. and was taken to the University of Cincinnati Medical Center in a state of unresponsive wakefulness (a severely brain-injured state).

Two days later, June 15, 2017, Otto's father, an articulate and intelligent-sounding man, spoke earnestly on national television. Absent from the broadcast was Otto's mother who remained on bedside vigil. "His spirit is with us and I can share my spirit with his spirit," Otto's father said. "And I am just so happy for that." I can imagine no one failing to understand the meaning of Otto's father's statement. His love for his son was clearly abundant and plain to see.

President Donald J. Trump

On January 8, 2019, the 45th president of the United States, signifying the importance of his address to the nation, spoke from the Oval Office of the White House on the need for a barrier or wall on our southern border. It was a sad, brief account of the harm done by some people who surreptitiously entered our country.

The president said he had held the hands of parents whose daughters and sons had been raped, murdered, even dismembered, by criminal illegal immigrants. Some of the victims have been police officers and people of all ages, including infants and children. There are no signs that the criminality of some of the illegal immigrants is decreasing. The president described the unlawful immigration at our southern border as a "humanitarian crisis, a crisis of the heart, and a crisis of the soul."

The Reality of the Human Spirit

Achieving spiritual fitness makes it necessary to continue our discussion of the human spirit and soul. The ancient Greek philosophers Socrates, Plato, and Aristotle could not agree on the meaning of the soul of mankind, yet its meaning seems obvious to me, at least in the context in which I use it here. I hope the reality of the spiritual realm in which we live, and the soul through which we experience our greatest happiness and our saddest moments, will become clear to you, as well, if it is not already apparent.

I included here in this chapter the tragic case of Otto Warmbier because his father told our nation that he was comforted by the presence of his son's spirit. To a grieving father, this invisible, immaterial, nonphysical presence was real and particularly meaningful. Otto's father saw his son's body. He could not communicate verbally with his son's mind. He could not know his son's emotions, but he experienced his son's spiritual presence. "I can share my spirit with his spirit. It is a great comfort," said Otto's father.

In a similarly earnest statement in an important time in our nation's history, President Trump used language that also referred to the invisible, immaterial, and nonphysical reality. His use of the terms, *crisis of the heart* and *crisis of the soul* was immediately understandable because so many of our citizens have suffered loss.

To a large degree, we are spiritual creatures with a soul, who deal daily with things we cannot physically see. These things are no less real than the visible world. Thus, we must remember that while wrong gratifies in the moment, good choices yield longstanding benefit. Each time we choose to make a good choice, we add to the human treasury of good by inculcating our values in others. Whether we are making choices for our own self or that of others in our local or global community, we can choose longstanding good.

The Reality of the Spirit of God

My understanding of the Spirit of God, as I look back on my life, came first from the reverence for

God that I learned from my mother, the strongest influence I felt as a youngster. I lived less than 100 yards from Burrows Memorial Baptist Church in Norfolk, Virginia. I grew up in that church, the only member of my family to attend. In that church I made a public confession of my faith and stated my belief that Jesus Christ was the long-awaited Messiah, the incarnation of God on earth. I was 12 years old. I attended Sunday school and the Baptist Training Union, sang in the choir, and grew up with my friends there. I was married in that church to a lovely young woman who also grew up in the same church.

In college, I attended the University Baptist Church in Charlottesville and sang in its choir. In graduate school, my wife and children and I attended St. Paul's Episcopal Church. We remained Episcopalians for many years before we joined Trinity Presbyterian Church, where we were inspired by Dr. Skip Ryan, the best minister I've known. Since then, Dottie and I have been Anglicans. Last week, I attended the Crozet Baptist Church, where I enjoyed singing the old Baptist hymns. I am also attending the Anglican Church of the Holy Cross in Crozet, Virginia where

Blake Johnson, a young man who reminds me of Dr. Ryan, is the pastor. Dr. Harold Bare, pastor of the Covenant Church of God in Charlottesville, is a friend and fine minister whose services and community work are inspiring.

My view of the Spirit of God is founded upon the Christian education described above. As of this time, I have found no non-Christian or nonreligious view of the Spirit of God and the spirit of man more acceptable or sounder than my own.

My spiritual views have also been informed and influenced by my professional career as a psychiatrist, with a subspecialty board certification in forensic psychiatry. Not only have I been privileged to meet and provide care for many patients over four decades, but I have examined prisoners on death row in a maximum security prison. I also evaluated numerous murderers, rapists, pedophiles, and men, women, and children who have committed unthinkable acts of violence. Remarkably, most of these violent people appeared ordinary, having much in common with you and me. Some, under the influence of voluntarily ingested mind-altering drugs, robotically stepped over those they murdered to steal their possessions, selling them for cash to obtain more drugs.

"The Spirit of God Moved Upon the Face of the Waters"

I do not wish to enter the creation versus evolution debate, but merely wish to state that the act of converting a void, dark, and formlessness into the Earth is consistent with an act of the Spirit of God. It seems to me that Moses, around 1450-1410 B.C, described the act in terms meaningful to him and to the scholars of his time. Moses wrote the first five books of the Bible. He elected to begin the Bible with the formation of the earth. It is a wonderfully told story, as meaningful to the literalists as it is to the skeptical mythologists today.

Moses wanted us to understand that God created mankind, so he described it in both the first and second chapters of Genesis, the first book of the Bible. In Genesis 1:26-27, we read in verse 26, "Then God said, 'Let us make mankind in our image, in our likeness ...,'" and in verse 27, "So

God created mankind in his own image, in the image of God he created them; male and female he created them."

What, you may ask, is the meaning of these important terms, *image* and *likeness* of God? If you accept Moses's depiction of creation told in Genesis, you are obliged to accept and believe that you are made in the image and likeness of God.

Suppose your resume contains the statement, "I am made in the image and likeness of God." Suppose you apply for a new position and have all the qualifications the position requires. Suppose you make it to an interview. The interviewer is likely to ask for an explanation of your statement, "I am made in the image and likeness of God." How would you answer the interviewer?

The "Image and Likeness of God"

Theologians continue debating the meaning of Moses's statement that mankind is "made in the image and likeness of God," but only God knows its true meaning (Hoekema, 1986; Hughes, 1989). One thing it does not mean is that God created little gods. Sometimes, we must remind ourselves that we are not God, but creatures of the loving God who is, thank God, also a forgiving God. As I ponder the words conveying that we are made in the image and likeness of God, I realize that no compliment could be greater. Further, no responsibility could be more demanding than dealing with us and others as creatures made in the image and likeness of God.

The uniqueness of our creation inevitably endows us with an unending instinct of longing for closeness to God. George Herbert, 1593 – 1633, a 17th century Church of England priest and poet, captures this longing in his poem, *"The Pulley."* Herbert opines that God gives us everything, except contentment. God pulls us closer to Him in our search for contentment, an inner peace not found apart from Him. Herbert calls the sought-after contentment, "this jewel":

"For if I should, said he
Bestow this jewel also on my creature
He would adore my gifts instead of me
And rest in Nature, not the God of Nature
So both should losers be."

Verse 3, The Pulley

If you accept, as I do, the Classical Greek tripartite view of mankind as having a mind, body, and spirit, then can we reason that God, in whose image and likeness we are created, must also have a mind, body, and spirit? As God is three parts in one, his creatures are also three parts in one.

The mystery of the Trinity is beyond full understanding. Christians accept the mystery of God the Father, God the Son, and God the Holy Spirit. Is it likely that God the Father is like the mind of God; that God the Son is the crucified body of God, and God the Spirit is the Holy Spirit that is the indwelling spirit of Christians? These are deep and weighty questions upon which I urge readers to reflect.

Moses describes the creation of man in Genesis 2:7 as follows: "Then the Lord God formed a man from the dust of the ground and breathed into his nostrils the breath of life, and the man became a living being." Thus, according to the history of the Jews and Gentiles, the creation of the Earth and creation of man were spiritual acts of God.

When God created man, he did not equip him with artificial intelligence, but with the capacity and potential for a sound mind able to choose good and evil. God did not create a robot; He gave us freedom of choice or *free will*. God soon observed that we are prone to behavior that is too often in our worst interests, but God permitted his creatures to do what they choose. In order for us to continue in disobedience, to live outside God's Perfect Will, he permits us to survive within his Permissive Will. God made it apparent that disobedience ultimately leads to death.

After entry into existence, mankind rebelled by disobeying God.

God mercifully provided hope and forgiveness to his evil-prone creatures: God gives forgiveness for us all through acceptance of his incarnated self,

Jesus Christ. Judgment will be tallied, based on our choices, at a future time after our death, according to the Gospels. God knows our flaws and weaknesses, and yet continues to love us unconditionally, holding eternity in mind.

Sigmund Freud

Freud, 1856-1939, an Austrian neurologist and the father of psychoanalysis, was one of the great intellectuals of the 20th century. He compared the human mind to an iceberg: Only a small part of it understands itself as conscious. The vast reservoir of the mind is beneath the level of consciousness. In this sense, much of who we are remains beneath the surface. In a few concise words, for the most part, we are an invisible, immaterial, nonphysical presence.

Although Freud did not discover the unconscious, he incorporated it as the center piece of his theory of mind and his treatment of patients with disorders of the mind. Freud was an atheist who strongly believed that his theories of the unconscious would ultimately be proven to have a physical basis. Nonetheless, his work was nearly entirely in the spiritual realm in as much as he treated disorders he believed grew out of the invisible, immaterial, and nonphysical, all subsumed under the term, *unconscious*. Freud's theory of the unconscious is described in his *The Interpretation of Dreams*, first published in 1898.

William James

William James, 1842 –1910, was an American philosopher, psychologist, and pragmatist. In 1890, he wrote *The Principles of Psychology*. James, the oldest of five children, grew up in an educated family. His father was a philosopher and theologian and his brother, Henry, became a renowned novelist. James was also an excellent physician and the first educator to teach a college psychology course in the U.S. He was a Harvard University professor. James's book entitled *Varieties of Religious Experience, a Study of Human Nature* (1902) is most relevant to our attempt to understand the spiritual side of human nature.

In the final chapter of *Varieties of Religious Experience,* James, broadly articulated the characteristics of religious life in the following ways:

1. "That the visible world is part of a more spiritual universe from which it draws its chief significance;
2. That union or harmonious relation with that higher universe is our true end;
3. That prayer or inner communion with the spirit thereof – be that spirit "God" or "law"–is a process wherein work is really done, and spiritual energy flows in and produces effects, psychological or material, within the phenomenal world.

Religion includes also the following psychological characteristics:

4. A new zest which adds itself like a gift to life, and takes the form either of lyrical enchantment or of appeal to earnestness and heroism.
5. An assurance of safety and a temper of peace, and, in relation to others, a preponderance of loving affections"

For me, William James's most valuable insight is revealed in his meaningful comment that we all "need to learn to give our little, private, convulsive selves a rest, and find the Greater Self.

When we find the Greater Self (God) our life and work take on a sense of lyrical enchantment". We will be humming through life, a soothing and encouraging thought. Our real and espoused values and priorities will be aligned. We will behave, acting in accordance with our purpose, our values.

The Human Spirit Versus Humanism

I want to emphasize in our discussion of the human spirit that I am neither engaging in a discussion of nor advocating *humanism*, the position that rejects supernaturalism and stresses the capacity, dignity, and value of individual self-realization through reason alone. In fact, my views contradict humanism, as I understand it.

My View of the Human Spirit and Depression

Of the three essential working parts of mankind, God created the spirit by giving us a soul, the life-giving part of us with which we most commonly listen to God and speak with God in prayer and study. It is our truest, most honest self, by which we know God and reflect our highest adoration upon Him by loving Him and our neighbors.

At the risk of oversimplification, I am using the terms *human spirit* and *soul*, nearly synonymously, intending to convey similar, but not precisely, the same meaning.

In some cases, not all by any measure, depression might be understood as a disorder of the human spirit. Persons with depression search for *inspiration*, or the condition of being inspired. They long for the experience of awe, reverence, and gratitude. While the ratios of biological, environmental, and genetic contributions that cause depression often remain unidentifiable, sometimes inordinate guilt and distance from God contributes to mental and physical distress.

In Proverbs 5:22 we learn that, "His own iniquities entrap the wicked man, and he is caught in the cords of his sin." This suggests that inadequate handling of sin needlessly complicates matters leading to deepening guilt and depression. Notwithstanding, guilt can be restorative when it brings one to a state of greater awareness and repentance. Just as we often make a wrong turn when driving to new locations, so too we often make mistakes in new emotional and spiritual territories. Yet rather than allowing guilt to destroy our relationship with others or our God, we can be prompted by guilt to return to concepts of grace and forgiveness.

Getting Right Spiritually

Despite convincing evidence of the importance of spiritual health, it is sad to observe that most of us neglect this aspect of the three parts of which we are comprised. Of the many possible explanations for the poor state of spiritual health in which many of us find ourselves, one clear reason is the difficulty scientists have in dealing with the human spirit or consciousness. Yes, I am, to a degree, suggesting that spirit and consciousness are one and the same. Our leading neuroscientists tell us that consciousness is the biggest problem they face; they simply cannot understand or explain consciousness. Yet implicit to this understanding is the fact that failure to observe a phenomenon (the supernatural), the ultimate goal of science, does not negate the rationale that some things are unobservable given our shortcomings as mortals.

Many people sincerely want to get and stay right spiritually. Religious people want to be on the right terms with God. Staying right with God is challenging even for the sincerest among us. Admittedly, had I been born in the East where Buddhism is practiced, or in the Middle East, where Islam is taught, my religious views today would likely be altogether unlike those described above unless I had converted to Christianity.

Christianity's roots are Hebraic. Jesus was a Jew educated in the Jewish temple, a confusing fact given that he was not seen as a Jew in retrospect; rather, he was viewed as the founder of Christianity. The four New Testament books of Matthew, Mark, Luke, and John tell the story of the life of Jesus. Therein, Jesus often quoted from the Old Testament scriptures containing the history of the Jewish people. Yet interesting is the fact that while he did not completely identify as a Pharisee or Sadducee, he was enough like both groups to connect with and debate the culture of both vociferously, highlighting his concomitant similarities and differences.

A lesser known Jewish prophet, Mica, a contemporary of Isaiah, asked and answered our question "How can I get right with God?"

> "He has shown you, O mortal, what is good. And what does the Lord require of you? To act justly and to love mercy and to walk humbly with your God" (Mica 6: 8 NIV).

Jesus's three-year tenure, shorter than most tenured professors, was spent teaching the importance of love. Never in the history of mankind had we been taught to love our enemies or to love our neighbors with the depth of love we have for ourselves. Jesus wrapped up "all the law and the prophets" by telling us to love our Lord God with all our heart, soul, and mind … and to love our neighbor as ourselves (Matthew 22: 37-40 NIV).

Jesus believed in a moral universe, an assertion that history increasingly bears out. While each generation has suffered its share of despots, each generation has also seen their demise and, along with them, their excess.

Why Get Right with God?

Imagine you are the newly appointed local director of emergency services. You have been informed on a secure phone line that our nation is likely to experience multiple nuclear attacks within hours, just as our allies, Israel, England, France, and Canada, were already attacked. Your assignment: "Do all in your power to prevent panic among our citizens!"

Having just read the 46th chapter of Psalms, the words take on a previously unknown but wonderfully realistic meaning in the following verses:

> 1. God is our refuge and strength, an ever-present help in trouble. 2. Therefore we will not fear, though the earth gives way and the mountains fall into the heart of the sea, 3. though its waters roar and foam and the mountains quake with their surging."
>
> 7. The Lord Almighty is with us; the God of Jacob is our fortress.

10. He says, 'Be still, and know that I am God; I will be exalted among the nations, I will be exalted in the earth.

You already have instructions that must be followed in the event of nuclear attacks. You must immediately notify the media, including the social media, to inform people to prepare by seeking shelter, remaining indoors for up to three weeks, taking a shower if outdoors when attacked, taking potassium iodide tablets to prevent accumulation of radiation in your thyroid gland, and not panicking.

Would you encourage people to read Psalm 46? Would you append the above verses from Psalm 46 to your emergency advisory of an immediately impending nuclear attack? Does Psalm 46:10 help you answer the question, "Why get right with God?"

Attachments and Losses

My mother, Johnnie Louise Beale (1893-1971), was the third of 10 children born to John W. Beale and Nellie E. Addison in Isle of Wight County, Virginia. Her mother died early. My mother was securely attached to her father. She loved and respected him, and she stood next to him as he sang to her dying mother, "We Will Meet on that Beautiful Shore." All her siblings held hands around the death bed. For the latter years of his life, her father was chronically hospitalized in the Norfolk Public Health TB Hospital.

On Christmas morning 1945, decades after my grandfather was widowed, my parents and I were joyful. World War II was over, my brother Randolph had served safely in the Navy throughout the war. In fact, he was entering Pearl Harbor aboard his cruiser, the USS Craven, on December 7, 1941, at the very beginning of the war.

A large turkey had been baked, hot eggnog was warming on the stove, and the fragrances of spice, cinnamon, and nutmeg pleasantly sweetened the kitchen, contributing to our warm Christmas spirit. My siblings and their families were joining us at noon for the traditional family Christmas celebration. It was an "all is right with the world" memory, still vivid though 74 years have raced by.

Our telephone rang. The phone was in an adjacent room. I ran to answer it. A somber woman said she was a nurse from the TB Hospital. "Is Louise Brown there? I'm afraid I have bad news for her."

"Mom, it's for you," I remember calling, omitting the "bad news" caution.

I passed the phone to my mother. "Merry Christmas," she happily said, "this is Louise Brown."

As if stabbed in the heart, my mother screamed and loudly wept inconsolably upon hearing the "bad news." I wondered if she would ever stop crying. It got worse during the funeral.

She had visited her father the day before his death. I went with her and Dad, but I remained in the car owing to my grandfather's contagious condition. Mother never learned to drive a car and never traveled on a passenger plane, but she was a take-charge person. Of all her siblings, she was the one the hospital called. She was deeply attached to her father. Even though her father was 75, a long life for a man born in 1870, her heart that had been filled with Christmas cheer was suddenly broken. No one during the funeral showed painful grieving that matched or came near hers.

But life must go on. Mother's crying gradually lessened. Outward, visible signs of grief slowly vanished. I am left to guess that inwardly, she slowly healed from the physical loss of her father, helped by the passing of time and the normal distractions of life. His death occurred before she became a Christian.

Attachment

As human beings, we develop attachments with caregivers to survive childhood and we form relationships throughout life. We are indebted to John Bowlby, MD and Mary Ainsworth, PhD for their keen studies of infants and toddlers that led to attachment theory. The showed us that each person provided with a caregiver will become attached, but that individual differences in relationship quality can differ significantly. This pattern of attachment evolves primarily from the mother-infant relationship. *Mothering person* is the more appropriate term these days for the person primarily interacting with the infant.

In 1970, Ainsworth identified three main attachment styles: secure, avoidant, and ambivalent. A fourth attachment style known as disorganized was later added.

Dr. Ainsworth's study of attachments was based on her *strange situation* paradigm. The strange situation is a laboratory procedure used to assess an infant's pattern of behavior with their mothering person following exposure to an unexpected threat. Toddlers studied in this experiment were 12 to 17 months old. Observers watched through a one-way window as each toddler was brought into a small room by his or her mothering person.

The mothering person interacted with the child in the new environment as the toddler was allowed to play on the floor with toys that were placed there. A stranger soon entered the room and attempted to interact with the toddler after a time. The mothering person then left the toddler and stranger alone in the unfamiliar room for a brief time. When the mothering person returned to the room, she attempted to comfort the toddler as the stranger left them alone in the room together. Next, the mother left the toddler completely alone in the unfamiliar room. The stranger returned and attempted to console the toddler. Finally, the mother returned and attempted to comfort the toddler. The total observational period lasts approximately 24 minutes.

The toddler was classified by its response to the return of the mothering person after exposure to threats (the presence of the stranger and the absence of the mother in an unfamiliar place). According to Ainsworth, three responses occurred: secure, resistant, or avoidant.

Securely attached toddlers were distressed when the mothering figure left, but were positive and showed signs of happiness when she returned, and effectively used the mother as a safe base to explore their environment. Resistant toddlers were intensely distressed when the mothering figure left, but were ambivalent to comfort from the mother when she returned, and explored the environment much less than the other children in the study.

Toddlers who were avoidant showed no sign of distress when the mother left, derived equal comfort from strangers and the mothering person, and was less interested in being reunited upon return.

Dr. Ainsworth, a fellow professor at the University of Virginia, told me, the avoidant toddlers were physiologically disturbed during the threat situation, as shown by rapid pulse rate, hyperventilation, and elevated blood pressure. It was if they had already learned that it was useless to approach the mothering person in times of emotional stress because doing so had no positive effect upon their ability to self-regulate. Parallel work showed that their mothers found it difficult to accurately read and respond to their toddler's needs. This was confirmed when Dr. Ainsworth and her colleagues visited their homes and observed the mothers' interactions with them.

With time, Ainsworth increasingly noted that the three-part classification system did not fully describe all toddlers. Some exhibited subtle stress manifestations before overt signs of distress became noticeable. Specifically, Ainsworth and colleagues observed tense movements such as hunching the shoulders, putting the hands behind the neck, and arching of the head—stress behaviors that preceded crying. These toddlers failed to exhibit coordinated behaviors that garnered proximity with the mothering person and were considered 'disorganized,' a condition that was putatively the result of a flooding of the neurobiological attachment system with fear and uncertainty. Later work showed that unresolved trauma or grief in the mothering figure impaired early dyadic interactions, causing mis-attunement in the dyad.

A person's style of attachment can be enduring throughout life because the perception of threat activates the same substrates for biological attachment in the brain regardless of age, although the system is not immutable. Different patterns of learning throughout life can alter patterns of activation for better or for worse. Extreme life events—such as divorce, death of a child, accident, military duty—can impair a secure attachment type.

Hence, a person's strategy toward relationships can differ depending upon timing, situation, and the people involved. Undoubtedly, a more in-depth understanding of our attachment style can help us leverage our strengths and vulnerabilities in relationships, particularly how we react to our needs and get them met. Moreover, an increased understanding of self can help to change our attachment over time, a slow and difficult process. A brief discussion of adult attachment styles follows.

Secure attachment style is the healthiest of all styles. A person who is securely attached easily and confidently displays interest and affection with others during interactions, a strategy that helps to meet their own needs and those around them. This pattern of attachment is characterized by a positive view of self and a positive view of others. These people are also comfortable being alone and independent. They draw clear boundaries around their life in accordance with values and priorities. Being reared by a mother who consistently responds to the infant's timing while feeding, for example, is critical to the process of becoming securely attached. It is the equivalent of being listened to. The skill of a symphony orchestra conductor comes to mind. The conductor and orchestra are responding to each other with a melodious outcome in the same way that a mother and toddler respond to each other for a harmonious outcome.

Undoubtedly, those with secure attachment style are likely to enjoy high quality relationships later in life. Research shows that securely attached individuals feel more supported, are less likely to be depressed, healthier, more successful professionally, and enjoy higher quality relationships.

Anxious-preoccupied attachment style, as its name suggests, is a less healthy style of relating to others, and is often referred to as *anxious-ambivalent attachment*. This pattern of attachment is characterized by a negative view of self and a positive view of others, causing them to exhibit needy behavior. People with this style of attachment are stressed and nervous about their relationships. They need constant reassurance and affection from their partner. People in this category exhibit high levels of emotional dysregulation and impulsiveness in their relationships. Their early caregiving is described as unpredictable.

Dismissive-avoidant attachment style is characterized by avoiding involvement with others, fears of closeness, and regrettably, in my opinion, a person with this attachment style is more likely to develop a pattern of unrewarding relationships. This pattern of attachment is characterized by a positive view of self and a negative view of others, causing them to exhibit arrogance and a fear of commitment. People in this category may work in excess as a means to avoid intimate commitment and tend to have an exit strategy. Their early caregiving is described as partially sufficient, but with gaps in need fulfillment. This type can benefit from being less judgmental of self and others.

Fearful-avoidant attachment style denotes an infant who shows no consistent behavior when separated or reunited with its mother. This pattern of attachment is characterized by a negative view of self and others, causing them to exhibit severe deficits in relationship functioning. People in this category are afraid of intimacy and commitment, and may distrust anyone who tries to get emotionally close to them. People who are fearful-avoidant spend much of their time alone or in abusive relationships. Research suggests this style of attachment may be passed from generation to generation by parents who struggle with unresolved trauma, having little tolerance for the range of emotions of their child. Their early caregiving is described as abusive or negligent.

By using this classification schema, you can begin to move toward cultivating more secure relationships by adopting a healthier concept of yourself and others. People who are anxious can work on creating healthy boundaries and more secure sense of self-confidence, keeping in awareness that anxiety comes from over-estimating danger while under-estimating your ability to deal with it. People who are avoidant can work on becoming aware of the value of others and the necessity and sheer pleasure of relating to others. People who are fearful can work on courage to face their fears, realizing that to get over them one must face them.

Loss

Losses come in many forms, such as the loss of a job, the loss of one's reputation, the loss of health, and numerous other kinds of loss. The meaning one gives to a loss is also determined by multiple factors. For example, religious people regard the life of the spirit to be eternal, and they anticipate a reunion with a lost loved one, thus lessening the burden of the loss.

Attachment style also influences how one manages the loss of a loved one. In reality, no relationship is entirely free of conflict. Of course, loss falls under the larger category of *change*. We know that change of any type is challenging. I treated professors who, surprisingly, became depressed following an academic promotion. A Middle Eastern prince became so depressed after a successful rhinoplasty correcting his crooked nose that his corrected nose had to be fractured and restored to its original abnormal state.

Reaction to loss is usually adequate when the reality of the loss is accepted. Normal grief is individualized, variable, and runs a course of about one year, about the same amount of time it takes to fully recover from major surgery. There are exceptions.

"Move to Charlottesville"

A middle-aged woman lost her husband to cancer. She submitted to his dominating personality, never considering it burdensome; in fact, hers was considered a comfortable role because he made all the difficult and important decisions.

During the days before his death, her husband left last-minute instructions for her on a tape recording: "Have my body cremated, sell the house, move to Charlottesville, and buy a house." Unfortunately, he left no instructions for the disposition of his ashes. A photograph of her husband rested on the mantle in the new home, his voice was on the tape recording, and his ashes were stored in the trunk of her car. Under these conditions, the reality of his presence was greater than the reality of his death. There was no need to grieve.

Linking Objects

Re-grief is a term defining a specific form of treatment for those who are unable to grieve. Vamik Volkan, MD, a former mentor and psychoanalyst, has made remarkable discoveries that are proving effective in the field of delayed grief treatment. He compares *transitional objects*— objects infants and young children cherish, such as a blanket or teddy bear, symbols of the mothering person— with *linking objects,* which are symbols of a lost loved one. Linking objects represent the decedent. As long as a linking object is used as a substitute for the lost person, there will be no grieving.

Photographs or personal possessions belonging to the deceased may have sentimental value to those who are grieving. Volkan's work is devoted to those who have not accepted the reality of the loss and have not grieved, a larger number of people than one might expect. Non-grievers who employ linking objects as cherished symbols for the dead loved one do so outside of their awareness. Consequently, initial inquiries about the linking objects may prove non-affirming when first taking the history of a patient with pathological grief.

Let me hasten to further distinguish between normal, psychologically healthy *security bridges* that serve as transitional objects— teddy bears for example— which aid in the process of separation and individuation in child development. Linking objects, on the other hand, are unhealthy substitutes in the disturbed reality-testing of those who cannot accept the reality of the loss. Admittedly, beyond the depth of our discussion, those who suffer from delayed or pathological grief have benefitted significantly from re-grief treatment introduced by Dr. Volkan (1966 and 1972).

An additional distinction is made between the normal, healthy role of objects having sentimental value or simply healthy reminders associated with the lost loved one and linking objects. In regard to healthy reminders, Dr. Phillips adds, "When a young teacher was killed at the start of a school year, the local administration and mental health team prohibited the removal of her reminders from the third grade. Instead, they reminisced and talked of her for the remainder of the year. Eventually, they planted a tree in a garden named after her ... and after a significant time moved on. From a balcony view, the approach appeared very healthy for these young children in the long-term."

Inquiring About Delayed Grief

Years ago, I was lecturing in Oxfordshire, England, to a group of teachers whose students were children of our military stationed in Europe. I was discussing linking objects as potential barriers to grief. A man in the audience stood up, opposing such a concept. He said, "Sir, my father died five years ago. I went back to the States and took care of all his affairs, including the funeral arrangements. I had no problems, then or now. Would you not agree that I handled his loss well?"

I asked, "Did you grieve for your father?"

"I was too busy for that. I selected the casket, purchased the burial place, and took care of all the expenses," he said.

"Do you have anything with you that belonged to your dad?" I asked.

"No, Sir."

Because the meaning given to linking and transitional objects occurs outside the awareness of those who need them, I reframed my question. "Do you have anything on your person that belonged to your dad?"

"No, I don't think so."

Still standing, he appeared fidgety and puzzled. He then said, "I'm sorry. I do wear my father's ring. I have worn it since his death."

Linking objects, like transitional objects, serve as substitutes for someone loved and valued, but who is unavailable. Suddenly, in front of a large audience of colleagues, he burst into tears, tears that had been dammed up for five years. It was an unforgettable moment. It was also a transforming experience for this man who had not grieved. His facial expression softened and saddened. He thanked me later and said it was "liberating" for him. He was then ready for the difficult task of grieving, an ideal candidate for re-grief work.

Linking objects are often kept in a special place and visited often, always reminding the non-griever of the deceased. Much more could be said about this fascinating topic, but it would not fit our objectives.

In summary, human grief is a complex biological, psychological, and spiritual process in response to a loss. It is germane to depression because grieving is painful and it is natural to avoid pain and suffering whenever possible. Major depression may result when grief is not permitted to run its course. The loss of a close loved one is the most difficult experience each of us faces. When it is not permitted to express itself, grief is complicated, prolonged, minimized, avoided, or pathological. In a word, it is the major exit event in the lives of those who loved and were closest to the decedent.

Heaven and Hell

According to the Pew Religious Landscape Study, 2014, most Americans believe in heaven and hell. Of the *religious affiliated*, 82% believe in heaven and 67% believe in hell, findings little changed since 2007. Of the *unaffiliated* group, 37% believe in heaven and 27% believe in hell. Of the atheists, 5% believe in heaven and 3% in hell. Agnostics indicated 14% and 9%, respectively, on the heaven versus hell question. *Heaven* in this study was defined as a place "where those who have led good lives are eternally rewarded." *Hell* was defined as a place "where people who led bad lives and die without being sorry are eternally punished."

Why Such Painstaking Detail on Spiritual Fitness?

In God's image and likeness, we are endowed with a body, mind, and spirit. I believe we have better physical and mental health when, perhaps only when, we have spiritual health. I know it is the case with me. I can neglect my spiritual health, even for long periods of time, and even while remaining physically and mentally fit, I am always brought back to the necessity and the reality of spiritual health. Using the terms *spiritual health* and *spiritual fitness* almost synonymously, I again point out that the meaning of the term *fitness* refers to being the best you can be, a notion that is devoid of striving. Underscoring this point, Exodus 14:14 tells us "The Lord will fight for you; you need only to be still," a notion reiterated in Psalm 46:10 "Be still, and know that I am God ..." (Psalm 46:10 NIV).

Jesus did not suggest or recommend, but commanded us, just as He told the Pharisees, "Love the Lord your God with all your heart and with all your soul and with all your mind. This is the first and greatest commandment. And the second is like it: 'Love your neighbor as yourself'" (Matthew 22: 37-39 NIV).

Can we fail to follow these operational orders and consider ourselves spiritually fit? I do not believe we can. Imagine how wonderful it is to live and die obeying God! Yes, a strong consideration of spiritual fitness is necessary to flourish in all dimensions of life.

References

Ainsworth, M. D. S., Blehar, M. C., Waters, E., Wall, S. N. (2015). *Patterns of Attachment: A Psychological Study of The Strange Situation*. New York, NY: Psychology Press.

Bowlby, J. (1969). *Attachment: Attachment and Loss.* New York, NY: Basic Books.

Hoekema, A. A. (1986). *Created in God's Image*. Grand Rapids, MI: Eerdmans Publishing Company, 1986.

Hughes, P. E. (1989). *The True Image: Christ as the Origin and Destiny of Man*. Grand Rapids, MI: Eerdmans Publishing Company.

James, W. (1890). The Principles of Psychology. New York, NY: H. Holt and Company.

James, W. (1902). *The Varieties of Religious Experience: A Study in Human Nature: Being the Gifford Lectures on Natural Religion Delivered at*

Edinburgh in 1901-1902. New York, NY: London: Longmans, Green.

Freud, S. (1913). *The Interpretation of Dreams (3rd edition). Translated by A. A.* Brill. New York, NY: The Macmillan Company.

Volkan, V.D. (1972). The linking objects of pathological mourners. *Arch Gen Psychiatry, (27)*2: 215-221.

Volkan, V., Showalter, C. R. (1968). Known object loss, disturbance in reality testing, and "re-grief work" as a method of brief psychotherapy. *Psychiatr Q, 42*(2): 358-374.

Wall, J.N. (1981). *George Herbert: The Country Parson and the Temple.* Mahwah, NJ: Paulist Press.

CHAPTER 18

ACHIEVING SPIRITUAL FITNESS

Nurturing Your Spirit

Suppose you achieved physical fitness and maintained it, adding years to your life. Suppose you also developed lasting mental fitness, freeing your thoughts of such common errors as prejudice and other destructive thoughts. Would you be fulfilled, needing nothing more to be at peace with yourself, your neighbor, and the world? I think not. Something important would be missing.

A large part of your life would be unrewarding. You would not have the almost indescribable feeling of spiritual transcendence, of being in touch with that which is exceedingly good, true, and beautiful. You may have good friends and a close family, yet repeatedly experience unfulfilled emptiness. There would be a hole in your life.

Years ago, our next-door neighbor hanged herself. It shocked all of us. I cannot say we were close neighbors, but we were friendly, greeted each other warmly when meeting on the street, and attended social events in each other's home. Her grieving husband talked to me about the death of his wife. "Her death," he said, "left a hole in my life that I walk around all day and fall into at night."

I imagine that a person without a nurtured spirit dwells in a hole not unlike my grieving neighbor suffered. His, I believe, will heal as grief runs its course, and the hole fills with the remembered love they once shared. Far too many of us dwell in an emptiness with an unnurtured spirit and an unrestored soul. John Lennon's song "Crippled Inside" comes to mind: "You can shine your shoes and wear a suit. You can comb your hair and look quite cute. You can hide your face behind a smile. One thing you can't hide is when you're crippled inside." The gifted musician's lyrics continue, "You can go to church and sing a hymn. You can judge me by the color of my skin. You can live a lie until you die. One thing you can't hide is when you're crippled inside."

The Spiritual Sphere

At this time in our journey into fitness, we leave the track and exercise mat. We are not seated at the table where a well-prepared meal awaits us and its fine aromas invite us, stimulating our appetites. We are entering the metaphysical, invisible, intangible, immaterial, yes, spiritual realm of daily existence.

The spiritual sphere is real. No rational person can deny it. Slam this book closed and throw it down if you are so inclined, or linger a little longer and see what the man is saying! If we were traveling by air, our present topic might alert us with the announcement, "Please fasten your safety belts and locate the nearest exit." But you are the pilot. I am your navigator. I believe our cooperative effort will assure us of a successful and informative flight and further prepare us for safe flights through storms yet to come.

Admittedly, our topic is difficult in part, because several of its relevant words and topics are archaic, used infrequently, and may conjure up unpleasant, even disturbing memories. Keeping it simple, I use the word *soul* as defined by the Oxford Dictionary, "the spiritual or immaterial part of a human being or animal, regarded as immortal." Taken from the same resource, *spirit* is defined as "the non-physical part of a person which is the seat of emotions and character."

The Development of the 21st Century Soul Concept

Considered by many to be the essence of life—a recurring theme in art, literature, and biblical texts—the concept of the human soul has a long history. Nearly 5000 years ago, Egyptians opined that magical forces within the world imbued every person, ultimately serving as the animating life force which left the body at death and traveled beyond. To assist with the process, *The Egyptian Book of the Dead* recounted a series of spells to help the soul navigate the afterlife, a safety mechanism placed in the tombs before sealing. Spell 125 describes the judging of the heart of the deceased by Osiris in the Hall of Truth, one of the best known descriptions from ancient Egypt, a narrative that alludes to the conjecture that the soul had to pass the weighing test to gain entry into paradise (Mark, 2016).

Nearly 2400 years ago in ancient Greece, Aristotle opined that the soul is a life-giving immaterial force present in all living things and is inextricable from the body, a force that had little to do with personal identity and individuality. He likened the soul to the body as a veritable stamp marked in wax, a metaphor that underscored Aristotle's notion that the soul was the name for characteristic modes and capacities of behavior in the living and, thereby, was not immortal. Contrasting Aristotle, Plato opined that the soul was immortal; it existed before birth and continued on after death (Ancient Theories, 2009).

At the heart of this difference in conceptualization is dualism, whether the body and soul can be separated. Plato viewed the soul and body as distinct and separable and, therefore, had no compunction with the notion of immortality.

During the time of Jesus, debates of dualism continued. The Sadducees (a group of priests and aristocrats who espoused a more literal interpretation as written in the Law of Moses) and the Pharisees (a group of commoners who espoused scholarly interpretations of the oral law given to Moses along with the Torah) differed on their view of the soul.

The Sadducees believed the soul ceased to exist after death, whereas the Pharisees believed in an after-life wherein God would reward the righteous and punish the wicked. The Roman Empire before Constantine rejected the idea of a human soul, certainly its eternal life, a fact that changed when Constantine became the first emperor to adhere to Christianity. Constantine issued the Edict of Milan in 313 A.D. that legalized Christianity and permitted worship throughout the empire. Later, he convened the Council of Nicaea to affirm that Jesus was a divine being. Perhaps affecting Constantine's conviction was the term *soul* that was referenced in 780 times in Old Testament, although it is not always rendered by the English word *soul* because of different contextual meanings. The effects of these actions were to promote religious tolerance and, as a central Christian belief, that the soul was eternal.

Modern day Christians often derive their view of the soul from scripture. The first literal appearance of the concept of soul is made early in the Bible in the book of Genesis 2:7 NIV: "Then the Lord God formed a man from the dust of the ground and breathed into his nostrils the breath of life, and man became a living being [soul]." Another familiar verse is referenced from Matthew 11: 29 NIV wherein Jesus referred to the soul in communicating His willingness to bear our worst burdens: "Take my yoke [wisdom] upon you and learn from me, for I am gentle and humble in heart, and you will find rest for your souls."

Interestingly, the Bible mentions often the secular history of Greece. According to Acts 17:21NIV, "All the Athenians and the foreigners who lived there spent their time doing nothing but talking about and listening to the latest ideas." Bolstering this notion, the work of Thucydides and Demosthenes firmly attest to the Athenian penchant for persistent conversation and debate. In Matthew 22: 37 NIV, we are bid to, "Love the

Lord your God with all your heart and with all your soul and with all your mind."

In Matthew 16: 26NIV, Jesus asked: "What good will it be for someone to gain the whole world, yet forfeit their soul? Or what can anyone give in exchange for their soul?" Together, these works bid us to revisit the Golden Mean as we attempt to consider the importance of the soul in relation to the mind and body. While doing so, must we rationally conclude that the soul is no less important to God than mind or the body? If so, do we all not have a solemn duty to care for our soul?

The United States, One Wide-ranging Nation Under God

The Pew Research Center reported on January 3, 2019, that "In the general public, 23% say they are atheist, agnostic or 'nothing in particular.' In Congress, just one person says she is religiously unaffiliated ..." However, "There are fewer Christians in the incoming freshman class [of Congress] than there are among incumbents ... Among the new members are the first two Muslim women in Congress ..." (Sandstrom, 2019), a veritable reification of real pluralistic values in the U.S. electorate.

Historically, America continues to uphold, even demand, religious freedom. I join others who appreciate this constitutional right. I trust it is apparent that I respect the right of all citizens to follow the dictates of their own heart in choosing the God they worship as well as their right to worship no God. Nonetheless, all citizens need to know that the human soul and the human spirit hunger for meaning, fulfillment, and truth. Physical, mental, and spiritual health are vitally connected. Optimal health and function are more likely achieved when we strive for fitness of body, mind, and spirit. Probably no one hungers more for meaning, fulfillment, and truth than those who suffer from depression.

Principles of Nurturing Your Spirit

1. Accept the fact that you are a human being with weaknesses, strengths, limitations, and potentialities.
2. As a human being you have physical, mental, and spiritual needs.

3. Your spirit needs rest, restoration, and inspiration.
4. Relax, let go, and accept grace in order to give your little private convulsive self a rest and find a Greater Self (James, 1902).

A Young Woman who is a Breast Cancer Survivor wrote:

"Sometimes inaction is the best form of action … meaning give oneself permission to stop comparing and striving and gradually come to the idea of being and enjoying. While I was recovering from bilateral mastectomies and trying to find my grounding, an older academic in town gave me a meaningful assignment: to imagine that I was there, that I had arrived, that I had made it and yet was the last to know. This idea challenged me to accept where I was, for better or for worse; to stop living for the future; and to more fully embrace the present. Referring back to your *Textbook for Mental Health*, I had failed to take a realistic assessment of my reality."

5. Merge the narrow private with a Greater Self (God) (James, 1902).

   The same young woman, upon reading this principle drawn from William James's *Varieties of Religious Experience* (1902), also wrote:

   "I played hide-and-seek with my Greater Self for years, largely because I didn't know what I was looking for. Perhaps this is where we define spiritual gifts as being the product of talents and prior experiences … and the idea of emotions as being guides to what we do and do not like … and what we need more of or less of."

6. When you find the Greater Self your life and your work will take on a sense of lyrical enchantment or an appeal of earnestness and heroism (James, 1902).

7. "Be still, and know that I am God" (Psalm 46:10 NIV).

8. Companionship and friendship are basic spiritual needs. According to Aristotle, "Man is by nature a social animal; an individual who is unsocial naturally and not accidentally is either beneath our notice or more than human. Society is something that precedes the individual. Anyone who either cannot lead the common life or is so self-sufficient as not to need to, and therefore does not partake of society, is either a beast or a god" (Aristotle, 1905).

9. Intentionally find ways to love others and, more challenging, be lovable.

Practical Spiritual Practices

1. Enjoy beauty spiritually.
2. Look for, and treasure, beauty in others and in your surroundings.
3. Discover art that spiritually entreats you.
4. Listen to music that touches your soul.
5. Identify the God you wish to worship. The earlier meaning of the term *worship* was

"worth." Is God of the greatest worth to you? Or does that attention too often go elsewhere?

6. "God is spirit, and his worshipers must worship him in the Spirit and in truth" (John 4:24 NIV).

7. Many Americans (36% of women and 26% of men) find a church to attend to worship and to find spiritual comfort.

8. Spiritual practices require thoughts and words, a unique mind and heart mixture, and action in the service of others.

9. In St. Paul's letter to the Philippians, written while under house arrest in Rome, 61 A.D., he listed worthy subjects on which to focus one's mind, convinced that one's thoughts significantly affect one's feelings and behavior. Those who intentionally follow St. Paul's advice will experience spiritual growth:

> "Finally, brothers and sisters, whatever is true, whatever is noble, whatever is right, whatever is pure, whatever is lovely, whatever is admirable – if

anything is excellent or praiseworthy –
think about such things. Whatever you
have learned or received or heard from
me, or seen in me – put into practice.
And the God of peace will be with you."
(Philippians 4:8-9 NIV).

Prayer and Meditation

In the same way that our physical needs must be
met daily, so also our spiritual needs must be met
daily. Moreover, just as physical exercise must be
scheduled to become habitual, so also must
spiritual practices be scheduled to become
habitual. Thus, find the best time of day and a
quiet place where uninterrupted reading and
prayer can be practiced and make it a part of your
daily schedule.

There are important differences between prayer
and meditation. They are by no means
synonymous, but each may have distinct spiritual
advantages. In prayer, a person calls upon God as
he or she knows him. St. Paul tells us in the
scriptures to "pray without ceasing"
(Thessalonians 5:17 NIV), to ask God for what we
need, and believe while praying that God is

listening and answering our prayers in His own way and in His own time. We find nourishment by communicating with God in prayer.

In meditation, we listen as the Spirit of God that dwells in us speaks. In so doing, we increase awareness of the thoughts that we need to hear in the present moment, as commanded in Psalm 46:10 NIV, "Be still, and know that I am God." Both prayer and meditation are equally essential parts of every spiritual communication. In prayer we speak. In meditation, we listen as the Spirit speaks.

Ideally, keep a double entry prayer and meditation journal. In the prayer journal, you can list the names and needs of those for whom you pray. In your meditation journal, make an attempt to be aware of and capture mental experience as it unfolds. A review of your journal over time can provide insight about your strengths and needs, and clues about how your practice impacts them. Relevant items include actual experiences that moved or touched you, and how those experiences were personally meaningful.

With time, journaling practice helps instill a focused effort where we can better connect and integrate our past, present, and future. To choose to keep a journal is to choose to stand guard at the door of our mind, body, and spirit and intentionally feed those elements in order to cultivate a more authentic life, a strategy that is essential to benchmarking growth that is needed to maintain or regain fitness.

Pascal's Wager

Blaise Pascal was a 17th century philosopher, scientist, and mathematician who spent time considering probability theory. He wrote in defense of the scientific method and religion. Blending these interests with decision logic, Pascal wrote an apologetic in *Pensees*, a posthumously published work that translates to the word *thoughts*. Therein, he equated the belief in the existence of God as the ultimate wager. His notion asserts that people bet with their soul when considering whether God does or does not exist. Pascal's logic asserts the notion of compulsory choice wherein the odds of benefit are high (eternal life in Heaven), but the odds of loss are low in matters concerned with belief in God's existence (Deem, 2011). Problematically, this logic contradicts the tenets of Christianity. Intellectual belief in God is not enough; commitment counts.

So, if you take the belief in the God side of the wager, how might you authentically become right with God? I can answer this from the Christian perspective, but I suspect that if other deities exist, the same answer applies: obedience. "Obedience" is so simple to say, yet so complex to follow owing to our nature of defiance. Adam had it all in the Garden of Eden, but he was incapable of obedience to God, with whom he walked in the quiet of the evenings. We too are like Adam. We are thinking and feeling people who are prone to disobey, a fact that is complicated by conscience.

Our conscience tells us when we do or think things inconsistent with accepted morality. In reality, this internal warning system alerts us to the presence of what Dietrich Bonhoeffer refers to as *cheap grace*. According to Bonhoeffer, "Cheap grace is the grace we bestow on ourselves. Cheap grace is the preaching of forgiveness without requiring repentance, baptism without church discipline, communion without confession...Cheap grace is grace without discipleship, grace without the cross, grace without Jesus Christ, living and incarnate" (Bonhoeffer, 1995).

Missing the Target, but Given New Arrows

Sincerely admitting our wrongful acts and faults is the first step in getting right with God. Truly intending to march steadfastly in the opposite direction of our offensive actions and thoughts is the second step in getting right with God. When steps one and two are sincerely taken, we are forgiven by a divinity that has a historically proven record of the greatest form of love and forgiveness.

I believe that God was incarnated in Jesus Christ and I know that I need forgiveness. I bet there is no one like Him. Jesus commanded us to fully love God and to love and forgive our neighbors in the entirely exceptional way we love ourselves.

The Power of Prayer

On February 6, 1986, President Ronald Reagan's birthday and our wedding anniversary, Dottie and I were privileged to hear President Reagan speak at the National Prayer Breakfast in Washington, D.C. President Reagan shared the following comments about President Eisenhower:

> "One night in 1952 during the Presidential campaign, Dwight Eisenhower confided something to one of his advisers, a close friend, Senator Frank Carlson. Eisenhower told him that during the war when he was commanding the allied forces in Europe, he'd had a startling and vivid spiritual experience—he had actually felt the hand of God guiding him, felt the presence of God. And the general told the Senator that this experience and the support of his friends had given him real spiritual strength in the hard days before D-day. Senator Carlson said he understood. He, himself, was getting spiritual help from the Members of a little prayer group in the Senate. And a few months later, the

general, who was now the President, asked Frank Carlson over to the White House. And he told him, 'Frank, this is the loneliest house I've ever been in.' Carlson said, 'Mr. President, I think this may be the right time for you to come and meet with our prayer group.' And Eisenhower did just that. In 1953 he attended the first combined prayer breakfast.

And ever since, Presidents have been coming here for help and assistance—and here I am."

Jesus has an open-door policy and He wants to hear from us on a daily basis, even more often if you sense the need to talk with Him. Praying is not easy for anyone. Barriers block prayer when our souls reach out to God. In *Hamlet*, we recognize a familiar situation: "My words fly up, my thoughts remain below: Words without thoughts never to heaven go" (III, iii, 100-103). In this key scene, the King prays not to ask forgiveness for his sins (killing his brother); rather, he prays that he will not get caught in the act. Unwittingly encapsulated in the Kings words were a lack of feelings of remorse for the actions that he committed and, therefore, he remained unrepentant.

There may be some occasions when you feel too distressed to pray. Jesus encourages us to "Pray without ceasing," but He understands when we are not capable of prayer. I hope those occasions are infrequent, but if that state of mind occurs, just breathe deeply and slowly while permitting the Spirit of God to hover over you and visualize the caring and protective love of God, the same love that hovered over the formless mass that became the Earth. That same Spirit of God remains available to those who recognize and call upon it.

When We Need the Right Prayer

When necessary, God will give us the prayer we need to pray. This happened to me in a vivid and convincing way. Many years ago, my wife and children and I attended a small Episcopal church in Charlottesville, the Church of Our Savior. The following week, my wife and I were scheduled to fly to the West Coast, where I would take an oral examination in neurology and psychiatry.

The exam loomed large over my head. A lot depended on passing the exam. Failure meant I could never become certified by the American Board of Psychiatry and Neurology. At that time, I would be required to perform a neurological exam in front of a neurologist. Also, psychiatric judges would oversee my interviewing of three psychiatric patients to ensure that I could make their correct diagnoses. The judges would seem to be nearly everywhere, coming and going, as they observed me interacting with the patients.

As customary, I knelt on my knees in prayer during the Sunday morning worship service four-and-a-half decades ago. On the way down from standing to kneeling, something undeniable happened to me. While standing, the prayer in my mind was, "Please dear God, help me pass this exam." I had taken a version of the exam the year before in Chicago and failed it.

My desperation was visible to God.

When my knees reached the floor, God gave me a different, more meaningful prayer, one that soothed my anxiety and literally transformed my thinking and demeanor. From my heart, I prayed, "Dear God, give me the wisdom to help my patients." It was an entirely new thought to me. I had been concentrating on the wrong thing. My worrying had been counterproductive. Thankfully, I took the exam with minimal anxiety. A week later, I received a letter informing me I had passed the exam.

Rejoice

I already mentioned the physical strength I experienced when fellow Soldiers shouted words of encouragement as I was being timed, running the last lap of the two-mile run for the "Army Physical Fitness Test." Without the inspiring words of Soldiers unknown to me personally, I would not proudly wear the patch awarded to those who match or excel the fitness maximum score. We all need encouragement. It can be inspiring, especially fitting when you are out of breath.

The Bible is filled with encouraging words and reasons for hope, as well as help and comfort for any situation, at any time. Imagine the power of the following words of encouragement:

"Rejoice in the Lord always. I will say it again: Rejoice!

Let your gentleness be evident to all. The Lord is near.

Do not be anxious about anything, but in every situation, by prayer and petition, with thanksgiving, present your requests to God. And the peace of God, which transcends all understanding, will guard your hearts and your minds in Christ Jesus" (Philippians 4: 4-7 NIV).

What it Means to Rejoice

Rejoice is not a commonly used word today. TV news channels are not rated on topics that give rise to the emotions associated with rejoicing, such as happiness, celebration, exultation, sheer delight, and joy. Plainly, the competitive prizes go to the channel that delivers the worst news the fastest. It is what we have come to expect.

Regrettably, we are conditioned to impatiently wait for the very worst news yet to come. We are also conditioned to expect violence in TV drama. As one astute person inquired, "If we have so much violence on TV, why do we have to have it real life?"

An antonym for *rejoice* is "be sad."

Our spiritual forefathers must have known that life events would distract us from rejoicing, our intended state, and provided reminders throughout the Bible to be happy: "This is the day the Lord has made; We will rejoice and be glad in it" (Psalm 118:24 NKJV).

What Gentleness Means

The incarnation of God into Jesus Christ, a humble, sinless human being with a birth certificate, was itself a remarkable act of gentleness. The most important journey in history began in heaven in love and gentleness and traveled to a manger in a stable in which the infant Jesus was placed. Our greatest role model, Jesus, tended to steer the various elements of his personality toward kindness and gentleness.

Juxtaposed alongside the love that Jesus felt was unmistakable anger. He loved those who suffered and staunchly opposed religious hypocrisy—leading him to at times comfort, rebuke, or threaten. Thus, we realize our persona of Jesus as gentle and kind emerged from his ability to maintain a tender heart, even when faced with challenge. Underscoring this endeavor was a persistent attention to retaining self-control, a characteristic that stood in contrast to timidity, weakness, or fear. Inspired by his example, and challenged by his commandments, we too strive to love one another—treating others with kindness, gentleness, dignity, and respect.

Unfortunately, far too many of us are indifferent to our neighbors. We are too tolerant of unimaginable genocide that continues around the world. If there is an antonym best suited for gentleness it is "war." We have been at war for nearly two decades in the Middle East. The great world wars of the 20th and 21st century was not about gentleness. For the US and her allies, the great world wars were about defending freedom.

Astutely affirming this position is Benjamin Ferencz, an icon whose story is expounded upon in the documentary entitled *Prosecuting Evil*. As a child, Ferencz was the child of Romanian immigrants to the U.S. Later, he studied law at Harvard and served in World War II. In 1945, Ferencz was headquartered with General Patton's Third Army and tasked with the collection of evidence from concentration camps for war crimes, a pivotal role that preceded his later appointment as chief prosecutor in the Eisatzgruppen case, or the trial for Hitler's killing squads, at the Nuremberg trials.

With a soul impassioned by the horrors he encountered in the concentration camps, Ferencz later laid out a legal process for dealing with war crimes at the international level. In July 2002, the International Criminal Court was established in Hague after it was ratified by 60 countries. Today, many countries still choose to use their own power in the ways and means that are compatible with their own desires as opposed to yielding to the power of international law.

Ferencz cautioned that war will inevitably make mass murderers out of otherwise decent people. Perhaps more than anything, Ferencz is a veritable moral conscious of what it means to exist in a global nation with a gentleness of spirit. Ferencz knows as much as anyone the dangers of moral relativism laced and delivered with charismatic rhetoric and skill, a remnant of the German atrocities no longer veiled after the end World War II.

What "Peace that Surpasses All Understanding" Means

According to a Pew Research Center report, January 21, 2016, Americans are becoming less religious, but more spiritual. From 2007 to 2014, those who responded that they "regularly feel spiritual peace, and sense of wonder," rose from 52% to 59% (Masci & Lipka, 2016). Based upon this research, it is fair to say that about half of the country know and experience spiritual peace, at least some of the time, although frequency was not delineated in the survey. "Not bad," some might say, but "not good" either, considering that real inner peace, the peace of God, is available to everyone who wants to experience peace that "surpasses all understanding." The unique peace that guards our hearts and minds comes from a single source.

As I read Jimmy Carter's book, *Faith: A Journey For All*, 2018, I am not surprised that his faith in God encouraged and helped him as president while dealing with the partial meltdown of a reactor at the Three Mile accident or afterwards while negotiating with North Korea to end their nuclear weapons program.

Carter's religious-based humanitarian efforts have prompted him to work diligently towards nuclear disarmament and the prevention of nuclear proliferation. How then is it that he and half our population can experience "spiritual peace" in the midst of stalled efforts for denuclearization? Perhaps the assured remember that "For he himself is our peace, who has made the two groups one and has destroyed the barrier, the dividing wall of hostility" (Eph 2:14 NIV).

The "Peace of God"

Recently, our youngest son spent five nights in the intensive care unit of our hospital. He suffered from an unexpected serious complication of a chronic illness, requiring emergency vascular surgery, and we are exceedingly thankful that he is mending well. The seriousness of his condition, combined with its unexpectedness and urgency, was difficult for all of us. We were not aware of it, but our son observed a difference between the way my wife and I were dealing with his illness.

"I can tell Dad is anxious, but Mom is calmer. I know you both love me," our son said, "but I want to be able to handle my stress more like Mom does. What is the secret?"

Dottie said she took all her worry about his illness to God in prayer and left it there. "God gave me an inner feeling of peace. God's hands are strong; it was such a feeling of relief," she said. From memory, Dottie smiled while quoting the following scripture:

"And the peace of God, which transcends all understanding, will guard your hearts and your minds in Christ Jesus" (Philippians 4:7NIV).

As a physician, I was giving my son medical information about his condition, some of which served to make me anxious. My son is perceptive. He saw the difference between his parents' ways of handling his illness. He knows I'm a Christian who believes in the eternal life of the soul and he knew I often quoted the same scripture to Soldiers and Marines suffering from depression and PTSD. But he was correct in this instance. He wanted the faith that his mother showed him through the darkest days and longest nights of his illness.

What Faith Means

Jimmy Carter wrote in his book, *Faith: A Journey For All*, that for him, "faith is not just a noun but also a verb," meaning he believes in the biblical statement that "faith by itself, if it does not have works, is dead" (James 2: 14-26 NIV).

At 94, former President Jimmy Carter is a living example of a person who believes and practices faith and works. I believe in this approach to life. I've seen Dottie's faith in action consistently over the years. It holds her life together like mortar holds bricks firmly in a sturdy wall.

What does it mean to have faith? Does one have faith in a chair, before sitting down, that it will provide a safe and comfortable seat? No, I think not. We are oblivious to most of our everyday actions. To introduce the term *faith* into that context is absurd, given the lack of conscious intent. Because we are aware that most people tend to operate in an unaware mode, we must guard against mindless thinking in favor of conscious actions that are in our best interest. For example, we make sure that the brakes on our car are functional and that it is mechanically safe. For decisions that are necessarily made on less evidence than is desirable, we can make a conscious decision to operate within a state of faith.

God is the most common source of faith, and belief in God is the fertile soil on which faith grows into meaningfulness. Of course, *faith* is a commonly used word in nonreligious contexts, but it is best used in the restricted sense described above. The Bible informs us that faith the size of a mustard seed, one of the smallest types of seed, is all that one needs (Mathew 17:20 NIV). One acquires faith by examining the evidence and then asking God for faith to believe and act.

I read and refer others to the Bible for wisdom and practical help and comfort. In these important regards, the Bible is the best reference, better than any other reference with which I am familiar, including textbooks of psychiatry, psychology, social work, counseling, theology, and philosophy. There may be exceptional situations in which you find yourself feeling too disturbed or incapable of reading the Bible or praying. Simply be still. If depression, anxiety, or any other condition severely consumes you, the Maker of your mind and soul understands and comforts you even if you cannot pray.

Review and Brief Summary

In my *Textbook for Mental Health: A Narrative Approach*, I listed Ten Steps for Enhancing Spiritual Health and copy them here for you:

1. Help someone without the expectation of appreciation or reward.
2. Practice and cultivate a habit of silence for 20 minutes each day.
3. Read about the practice and meaning of prayer.
4. Ask a trusted friend or relative to write a letter to you addressing their perceptions of you as a person. Write yourself the same type of letter. Read both letters in a special, quiet place where you can reflect earnestly on them.
5. Listen on a regular daily basis for at least one week to music you find inspiring. Let nothing but the music attract your attention.
6. Attend a religious service each week for at least one month.
7. Write a letter to someone who has influenced your life.

8. Ask someone whose opinion you respect to describe where they are now on their spiritual journey.
9. Read a brief history of one of the world's great religions.
10. Keep a reflection journal in which you write about the people and events that are having a spiritual influence on your life (Brown, Snyder, Peterson, 2002, p. 372).

Many years ago, my son Clinton and I drove from Charlottesville to Los Angeles in a pickup truck en route to the Musicians Institute. He spent a year there studying guitar and voice, and later he studied audio-engineering at Middle Tennessee State University. It was a significant time in Clinton's life and his first time away from home.

All the way to the West Coast, I pondered what I would say to my son as I departed for home. I came up with nothing suitable to say, so I decided to leave Clinton a note in which I would write about the important issues a young man faces. I wanted life to be good for him and I wanted him to make a good effort.

I identified with Penny Baxter, the role Gregory Peck played in the movie *The Yearling,* based on a book by that title by Marjorie Kinnan Rawlings, 1938. The principal characters in *The Yearling* are Ory, the mother, emotionally calloused by loss of three young children, Penny Baxter, the father, and Jody, their pre-adolescent son.

Jody adopts an orphaned fawn after shooting its mother to harvest its heart and liver as an antidote for a rattle snake bite. He cared for and increasingly loved the fawn, but as it grew and invaded the family garden, Jody's mother shot the deer to ensure survival of the family over the winter. Her bullet did not kill the young deer; it wounded him. Jody had to put the deer out of pain, killing the pet he loved dearly. Penny was in bed with a broken ankle at the time.

Jody, shaking with grief over the slaughter of his fawn, ran away from home and encountered hunger and hardship alone for a brief time. Upon returning home, Penny was still confined to bed from his injury. The reunion dialogue captured my feelings as I left Los Angeles to fly home. Here is the script of the reunion as Penny Baxter spoke knowingly, with compassion, from his sick bed to his son Jody:

> "I've wanted life to be easy for you.
> Easier'n 'twas for me.
> A man's heart aches, seein' his
> young uns face the world.
> Knowin' they got to get their guts
> tore out, the way his was tore.
> I wanted to spare you,
> long as I could.
> I wanted you to frolic with your yearlin'.
> I knowed the lonesomeness he eased for
> you.
> But ever' man's lonesome.
> What's he to do then? What's
> he to do when he git knocked down?
> Why, take it for his share and go on."

Curiously, I never said or wrote my feelings to Clinton when we parted in Los Angeles. Long after he resettled in Charlottesville, I told him what I had wanted to do, but could not do when I left. "I'm glad you didn't give me that kind of fatherly advice. I would not have listened," Clinton said.

Thus, I complete this chapter wondering if I should say more, give more helpful suggestions, or sincerely say that I want all depressed people and all others who read this book to discover the joy of being the best they can be physically, mentally, and spiritually. In the words of Winston Churchill, "Never give in. Never, never, never give in..."

References:

Ancient Theories of Soul. (April, 2009). Retrieved from https://plato.stanford.edu/entries/ancient-soul/.

Aristotle. (1905). *Aristotle's Politics*. Oxford: Clarendon Press.

Bonhoeffer, D. (1995). *The Cost of Discipleship*. New York, NY: Touchstone.

Brown, R., Snyder, D.M., Peterson, D.W. (2002). *Textbook for Mental Health: A Narrative Approach.* Boston, MA: Pearson Publishing.

Carter, J. (2018). *Faith: A Journey for All.* New York, NY: Simon and Schuster.

Deem, R. (2011, April). *What is wrong with Pascal's wager?* Retrieved from http://www.godandscience.org/apologetics/pascals_wager.html.

James, W. (1902). *The Varieties of Religious Experience: A Study in Human Nature: Being the Gifford Lectures on Natural Religion Delivered at*

Edinburgh in 1901-1902. New York, NY: London: Longmans, Green.

Mark, J.J. (2016, March). *Egyptian Book of the Dead*. Retrieved from https://www.ancient.eu/Egyptian_Book_of_the_ Dead/.

Masci, D., Lipka, M. (2016, January). *Americans may be getting less religious, but feelings of spirituality are on the rise*. Retrieved from https://www.pewresearch.org/fact-tank/2016/01/21/americans-spirituality/.

Rawlings, M. K. (1938). *The Yearling*. New York, NY: Charles Scribner's Sons.

Sandstrom, A. (2019, January). *Five facts about the religious makeup of the 116th congress*. Retrieved from https://www.pewresearch.org/fact-tank/2019/01/03/5-facts-about-the-religious-makeup-of-the-116th-congress.

CHAPTER 19

START MOVING: BECOME THE HERO OF YOUR LIFE

How to Start Moving

Charles Dickens, one of my favorite authors, wrote no autobiography. However, those whose careers are spent as Dickens scholars suggest that *David Copperfield* contained many autobiographical elements. Its opening sentence intrigues me: "Whether I shall turn out to be the hero of my own life, or whether that station will be held by anybody else, these pages must show."

The fundamental concept of becoming the hero of your own life will serve to narrow the focus of our final chapters. The word *hero* is used as a description of someone who overcomes obstacles to achieve good, with *good* necessarily referencing the universally accepted good for others. Certainly, *heroic* and *self-interested* are not mutually exclusive terms. A byproduct of heroic behavior is positive self-regard.

Countless studies have shown that people who participate in meaningful activities feel happier and develop a greater sense of purpose in contrast to those who pursued wealth, fame, or pride. One particularly interesting study was conducted by Harbaugh and colleagues (2007) wherein it was demonstrated that altruistic giving produces increased activity in the nucleus accumbens, a portion of the brain that is responsible for feelings of reward and pleasure. So, while heroes by definition espouse an outwardly facing altruistic orientation, they do, nevertheless, derive considerable benefit from the process.

Undoubtedly, most people, if not everyone, have accomplished something heroic. Initially people may reject this notion, largely because they unconsciously relegate hero status to epic poems of yesteryear. Notwithstanding, it is a known fact that the mind, body, and spirit are endowed with the unique ability to rise to a challenge and work selflessly in the face of adversity. In fact, we hear daily of others who are putting themselves in the fray while working tirelessly to minister to the sick or downtrodden. Given this potentiality, it becomes obvious that we must prepare ourselves to act in times of need, particularly by guarding against our tendency for social paralysis in the presence of others (the bystander effect). By honing ourselves to be active bystanders, we can learn to feed the hungry, comfort the sick, and necessarily standup for unpopular ideas that benefit others.

While memories of being heroic are a vital source of self-respect, many good memories, including memories of heroism, are purged from the brains of people affected by depression. This state is further complicated by the fact that memories of cowardly conduct, mistakes, or past wrong remain painfully seared in awareness of the depressed mind. J.B., the depressed wealthy businessman in Chapter 13, for example, said convincingly that he was a total and complete failure. He had forgotten a number of rather heroic deeds he had been a part of. When I asked him what he was proud of, he recalled some undeniably heroic tasks he had successfully completed. As he recalled them, these forgotten memories enlivened him, and lifted his spirit, bringing a smile to his face.

Become the Hero of Your Own Life

You will feel heroic as you overcome the obstacles to fitness, proud of your achievements. If you love your family, you will try to be healthy. If you love your country, you will not add to the crisis of health care costs, the largest burden of which is self-inflicted lifestyle diseases. If you want to reduce the risk of a heart attack, cerebral vascular stroke, or debilitating depression, you can work earnestly on becoming fit, staying active, and learning to manage stress. There is no secret shortcut to successful fitness. Consider these common-sense principles and if you agree with them, give them a try.

Basic Physical Fitness Principles

1. Schedule a specific time to exercise and stick to it, come hell or high water.
2. Avoid boredom by varying your exercise, location, and route.
3. Start by walking on a level surface either indoors or on a track.
4. Start low and go slow.
5. Some exercise is better than none.
6. Too much exercise is worse than none.
7. If possible, get an exercise partner.
8. If you can afford it, join a gym or find an exercise class.
9. No exercise equipment is needed, with the exception of a good pair of shoes.
10. Stretch for at least 10 minutes while still warm after exercise.
11. Progress to tolerance.
12. Remember that your outcomes reflect your targets, so plan for endurance, strength training, and flexibility exercises accordingly.
13. Vary your activities and routine to prevent boredom.

14. Expect that you will "fall off the wagon," and make a plan to get back into the routine once this happens.

Basic Mental Fitness Principles

Your thoughts powerfully influence your feelings and behavior. As you start to move your body and become more aware that exercise is improving your brain's activity, observe what you are thinking. The effects of your thoughts while exercising is important. You may make matters worse when you start exercising in a bad mood stemming from disturbing thoughts. But if you are knowingly exercising primarily to "blow off steam," that can be accomplished. Become aware of the body-mind connection during exercise because it is noticeably influential. Before exercising, try to clear your mind of bitterness, grudges, and conflicts. After exercise, you may find it helpful to meditate or pray quietly. Doing so may enhance the body's post exercise relaxation response.

Facebook greets me each day with the following question, "What's on your mind, Bob?" Why not ask yourself the same question as you begin your workout? Of course, if you have an exercise partner, your thoughts become audible and you and your partner influence each other's thoughts. Knowledge of this fact is important. Use the time to capture pleasant memories. Just as you start low and go slow physically in the beginning of a serious commitment to regular exercise, follow the same model for your thoughts. I'm asking for multitasking, but you may not be ready for that in the beginning.

Other Fitness Considerations

The first and foremost principle while planning for exercise is, "Above all else, be safe." In regard to safe outdoor exercise, headphones/ear plugs may be hazardous while jogging. They are prohibited on military posts. Also, regarding safety, I strongly recommend having an exercise partner. Choose someone you know well who is motivated to stay healthy and who agrees to exercise with you at least 150 minutes a week. Walking on a level surface is a natural exercise for beginners. The social advantages from exercising with a partner provide extra benefits for your brain as well as protection from danger. Having an exercise partner is also an important way to stay motivated to exercise.

For years, David Ibbeken, former Director of the UVA Law School Foundation, Dennis Womack, UVA baseball coach for 26 years, and I walked around the perimeter of the University athletic facilities at noon. For 30 minutes, five days weekly, we solved many world problems, and family issues, and talked about the personal quirks of our friends. These honest discussions focused our attention and seemed therapeutic. It was good to be with each other, catch up on each other, and exercise mid-day. We were sad to see it end due to inevitable life changes.

Research shows the greatest antidepressant benefits of physical exercise are oftentimes greater in social contexts. Research shows that high intensity training in competitive athletes affords antidepressant effects. Studies in older adults repetitively show that walking groups for seniors are better than solo exercise. Also, there are distinct advantages to rehab exercise programs for patients recovering from heart-disease treatments, including surgery.

Furthermore, degree of social connections that a person has is related to depressive symptoms. After studying research supporting both regular physical exercise and social support, I believe exercise with other people is of extreme importance to people who are prone to depression. Accountability to others and to yourself is a fringe benefit that is improved with exercise partners, trainers, and coaches.

Reasons for Wanting to Exercise

Joe is an "Army buddy," a synonym for *close friend*. He served nearly 40 years in the military. Joe is 67 years old, one of eight children born and reared in the Mid-west by hard-working parents. Years ago, we met in the gym of an Army post, actually in the shower, where for years we compared our aches and pains after our workouts. Nothing kept us from our workouts.

Today, Joe, retired, spends hours in the gym near where he resides in Louisville. Last year, he ran three sub-marathons (13 miles) each with a faster time than the one before, and one marathon (26 miles). Joe's wife of many years is a school teacher in a Jesuit school and their two adult children live independently; one is in Atlanta, while the other lives abroad. Joe is health-conscious and served as commodore of his neighborhood sailing club.

Only one of Joe's siblings exercises and takes care of himself, and none are seriously health conscious. The comparatively health-conscious brother wrestled and played football in high school. "He would work out more now if his work schedule permitted it," Joe said.

What Makes Joe Run

"I never gave much thought to my health," Joe said, "until I was older … like 45 or 46 years old. My mother-in-law was ill in the hospital on a ventilator. She told the doctor, 'I don't want to live this way' and she pulled the plug on herself. Her death made me think how I wanted to live longer and avoid dying as she died. I wanted to feel better, look better, and have better lab results.

"It was the first time I ever seriously considered just how important my life is. I don't think taking the Army Physical Fitness Test every six months had much to do with it. I could always run. I've never been really heavy or thick like my brothers. We lived near the school I attended, and I had an hour off for lunch. I ran home for lunch every day, and sometimes during lunch I had to run to the store for bread and cheese so I could have a grilled cheese sandwich for lunch."

In addition to Joe's dedication to a healthy physical lifestyle, I've observed over the years of our friendship that he also leads a healthy fiscal lifestyle, and he has an affinity for assisting the elderly. Occasionally, Joe will travel across the country to assist an army buddy who is seriously or terminally ill. Several months ago, Joe flew to a western state and spent a week cutting firewood, mending property, and comforting his friend. I know he provides information and recommendations, managing the portfolios of several elderly widows, never charging for his help and never accepting gifts.

What Makes Joe Fiscally Fit

For several years, I had dinner with Joe one night a week at a small Italian family- owned restaurant near Fort Lee, Virginia. The stock market was one of our favorite topics of discussion; Joe was the teacher, and I was his student. Over time, I came to respect his knowledge of the market. Joe discovered that I had a lot to learn and described me as "fiscally impulsive" and prone to operate without a plan. His observations were unflattering, but accurate.

Patiently and kindly, Joe helped me correct some of my errors. I guess it was fortunate that my holdings were small and limited to an individual retirement plan. Interestingly, I never knew how Joe acquired his financial wisdom even until today, at least 10 years since we met in the shower at Fort Lee. It fascinated me that Joe's commitment to physical fitness was soon followed by his commitment to fiscal fitness.

"About the time my mother-in-law died, a fellow Sergeant Major, Donovan, asked what I planned to do when I retired. He just asked out of the blue one day," Joe remembered. "I already had spent more than 20 years in the army. I told Donovan I would live on my retirement pay, but Donovan said I better rethink my retirement plans. Army retirement pay would be about 50 percent of my base pay. And I would no longer receive pay for housing or clothing.

"Donovan's comment came at the time I was seriously wondering how long I would live, not how I would support myself and my family. It made me think. I remained in the army another 14 years, but the retirement pay would still not meet our needs. I started reading about investments. I am still learning. I have invested in index funds and in equities with histories of consistently good dividends. It's paying off. As I look back on it, I decided to work on becoming physically and fiscally fit at the same time. It feels good knowing that I'm doing the right things with my life, no matter how long I live."

Joe continued, "I know in so many ways that I'm doing the right things with my life; I can feel it in so many different ways. I sleep soundly and when I wake up in the morning, I feel rested, ready for the day. I'm so tuned-in to my body; I can tell when the slightest change occurs. I have enough energy to do all the things I want to do, from cutting up trees blown onto my deck during the last hurricane, to frequently flying with Charlene anywhere in the world. I can honestly say that I feel better now than at any other time in my life."

Following our discussion about Joe's turning point, deciding to become the hero of his own life by overcoming obstacles and taking his share of control of his destiny, he sent me the following e-mail message:

> "As the oldest of eight children, I probably pushed myself more than the others, and still do. Two other brothers work out when they can. It's not important to my other brother and four sisters."

Joe's statement, "I pushed myself," is the truth underlying the meaning of the word *hero* that I want to convey in this text. I wonder if I am adequately pushing myself when it comes to fitness of body, mind, and spirit. Will my readers understand and push themselves? Am I contradicting what I wrote earlier about the misconception of depression— "the depressed need to try harder?" At the risk of being self-defensive, there is a place for trying harder and pushing oneself in healing from depression. The *pushing* that helps in healing depression is a matter of degree.

The depressed have to push themselves to get out of their warm bed each morning, wash and dress, eat reasonably, go for a walk, and accept the common miseries of life. Push yourself. Push by degree. A little pushing is better than none. Pushing too hard does not help. It is violating the "healing by degree" principle.

The Role of Inspiration in Healing by Degree

Bill Story is the first person associated with inspiration that pops into my mind. Yes, there are others who inspired me, but none like Bill Story. He was the assistant principal of Maury High School, Norfolk, Virginia, in 1948; but in his heart, he was a coach and had an unmatched winning record at Granby High School before becoming a school administrator.

He was a southern gentleman when that term was respectable and meant admirable and honorable. He was a handsome man. His three-piece gray flannel suit covered a tall, strong frame topped with a full head of gray-streaked brown hair.

Most of all, he stood erect. He was a gifted after-dinner speaker. I recall many of his banquet addresses and poems he recited on the field. I kept a letter of encouragement he sent me after a Maury High School football game our team won. He was complimentary of my performance on the field, but mainly he was asking me to push myself harder in the classroom.

He had a unique way of commanding respect while letting us know he cared about us. Years later, I learned that Bill Story sent letters to players wherever he coached. I can say with conviction that my motivation as a player and student knew no human limitation the few times he coached me on the field. I believe there is no meaningful motivation like that which is inspired by someone we respect and who cares for us. The inspirational role can be assumed by parents, teachers, coaches, counselors, ministers, friends, or others. When that role is unoccupied, we must reach deep inside and push ourselves and keep pushing.

The President's Council on Sports, Fitness and Nutrition

In 2017, the U.S. Department of Health and Human Services' President's Council on Sports, Fitness and Nutrition soberingly reported discouraging news about our nation's fitness and nutrition, even sadder because it is becoming worse:

1. Only one in three children is physically active every day.
2. Fewer than five percent of adults participate in 30 minutes of physical activity each day.
3. Only one in three adults receives the recommended amount of physical activity each week.
4. Children now spend more than seven-and-a-half hours a day in front of a screen (e.g., TV, videogames, or a computer).
5. Americans eat less than the recommended amounts of vegetables, fruits, whole-grains, dairy products, and oils.

6. About 90 percent of Americans eat more sodium than is recommended for a healthy diet.
7. Reducing the sodium Americans eat by 1,200 milligrams per day could save up to 20 billion dollars a year in medical costs.
8. Since the 1970s, the number of fast-food restaurants has more than   doubled.
9. Recent reports project that by 2030, half of all adults (115 million adults) in   the U.S. will be obese.
10. Obesity is also a growing threat to national security—a surprising 27% of young Americans are too overweight to serve in our military. Approximately 15,000 potential recruits fail their physicals every year because they are unfit (U.S. Department of Health & Human Services, 2017).

These statistics underscore the fact that far too few of us are like Joe, my Army buddy and financial advisor. Rather, our tendency as a nation is to over-eat and under-exercise. Unfortunately, a person can't outrun a bad diet any more than they can outrun faulty thinking.

Such is problematic because caloric excess over time feeds obesity: It only takes an excess of 100 calories a day to induce a gain in 10 pounds in a year. So how does this relate to depression? Obesity induces a state of low-grade inflammation in the body that, in turn, increases or worsens depressive symptoms.

Feast, Famine, or Nutritional Fitness

The ancient golden mean advises *moderation* in all things. The classical Greek architects followed this rule in building their magnificent structures by consciously emphasizing simplicity, proportion, perspective, and harmony. Classical Greek philosophers advocated the use of rational choice as a means to limit excess chaos in life and echo divine harmony. Classical Greek physicians also ascribed to calls for a limit of excess to maintain a healthy mind in a healthy body.

The principle of moderation is central in our pursuit of physical fitness. For many people, the habit of overeating is a common problem before one makes a commitment to the habit of exercise. Once the habit of regular exercise is established, the habit of overeating weakens and fades away, the putative result of Brain Derived Neurotropic Factor (BDNF)'s anorexigenic effects.

We further increase this effect by remaining cognizant of our eating habits. My Army buddy Joe follows the 80:20 rule: A person who eats healthy 80 percent of the time can eat almost anything else 20 percent of the time. If you chronically struggle with excess weight, I recommend that you apply the golden mean or moderation rule to the 20 percent of what you eat in Joe's suggested 80:20 ratio.

The notion of sensible nutrition can easily be extended beyond ourselves. The U.S. has been a leader on international efforts to reduce food insecurity, particularly by funding Food for Peace. In 1961, President John F. Kennedy appointed Senator George S. McGovern to be his first director of the Food for Peace Program.

Senator McGovern accepted the post in preference to secretary of agriculture, a position also offered to him, sensing its enormous potential to help feed the hungry worldwide. Functioning as the largest food assistance platform, the program has provided life-saving assistance to more than four billion people since its inception. Efforts like Food for Peace underscore the outcomes of organized altruistic endeavors on the global stage.

Senator McGovern and his wife, Eleanor, and their children were a fine family. We were honored to know them and particularly proud that Eleanor McGovern was the god-mother of our children. Senator McGovern was a man that moved tirelessly across many platforms to improve nutritional fitness for the nation's most vulnerable population, recognizing that both under- and over-consumption impaired fitness of the mind, body, and soul.

The Golden Mean in Fitness

Follow the "golden mean" in pursuit of physical, mental, and spiritual fitness!

We are at our best as doing, thinking, and feeling beings. A sedentary life worsens our tripartite natures. Frank Finger, a truly remarkable gentleman, was professor of psychology at UVA for many years. A quiet man, Professor Finger avoided attracting attention to himself. In his mid-80s, he held several national records in track, and some are still standing.

When Professor Finger spoke to my Mental Health class each semester, his presentations received resounding applause. As part of his introduction I always sang, "Did I ever tell you you're my hero?" from "You Are the Wind beneath my Wings."

Dr. Finger was unique in that his return to renewed youth via competitive running occurred when he was 61. Realizing his weight had spiraled out of control, he committed to a serious life change. Initially he began running at University Hall a few laps a day and, quickly buoyed by the positive comments from onlookers. He soon progressed to running six to eight miles a day—a feat that left him physically and emotionally uplifted.

At a time when he was basking in the glow of his new found abilities, he read in the *Daily Progress* a recount of a new state record for the Masters group (men over the age of 40 or women over the age of 35) in the mile. Most surprised he was to realize that he had been running six miles at a faster pace! Determined to erase the frustrations of his earlier athletic pursuits, he became determined to set a new record. Entering the race at Lannigan Field, he completed the race more than a minute faster than the record, an event that spurred him to enter a series of other races all over the state, eventually completing a ten-mile run at age 62. During the process he reconstructed his identity in a manner that revealed a "successful competitive athlete," an identity constructed on knowledge that his body was far more capable than he ever realized.

Yet in a turn of bittersweet irony, pride goeth before the fall, a characterization suggested by Dr. Finger himself. His hyper-focus on physical activity amidst a lack of attention to diet eventually contributed to a heart attack wherein a major artery supplying life-giving blood flow completely narrowed. Luckily, he survived, a testament to the effect of vessel collateralization that had developed in response to an active lifestyle. Nevertheless, his heart was sufficiently damaged in a way that prohibited him from ever running a 10-mile race, or even 1-mile race, again. Faced with this knowledge, he rechanneled his voracious appetite for goal setting and achieving not only towards sprints and hurdle events, but also toward rationale nutrition, a strategy that continued to pay dividends for another 15 years.

Chief among Dr. Finger's new focus on dietary habits were restrictions on saturated fat, refined sugars, and adequate consumption of fruits and vegetables. He realized there is a crucial relationship with sensible nutrition, physical activity, and health. Dr. Finger tended to emphasize the fact that lifestyle habits in middle age exert tremendous influence on the quality of life in older age, a key point that has traditionally been under-emphasized in American medical practice.

Fortunately, readers of this book find sufficient impetus to adhere to the sage advice of Dr. Frank Finger. He was a man whose enduring legacy for education and lifestyle choice prompts us to adopt holistic personal fitness. If we are to learn from his example, we must learn to incorporate rational nutrition and physical activity into our daily lives.

What Time Are You Exercising Today?

Inevitably, what stuck in our minds after Frank Finger spoke to our Mental Health class was his reference to his wife: "Early on, she used to ask if I was going to exercise today, but as time went on, she always asked, "What time are you exercising today?" We would do well to ask ourselves the same question and subsequently adopt habits that help us achieve this aim. By design, we can do just that by using and extending Dr. Finger's formula for success.

Develop an Exercise Plan

1. **Start today.** William Jennings Bryant reminded us that, destiny is not a matter of chance; rather, it is a matter of choice. Given that there are 1,440 minutes in the day, it really is a small tribute to fitness to choose to dedicate a few minutes a day to physical activity and sensible nutrition. In order to solidify this commitment, think about ways to adopt a healthful routine.

    For many, walking is an ideal type of structured physical activity that can be used to treat depression. This mode of activity requires very little learning and equipment to be effective. Rather, one only needs to make a conscious decision to get up and start moving in order to break the inactivity cycle. As an added bonus, walking is a low-impact exercise and doesn't require recovery time, which means you can exercise the next day.

Notwithstanding, you should also consider whether other activities would be more preferable, taking into account the timing of the activity. Might you be more likely to do some gardening in the evening, start your day with a morning walk, or join a friend at the gym for group exercise?

2. **Actively work out the logistics in advance.** Will you have an exercise partner? If so, who? Where will you exercise? What exercise goals do you and your exercise partner have? Will you be sensible about the intensity and duration of your exercise? Can you remember the rule, "start low and

go slow"? Do you know what that means and will you try to follow it? Finally, schedule a time to exercise for at least 30 minutes for at least five days a week.

Plan to escalate slowly to mitigate undue soreness and frustration. The goal should be to take several lengthy walks at a doable pace and patiently wait to realize the mood-lifting effects. Patience becomes paramount because people who have been sedentary tend to take four to eight weeks to see noticeable increases in coordination and to feel that physical activity is becoming easier.

"So, how often should I walk?"

Generally speaking, everyone should have a goal of walking three to five days a week at moderate intensity for a minimum of 150 minutes a week. For those with depression, Trivedi prescribes aerobic exercise—which can include walking, jogging, cycling, or biking—three to five times per week for 45 to 60 minutes per session (American Medical Association, 2013). Aiming for consistency is important because it is a key factor for mitigating depressive symptoms. These guidelines hold for persons with depression; however, most exercise neuroscientists agree that some exercise is better than none, particularly among people who are very sedentary and depressed.

"How fast should I plan to walk?"

If you are cleared by your doctor for physical activity but have a history of cardiovascular disease, then you plan, in collaboration with your physician, to walk at 2 to 2.5 mph—a target that translates to 71 to 90 steps per minute. If that feels like too much, then set your own optimal pace while remembering that if you are out of breath, then you are probably going too fast. A good rule of thumb is that you should be able to talk while walking. For those who are depressed but otherwise healthy, 2.5 to 3 mph is recommended, or 91-110 steps per minute. If you do not want to count steps, you can keep track of minutes that you walk each day with the goal of getting 30-45 minutes of physical activity every day 5 days per week. While building up, your goal should be to increase the length of time and distance initially, and later increase pace.

In the beginning of your training, are you willing to limit yourself to walking on flat surfaces? Will you try to avoid exercising near heavy traffic where exhaust fumes from cars and trucks may be toxic? Will you use a cane or walking stick if you have balance problems or a tendency to have gait issues? Will you phone or see your family doctor for his or her approval before exercising? Never leave home without your cell phone!

3. **Make a regular, concerted effort to commit to the plan, realizing that your personal credibility is at stake.** To aid in doing so, keep reminders of your commitment visible in your immediate environment. Visible workout gear tends to be a good reminder that your workout

awaits. For additional personal accountability, track your progress in a journal or app—an easy way to objectify the calories you burn in relation to the calories that you consume. Be sure to record the time of day that you participated, the type of physical activity, the length and intensity, and your post-activity mood. Keeping a record will help you to identify your progress so that you can give yourself credit for every step in the right direction. Acknowledging your record of success can motivate you to continue.

To maintain your motivation over the long haul, it's important to not think of physical activity as a chore. Rather, you **think of physical activity as a form of self-care that can help you get better and stay better.** Along those lines, it's helpful if you intentionally plan your exercise times and set realistic, achievable goals.

Along the way, add elements that make physical activity enjoyable. If you are an introvert, think about whether you might enjoy listening to music, podcasts, or audiobooks on longer walks. Alternatively, you can think about aesthetics and new places where you might be able to walk safely. The process of taking in views of nature while strolling in a local park or along the beach can invoke a mood-elevating effect. If you are an extrovert, consider finding a buddy that could enjoy the effects of walking or, alternatively, consider joining in a group-fitness activity. It's often easier to maintain an exercise routine when you have an accountability buddy to walk with. Regardless of whether you would rather walk solo or with a buddy, do plan for inclement weather. Many people resort to treadmill walking when bad weather prevails. Others find an indoor path to walk at a local mall.

4. **Gradually increase your performance target each week, but keep your targets realistic.** Initially, you may find it helpful to use a step counter (e.g., a Fit-bit or GPS on a phone or app) to gauge your current

activity level. Many people get about 4,000 steps during their regular daily routine. Because the general guidelines suggest that all people should get at least 10,000 steps per day, persons with a 4,000 daily step count will need to budget an additional 6000 steps per day to meet the guidelines for mental and physical health.

If a person is truly sedentary—meaning that they get 2,000 steps or less a day—then they need to slowly increase their daily average by an additional 10 to 20 percent each week. So, if a person found that they averaged 2,000 steps their first week, they could aim for 2,400 steps per day the following week. The goal could then be to keep adding 20 percent more steps each week until they achieved the 10,000 steps per day recommendation.

5. **Adhere to your routine regularly.**
   Recognize that half the battle is showing up and going through the motions. Thus, we challenge you to keep to your scheduled

plan like it was an appointment with the doctor.

If you work too late to get to a gym, keep a set of tennis shoes and weights at home. If you can't work out for longer periods of time, break the sessions into shorter bursts of time. Daily live in the present while attacking your plan, realizing that "now" is the time to hone your routine. In order to expand your degrees of fitness, you might also consider exercising in charitable events. Paying for these events ahead of time is a good motivator to remain steadfast and completing the events will pay multiple mental benefits. Once it becomes a part of your routine, you won't have to think about it. Your positive habits will be entrenched as a regular part of your day.

What Are You Doing to Improve Your Mental Fitness?

We are endowed with unique and precious gifts to think, understand, be understood, and communicate our thoughts and understanding. When those we know and love lose these gifts, even to a small degree, it is frightening and despairing. Without these gifts they are no longer who we knew. You may have experienced the feelings of helplessness when a family member or friend developed cognitive impairments known as dementia, such as Alzheimer's disease, or severe traumatic brain injury. Fortunately, neuroscientists are diligently searching for the cause and treatment of all forms of cognitive impairment. Our purpose is to address ways of living more fully cognitively and to examine the association between fitness and optimal brain function.

Practical Ways to Improve Mental Fitness

1. Seek daily opportunities to interact with people and be helpful to others.
2. Do all you can to rid your thoughts of the fear of dementia.
3. Discover the pleasure of reading.
4. Read books about things that interest you.

5. Realize that recurrent aerobic exercise coupled with mentally stimulating activities (e.g., crossword puzzles, learning a new language, social interaction, crafting, etc.) will help preserve your mind.
6. Aerobic exercise of moderate activity is needed to elicit the beneficial effects of BDNF in the hippocampus, as described in Chapter 6.
7. Intermittent caloric restriction and dietary modification have been shown to optimize hippocampal BDNF.
8. Isolation reduces hippocampal BDNF and impairs memory; by contrast, social interaction is associated with higher levels of BDNF and cognitive and emotional health. Recognizing this, work to strengthen relationships with family and friends.
9. Conscientiously try to be positive, not negative, in your thoughts and attitudes.
10. Have fun! It's a sure way to slow down aging.

11. Learn to dance and dance for exercise and pleasure.
12. Relax with good classical music in addition to the Beatles, or Perry Como, my favorites.
13. Keep a journal, recording highlights of how you spent the day.
14. Keep a prayer, meditation, or gratitude journal, noting why you are thankful.

Metacognition: Thinking About Thinking

Assume, as I do, that our thoughts give rise to our feelings and actions. It is a sound assumption, forms the basis of cognitive behavioral therapy (CBT), and sets us apart from other creatures. Thus, it is immediately apparent that our best thoughts are those that are free of errors. At this point, I want to return to the references made in John's case, "Intuitive Treatment of Depression," Chapter 1; Jim's case, "A Depressed College Student," Chapter 12; and J.B.'s case, "Depressed Wealthy Businessman," Chapter 13. All three men improved when they got their "thinking straight."

Dr. Aaron T. Beck is the father of CBT. He is a quietly calm and persistent person who helped beyond psychoanalysis, a method in which he was trained and fully qualified. Essentially, he replaced analysis with a treatment method (CBT) that readily lends itself to measurable evidence of its effectiveness in the treatment of depression and some other mental disorders. As its name suggests, CBT helps patients identify their cognitive mistakes and correct these mistakes, feelings, and resultant behavior that occur as a consequence of cognitive errors. CBT is not a resurrection of the once popular Power of Positive Thinking movement of the past. It is about thinking clearly and rationally.

Dennis Greenberger and Christine Padesky, Dr. Beck's former students, wrote *Mind Over Mood: Change How You Feel by Changing the Way You Think.* Let me urge you to obtain a copy of this workbook. You will discover the common errors in your thinking if you read the workbook and complete its exercises. Dr. Padesky describes how to keep a record of your thoughts and also teaches you, in clear and simple terms, how to identify and correct your cognitive errors. It is a "must read" for depressed people. I recommend it for the nondepressed as well, because they also make their share of cognitive errors in thinking.

Journaling

It is never too late to start keeping a journal. Absolute honesty renders the most usefulness in journaling, but this means it must be kept confidential. You can work out the details of this challenge. I started journaling in 1968, inspired by the James Boswell, a well-known eighteenth-century Scottish diarist, lawyer, and biographer. Boswell's keen interest in maintaining a diary can be captured in his comments that, "I should live no more than I could record; it is a waste of good if not preserved." Not surprisingly, Boswell recorded his own ups and downs as well as those around him in a particularly dramatically unique style. He wrote each event as if he was living it, with his characters actively talking and gesturing. Part of Boswell's obsession with the written word lay in the knowledge that the process allowed him to capture various states of observations and mind that could later be analyzed and enlarged.

Indeed, sentiments captured by Boswell from the age of 22 to 55 portray the dual mind of a man haunted by a penchant for adventure, yet duty-bound to familial obligation and, thereby, working toward a career in Scottish law. Addressing his tendency to wonder, Boswell's father, a rather severe and grim man, inscribed a phrase by Horace on the façade of the family home in rebuke: "If you be of calm and contented mind all that you seek is here, even in this remote place." Unmoved by Horace's sentiment and rarely given to calmness or contentment, Boswell feared that his persistent mental highs and lows would be his undoing, a notion deepened by his brother's commitment to an asylum.

In 1776 he wrote, "I was so afflicted with it, that's to say with the black mood of the day, that I had no just ideas or sensations of any kind. I was anxious to be with Dr. Johnson." Dr. Johnson, known formally as Samuel Johnson, a great friend and confidant who was 31 years his senior, also suffered from a depressed mood. Their heartfelt discussions on the topic were deeply gratifying, "It gave me great relief to talk of my disorder with Mr. Johnson, and when I discovered that he himself was subject to it I felt that strange satisfaction that human nature feels at the idea of participating in distress with others."

The stories of Johnson's achievement have become legendary. Johnson came to London in 1737 after writing a tragedy that was lacking in stage craft. He desired to be a playwright, but after that attempt failed, he wrote to Edward Cave who was editor the *Gentleman's Magazine* and asked for employment. Cave gave him his first literary employment (1741-1744), publishing much of his work anonymously. However, Johnson soon wanted more.

For 13 months, Johnson had attended Oxford before dropping out due to financial considerations. With time, he came to realize that many people that held the stations that he coveted were at best independently wealthy, but without special skills and ability, a source of growing resentment because he was blocked from the professional life that he desired. After his dreams prematurely forestalled, he sought alternative writing venues, which ultimately resulted in the authorship of squibs, essays, pamphlets, and biographies. Eventually, a famous bookseller of the time, Robert Lee, befriended Johnson and later proposed the dictionary assignment.

At the beginning of the undertaking, Johnson, a mere 46 years of age, had a nominal reputation at best, a fact that changed when he published *A Dictionary of the English Language*, a work that is considered as one of the most authoritative dictionaries of the English language for over 173 years. Johnson compiled the dictionary with only the help of assistants, a work that spanned 42,000 definitions and 116,000 illustrative quotations. Undergirding Johnson's approach was a plan to derive the list for the dictionary from books in his and his friends' possession. This approach prompted him to define all words in context.

Yet nearly 3 years into the work, Johnson figured out that his original strategy had failed and he had to reformulate a new strategy. Recognizing that fact, he was plagued by anxiety and questioned whether the work would ever be completed. To quell these emotions, he frequently reminded himself that someone above was keeping score and that He required only that a person do their best and persevere. Finally, after 9 years of persevering, Johnson produced a comprehensive dictionary, a work that took 6 years more than his original estimate, but a feat that still loomed large. France had required the help of 40 academicians to complete a similar work.

With the work completed, Boswell later questioned whether Johnson knew what he was getting into. Johnson retorted that he knew very well what he had undertaken, how to do it and, ultimately, he had done it very well. With age and success, Johnson increasingly accepted a mood of peace, one that was readily received given the length of time it took to come.

Reading about Samuel Johnson over the years, up to and including the present, has been a steady source of pleasure. We are indebted to the Yale University Editions of the Private Papers of James Boswell, a collection that was beautifully edited by Frederick A. Pottle (1966). Add John Wain's *Biography of Samuel Johnson*, 1974, to the Pottle collection and you will join me in discovering a remarkable hero.

Your memory is bound to improve as you keep your journal, recording how you spent the day and how it affected you. It also documents that you are doing the things listed above in the subsection entitled, "Practical Ways to Improve Mental Fitness." You will enjoy journaling once you begin doing it on a regular daily basis. I learned a lot about myself from my journal, things that pleased me and things I needed to change.

Your Journal

Buy a journal-size book and get started. Don't think about it; just do it! Journal! I write about what seemed important about the day; thoughts that lingered around in my mind that seemed important to settle. I've kept these journals over the years. When I read them now, I am struck by the importance of relationships with my family and friends and by people I hardly knew that affected me in ways I needed to explore.

References

Beck, A.T., Rush, A.J., Shaw, B.E., Emery, G. (1979). *Cognitive Therapy of Depression.* New York, NY: The Guilford Press.

Boswell, J., Morley, C., & Pottle, F. A. (1950). *Boswell's London Journal, 1762-17633: Now first published from the original manuscript.* New York, NY: McGraw-Hill.

Boswell, J., Morley, C., & Pottle, F. A. (1950). *Boswell's London Journal, 1762-17633: Now first published from the original manuscript.* New York, NY: McGraw-Hill.

Cotterell, N. (2016). *Values can be an antidote to suicide.* Retrieved from https://beckinstitute.org/values-can-be-an-antidote-to-suicide/.

Dickens, C. (1850). *David Copperfield.* London: Bradbury and Evans.

Greenberger, D., & Padesky, C. A. (2016). *Mind Over Mood: Change How You Feel by Changing the Way You Think (2nd ed.).* New York, NY: The Guilford Press.

Harbaugh, W.T., Mayr, U., Burghart. (2007). Neural responses to taxation and voluntary giving reveal motives for charitable donations. *Science* 316; 1622-1625.

US Department of Health and Human Services' President's Council on Sports, Fitness, and Nutrition (2017, January). *Facts & Statistics Physical Activity.* Retrieved from https://www.hhs.gov/fitness/resource-center/facts-and-statistics/index.html.

Wain, J. (1975). Samuel Johnson: A Biography. New York, NY: Viking Press.

CHAPTER 20

DEPRESSION, RATIONAL THOUGHT, SPIRITUAL HEALTH

Mens Sana in Corpore Sano

Mens sana in corpore sano is a Latin phrase attributed to a 2nd-century Roman poet named *Juvenal*. He used the phrase at the top of his list of what we should pray for, a healthy mind in a healthy body. In a few words, his poem cautioned that wrong desires were the source of suffering. Recognizing this, he instructed his fellow Romans to pray for virtuous behavior and, thereby, established physical and mental health as the root of happiness. We have highlighted this premise In *Healing Depression by Degrees of Fitness* by reviewing the literature and case histories that scientifically confirm this ancient truth.

Juvenal's Poem

> It is to be prayed that the mind be sound in a sound body.
> Ask for a brave soul that lacks the fear of death,
> which places the length of life last among nature's blessings,
> which is able to bear whatever kind of sufferings,
> does not know anger, lusts for nothing and believes
> the hardships and savage labors of Hercules better than
> the satisfactions, feasts, and feather bed of an Eastern King.
> I will reveal what you are able to give yourself
> For certain, the one footpath of a tranquil life lies through virtue.

Thales (624/623 – 548/545 BC), a pre-Socratic philosopher and the first scientist of record, expressed a similar thought: "What man is happy? He who has a healthy body, a resourceful mind, and a docile nature." If there is a better definition of happiness than these words, written over 2500 years ago, then I have not discovered it. It's the kind of note I would place in a bottle and launch out to sea for those seeking happiness.

Sir Roger Bannister

Many have told the remarkable story of Roger Bannister, the first person in history to run a mile in less than four minutes. Bannister was a medical student on May 6, 1954, when he ran a mile in three-minutes and 59 seconds, a feat largely thought impossible at the time (Bascomb, 2004). I distinctly remember the excitement of the news about this event. His competitors were professional athletes; Bannister was an amateur.

His victory was the result of long, hard, calculated training, and something else required of all who train to win, the unquenchable drive for victory. Bannister conceptualized the task as a "challenge of the human spirit." Speaking of the feat in a

2012 interview with the Associated Press, he recounted, "There was no logic in my mind that if you can run a mile in 4 minutes, you can't run it in 3:59 ... I knew enough medicine and physiology to know it wasn't a physical barrier, but I think it had become a psychological barrier."

Among his many legacies, Bannister taught us that much can be accomplished when a person puts their mind, body, and spirit to the task. In his 1955 book, Banister shared with us, "The aim is to move with the greatest possible freedom toward the realization of the best within us" (Bannister, 1955).

Many years after Roger Bannister's world record, I was privileged to hear him address an audience of neurologists and psychiatrists in London. At that time, he was already knighted by Queen Elizabeth and was a professor of neurology. We spoke briefly after his presentation. His daily exercise at that time in life was riding a bicycle. I recall the honor of meeting him as one of my fond memories. I was particularly impressed by his warmth and his gift of humor.

Sir Roger told the following story, alleged to be true, of a very competitive sports store owner in London. The next-door sports store owner seemed to have many more customers. That store's motto was printed over its display window in large, golden letters, "Mens Sana in Corpore Sano." That sign, he reasoned, is attracting more customers. So, he installed the following sign, "Mens and Womens Sana in Corpore Sano." Obviously, Sir Roger said, that proprietor had not won his school's Latin prize.

> "I will reveal what you are able to give
> yourself
> For certain, the one footpath of a tranquil
> life lies through virtue."

To the scientists go the credit for the unsurpassed and unquestionable evidence that a reasonable amount of physical activity has major beneficial effects upon the brain. This is true for everyone. It is particularly relevant for those who suffer from major depression because depression is best understood today as essentially a disorder of the brain. Major depression is toxic to the brain, but the very good news is that regular, accumulative physical activity heals the brain damaged by depression. This is absolutely true, yet its simplicity often leads to the fact being denied, neglected, or placed outside awareness.

To the philosophers, theologians, and coaches go the credit for inspiration that results in sustained effort. They help us all to journey into the inevitable problems of life so that we can more fully understand abilities, possibilities, self-determination and relationships that give meaning to life. By holding firmly to the ones that have gone on before us, we can internalize these messages to inspire ourselves also.

To the mental health professionals go the credit for sustaining those in the throes of emotional pain and, while doing so, helping to reframe the common miseries of life as opportunities for growth and vitality. By understanding what recovery feels like from the outside in, mental health professionals provide guidance for authentic healing, a process that involves the identification of key feelings, attitudes, and values as well as the inculcation of hope, identity, meaning, and personal responsibility.

By harnessing the lessons from each domain, all people, particularly those with depression, can learn to develop new meaning and purpose in life. Doing so is paramount for re-engaging in life in a manner that honors personal goals and strengths. Admittedly, re-engaging in life often involves a long and painful, but necessary, process. Health problems are frightening and often prompt people adopt "quick-fix fitness," but these do not last. Rather, it takes time to establish key habits and dispositions that are necessary for us to lead a virtuous life.

"The Answer, My Friends, Is in Your Hands"

Two adolescent boys found a baby bird and tried to use it to trick a wise old man. "We found a baby bird, Sir," they boasted. "Tell us if he is alive or dead." If the wise old man answered, "He is alive," they planned to squeeze the life out of the baby bird. If he guessed the bird was dead, they planned to release it into the sky. The wise old man peered keenly into the eyes of the youths. "The answer, my friends, is in your hands."

We have provided you with the evidence that major depression damages the brain. Some may even say we have overwhelmed you with the evidence. Nevertheless, review the following information and reflect on it, and see if you agree with the wise old man that the answer to self-mastery is in your hands.

The Depressed Brain: A Summary

1. The depressed brain is chronically stressed.
2. Chronic stress impairs the normal functions of the brain and interferes with its healing tendencies that would occur under normal circumstances.
3. The stressed brain is biologically and psychologically unable to divert its attention away from negative stimuli.
4. Focusing on negative stimuli causes internal conflict, worsening stress.
5. Physical stressors such as chronic inflammation, obesity, or traumatic injury elicit hormonal changes that impair mood regulation.
6. Psychotherapy, antidepressant medications, and lifestyle changes can reduce stress and its adverse effects on the brain and repair the stress-caused damage to the brain.

7. Maladaptive thoughts and behavior contribute to stress-related brain processes.
8. Improving your thoughts and behavior can protect your brain.
9. Chronic stress kills brain cells in specific parts of the brain and damages connections between cells in the brain. Destruction of brain cells and synapses alter communication between brain cells.
10. Neurotransmitters are chemical messengers released at the synapses; serotonin is one of neurotransmitters widely studied.
11. People with stress-related low levels of serotonin and fearfulness have higher rates of suicide.
12. Neurotransmitter levels and synapses, along with their communication centers, are dysregulated in the depressed brain.
13. Genetic background contributes to depression in about 30 to 40 percent of cases.
14. Stress hormones reduce BDNF, a growth hormone that helps convert stem cells in

the brain to new brain cells. Physical
activity increases BDNF.

15. Depression damages the brain's cognitive
function as well as emotion.

Yes, there is strong scientific evidence that the
brain is significantly impaired by major
depression. The question now before those who
are depressed is, "What can I do to repair my
depression-damaged brain?" You can worry
about it, adding further damage to the brain.
Alternatively, you can make a plan to live a
virtuous life by sensibly increasing your physical,
mental, and spiritual fitness.   Then resolutely, you
can commit yourself to follow the plan.

**Physical Activity and Depression: A Summary of
the Research**

In Chapter 6, Dr. Phillips provides a
comprehensive review of the studies of the
positive impact of physical activity on the brain. I
summarize Chapter 6 for your consideration:

1. Physical activity reduces inflammation and the risk of cancer, heart disease, and diabetes.
2. Physical activity is important for brain health.
3. Physical activity enhances emotional and cognitive function.
4. The mind and movement are strongly linked together.
5. We are increasingly becoming more sedentary with more jobs requiring less physical movement. Notice how home delivery is rapidly expanding.
6. As more things are done for us, we need more daily exercise.
7. Vast numbers of people die from decreased physical activity.
8. Physical activity can reduce adverse effects of stress, improving physical and mental health.
9. Physical activity optimizes neurotransmitter level and function.
10. Physical activity optimizes BDNF, a brain growth hormone that helps convert stem cells into brain cells.

11. BDNF helps restore brain cells destroyed or damaged by depression.
12. Newly formed brain cells mature and assume normal brain function, increasing memory.
13. Moderate-to-high training intensity physical activity best stimulates positive effects, although a little activity is better than none.
14. Thirty minutes of moderate-intensity exercise most days of the week is an important goal for those whose physical health will permit it.
15. Walking, cycling, rowing, stair climbing, dancing, swimming, tennis, or household chores can enhance mental health.

Reminders: How to Make Exercise Nearly Ideal

1. Find an exercise partner who will reliably exercise with you.
2. Join an exercise class run by someone informed about exercise.
3. If you can afford it, retain a coach or trainer.
4. Well-trained physical therapists make excellent coaches.

5. It may be worth the expense to join a gym, eliminating the problem of inclement weather, while you enjoy the enormous social benefits.

On the Importance of Thinking Clearly

According to Dr. Phillips's discussion of the neuroscience of the normal adult brain, Chapter 4, and the depressed brain, Chapter 5, research assures us that the brain's repair and health depends upon a reasonable amount of physical activity. I believe that the most conclusive observation one can make is that depression damages or destroys brain cells and dysregulates brain function. Physical activity significantly contributes to restoration of brain health in a variety of important ways, one of which is neurogenesis–the production of new brain cells.

We are also reminded by Dr. Phillips that, "Fascinatingly, the outcome of the whole process of neurogenesis (creating new brain cells) is contingent upon ongoing active learning. Exercise makes the cells available, but intellectual engagement ensures that they are incorporated into the circuits. Admittedly, neurons elicit BDNF in an activity-dependent manner; thus, some hypothesize that the very act of thinking increases neuronal health by eliciting BDNF. I believe the latter, but with the caveat that the proportional increase is greater with exercise."

What We Think Powerfully Affects Us

Chapter 5 reviewed the research showing how the brains of depressed people focus on negative stimuli. I presented a clinical case history demonstrating how J.B., a millionaire, attempted suicide twice, mistakenly believing he was a failure. When he correctly recalled that he had actually been successful, he felt better immediately. Indisputably, what we believe, true or not, powerfully influences how we feel and what we do.

While practicing military psychiatry, I saw an Army captain who had not slept for three months. "Why can't you sleep?" I asked. "There's a picture, Sir, I can't get it out of my mind," he replied. He was reluctant to describe the picture afraid it would worsen his insomnia. With encouragement, and a promise not to be judgmental, he shared the following story.

"We had been in Iraq for a year, a very bad year. I am the commander of a logistics company. The day that haunts me was a good day, up to the time of the incident. I had not lost a man in combat, and no one in my company was injured. It was the end of what I had thought was a good day. I left my vehicle in the motor pool, and I took a short-cut. I was covered with dust and mud.

As I walked past the medical aid station, two Soldiers came up dragging another Soldier between them. "Save our brother, save out brother," they pleaded, mistakenly thinking I was a medical officer. I looked down at the Soldier being dragged. I could see brain matter coming out of his head. I froze for a moment. That's the picture, Sir. It's very disturbing. Whenever I close my eyes, I see it. It's why I haven't slept in three months."

"What happened to the two guys who were dragging the Soldier?" I asked.

"It's funny you should ask about them," he replied.

"Why is it funny?"

"Because they would not leave me."

"What do you mean, they would not leave you?

"They stayed with me. They would not leave me. Their commander told them to move on, but they stayed with me. My commander told me to move on, but I did not obey her, Sir."

The captain said that the two young Soldiers spent the night talking about their buddy. "He was only 19 years old, grew up on a farm, and had a girlfriend back home."

"Captain," I asked, "Do you think you were there to save the Soldier whose brain matter was protruding out of his skull?"

"Yes," he said dropping his head in painful guilt. "That's what I've been thinking."

"Captain," I said, "You are a good officer. You care deeply about the Soldiers you command, but no one could have saved the injured Soldier's life. Had he been in the Army's best hospital with brain surgeons surrounding him, that Soldier's life could not have been saved; not by specialists, not by the best hospitals, and certainly not by you."

The sleep-deprived captain stared at me. He was in a daze, not yet capable of fully understanding that he believed something that was not true.

"You were not there to save the Soldier's life. Freezing for a moment made no difference.

"If you were not there to save the Soldier's life," I inquired, "What else could you have been there for?"

"I don't know," he replied, still puzzled.

After a long pause, he asked, "Was I meant to be there for those two guys?

"You tell me," I said.

With an entirely different facial expression, the one seen when understanding and truth brightens the mind, the captain said, "Yes, that is what I was meant to do. Those two Soldiers needed me. Yes."

With a high level of confidence, I said, "They will never forget you."

For the first time in three months, the captain slept that night.

Active Learning

Dr. Aaron T. Beck was a trained psychoanalyst—the quarterbacks of psychiatry— but he was disappointed with the results of highly valued psychoanalysis. He observed that his depressed patients had negative thoughts about their past, their future, and themselves. Much of what depressed people thought was not true. They needed to reduce the errors in their thinking. Dr. Beck developed a treatment method showing depressed people how they can actively learn the truth about their past and themselves. Dr. Beck's approach is now called CBT or cognitive behavioral therapy, but initially it was known as cognitive therapy.

To his credit, Dr. Beck was able to reduce his treatment method to a manual that other professionals can read; they then can attend workshops at his center in Philadelphia and master the technique, earning certification in CBT when they complete rather arduous training. Today, no other form of psychotherapy for depression or other psychological disorders is established upon nearly as broad a research foundation. CBT has been proven to effectively treat major depression.

It is necessary, but not sufficient, for a depressed person to become physically fit while on their road to healing. But the newly formed brain cells that result from physical activity must learn to take their place in the brain's complex network. This is accomplished by learning. In the most basic form, learning is a change in behavior as a result of experience. In the brain, learning means more synaptic connections are formed, a fact that is well-established.

For the body, stay physically fit. You will feel better, look better, live longer, and ward off common health problems of heart disease, diabetes, stroke, and depression. The conspicuous absence of cautions against smoking, substance abuse (including alcohol), overeating, and poor sleeping habits is intentional. Becoming and sustaining physical fitness, it seems to me, already eliminates unhealthy lifestyles. Integrity is a must. Perhaps you've heard this old joke, "If you think a fisherman lies about the number of fish he caught, ask a jogger how far he runs!" The proof of physical fitness is in one's appearance. It is the case where you can judge a book by its cover.

For the mind, become a student. First, become a student of your own thoughts. It may feel unnatural at first, but there are ways of learning to think about what you are thinking. I agree with Dr. Beck about the cognitive aspects of depression. Professionally, I respect and admire him and personally I like him. I spent two years as one of his extramural fellows. Dr. Judy Beck, his daughter, supervised my treatment of depressed patients by weekly reviewing recordings of my sessions with patients and consulting via phone weekly for two years.

Yes, depression significantly involves a remarkable sensitivity to the negative. The gloom associated with such negativity is remarkable. The relief experienced by the depressed patient who corrects errors in his or her thoughts is even more amazing. It is clear, based on brain research over the past two decades, that brain health requires learning.

For the spirit, acknowledge God, worship him with those who share your beliefs, and educate yourself, learning all you can from regularly studying the Scriptures. I explained earlier how my religious perspective is Christian. In the words of William James, it has added a "new zest for life," a guiding light, and a major source of inspiration.

Our curriculum for *Healing Depression by Degrees of Fitness* is composed of three separate but interacting major components: body, mind, and spirit. The theme for all three functions is fitness.

For the definition of fitness, we mean trying to do or be the best you can for your unique set of circumstances or situation. The second part of our definition of fitness refers to trying to sustain your best level of fitness for your body, your mind, and your spirit.

The Living Soul

Christians believe the life of the soul is eternal and the body will be resurrected in the future, after death occurs. In the midst of Job's loss of all that he had, he convincingly said, "And after my skin has been destroyed, yet in my flesh I will see God" (Job 19: 26 NIV).

Human nature, unfortunately, is prone to disobedience, obstinance, pride, and rebellion. While seeking pleasure and avoiding pain, we often fail to recognize that we incur much pain and suffering through excessive pursuit of pleasure. Turning our back on our God-given moral conscience, endless varieties of pleasure are employed to regulate our feelings. Misuse of sexual pleasure comes to mind as an example of a wholesome and special element of normal relationships that becomes frenetic when it is robbed of its chief spiritual functions.

I wish to offend no one's faith, religion, or nonreligious practices, but I want to remind depressed people that faith is a great resource for them. For example, words of encouragement to be faithful are abundant in the Bible. Paul was imprisoned by Nero for disturbing the peace in the years 66 to 67 A.D. In spite of his circumstance, Paul mustered a positive spirit. During this time, he wrote a letter to Timothy, a co-worker with whom he had a father-son-like relationship. Realizing his own execution was imminent, Paul attempted to instruct Timothy to maintain strength when facing challenges. In his letter to Timothy, Paul wrote, "For the Spirit God gave us does not make us timid, but gives us power, love and self-discipline" (2 Timothy 1: 7 NIV).

Jesus Knows Depression

Imagine that Jesus was leading a group-therapy session for depressed people. I believe His tender love and kindness would be heart-touching. He would gently smile at each person, calling them by name and saying, "I knew you before you were born. I loved you then and I love you now."

I believe all of this is implied by what Jesus said as reported in the book of Matthew: "Come to me, all you who are weary and burdened, and I will give you rest. Take my yoke upon you and learn from me, for I am gentle and humble in heart, and you will find rest for your souls. For my yoke is easy and my burden is light" (Matthew 11:28-30).

Group Therapy Session of Depressed Patients Led by Jesus

Bill: "Tell me, Jesus, how to bring my depression to you. You are correct. Depression is a very exhausting condition. I would love to bring my depression to you, but I don't know how.

Jesus: "Start by loving me with your whole being."

Keith: "I'm sorry, Jesus, but I really don't know how to love you."

Jesus: "Begin by keeping my commandments."

Shirley: "What are your commandments, Jesus?"

Jesus: "Bob, do you know my commandments?

Bob: "Yes, Jesus, I know your commandments. I confess and regret that I don't always keep them or follow them, but I know them."

Jesus: "Bob, I think the members of this group of depressed people, all good in their own way, want to hear you tell them my commandments.

Bob: "When an expert in the law asked you, Jesus, 'Which is the greatest commandment in the law?' You said, 'Love the Lord your God with all your heart and with all your soul and with all your mind. This is the first and greatest commandment. And the second is like it: Love your neighbor as yourself.' All the Law and the Prophets hang on these two commandments" (Matthew 22: 36-40).

Jesus: "Yes, thank you, Bob, that's what I said. I also said if you love me you will keep my commandments."

Jenny: "Jesus, those words are familiar to me, but I'm so depressed I don't feel like I can love anyone, including myself. Often, I feel just the opposite. I hate myself."

Jesus: "Dear Jenny, I know how you feel, but I believe love is more about thoughts and action. It is less about feelings."

Jenny was suddenly the center of attention in the group—it's called being on the *hot seat*. Her anxiety level suddenly shot up. Her face reddened. She could hardly catch her breath.

Jesus: "Do not be alarmed, Jenny. Your statement was honestly and courageously made. I believe the group itself has the same problem with love. Thank you for speaking up.

"Let me see if I can clarify the meaning of love. It is at the very core of all Scripture. It is essential that everyone understands the true meaning of love."

"A man was going down from Jerusalem to Jericho, when he was attacked by robbers. They stripped him of his clothes, beat him and went away, leaving him half dead. A priest happened to be going down the same road, and when he saw the man, he passed by on the other side. So too, a Levite, when he came to the place and saw him, passed on the other side. But a Samaritan, as he traveled, came where the man was; and when he saw him, he took pity on him. He went to him and bandaged his wounds, pouring on oil and wine. Then he put the man on his own donkey, brought him to an inn and took care of him. The next day he took out two denarii, and gave them to the innkeeper. 'Look after him,' he said, 'and when I return, I will reimburse you for any extra expense you may have.'"

"Which of these three do you think was a neighbor to the man who fell into the hands of robbers?"

"The expert in the law replied, 'The one who had mercy on him.'"

Jesus: "Go and do likewise" (Luke: 10: 30-37).

Jenny: "Thank you, Jesus. Love is not just a sentiment. It is clearly expressed in the action we take on behalf of someone else. The story of the Good Samaritan, an otherwise nameless man, shows that he loved the stranger who had been beaten and robbed by taking care of his needs."

Jesus: "Yes, Jenny, but love is not necessarily devoid of sentiment or emotion. You may recall reading that I cried when my friend Lazarus died."

Keith: "Jesus, I was moved when I read that you wept. Up till then, I thought that real men don't cry, but I was wrong."

Bill: "I felt the same way until now."

Bob: "I felt I was on sacred ground when Soldiers shared their combat trauma stories with me. Sometimes, I cried with them."

Jesus: "All of you are made to feel and to understand what others feel, but it must not stop with the feeling. When possible, become a part of the solution. Throughout the Bible, good Soldiers and fit athletes are held up as models to emulate."

Jesus Knows Anxiety

Jesus does not want us to be anxious or depressed. The admonishment *fear not* is used 365 times in the Bible. Jesus does not want us to be anxious for any reason. According to the Scriptures, Jesus wants us to have the peace of God, a peace that surpasses all understanding.

The peace of God is a unique state of mind and nearly beyond human conception. The peace of God is based on the confidence that your past mistakes are blotted out because Jesus keeps no record of wrongs when you acknowledge them and walk away from them.

Final Thoughts

If you want to learn the meaning of unconditional love as a unique way to think and act, learn about the life of Jesus Christ. He is predicted and depicted throughout the Old Testament of the Bible. His three-year ministry is documented in each of the four gospels of the New Testament of the Bible.

Since my 12th year of life I have been exposed to Christian teachers and ministers. Today, I begin each morning reading a Christian book of Bible verses and thoughtful prayers from a book given to me by my best friend in college, Ed Weise, who is now a pediatrician in Florida. Our friendship began in 1950 and becomes more precious and more meaningful each year.

In the 75 years that I have been a Christian, I have never been taught that *sin* causes diseases. Certainly, I do not believe that major depression is a punishment for sin. I hold the view that God does not punish people in this life for falling short of the goal he would like us to achieve.

Jesus taught in parables, or stories, not for entertainment but as a good way to teach. Many stories Jesus told were about God's love for everyone, especially for those who do wrong. Such a story is told by Jesus, recorded in Luke 15:11-32, about the prodigal son. It's a touching story about a man who had two sons. The younger son demanded his share of his father's inheritance, unheard of in those ancient days. His father did not object. The son left home and squandered his money, only to end up starving, longing to eat what was fed to swine.

The son came to his senses and returned home to beg his father to hire him as one of his servants. Instead, his father showed his forgiveness by kissing his son, placing a ring on his finger, and giving him a lavish party after stating, "...for this son of mine was dead and is alive again; he was lost and is found" (Luke 15:24 NIV).

I know of no story of a father's forgiving love more compassionate, except "For God so loved the world that he gave his one and only Son, that whoever believes in him shall not perish but have eternal life" (John 3:16).

Friday Mornings

Attending the weekly exercise class, led by Rick Moore, my physical therapist, is one of the highlights of my retirement. The members in our class enjoy different states of fitness, but the class is open to anyone choosing to attend. The social benefits are immeasurable. I suspect the age range of our members is 70-88 and, on some occasions, we are joined by a fit 93-year-old man.

At the end of each class, Rick walks around behind our chairs, arranged in a circle, and gives each of us a soothing, gentle neck massage. With our eyes closed, breathing deeply and slowly, we repeat out loud Rick's words, and we come to believe them: "I am safe. I am happy. I am healthy, and I live with ease." Someday, under similar circumstances, I hope you can say, "I am safe. I am happy. I am healthy, and I live with ease." When you are ready, I want you to add, "I am physically fit. I am mentally fit. And I am spiritually fit."

May you have a sound mind in a healthy body inspired by the Spirit of God and may you fully experience the healing of depression by degrees of fitness.

Robert S. Brown and Cristy S. Phillips

References

Bannister, R. (1955). *The Four-Minute Mile*. New York, NY: Dodd, Mead.

Bascomb, N. (2004). *The Perfect Mile: Three Athletes, One Goal, and Less than Four Minutes to Achieve It*. New York, NY: Houghton Mifflin Company.

Made in the USA
Middletown, DE
23 July 2019